ALEXANDER MEIKLEJOHN

Teacher of Freedom

*The primary social fact which blocks and hinders
the success of our experiment in self-government is that
our citizens are not educated for self-government.
We are terrified by ideas, rather than challenged and
stimulated by them. Our dominant mood is not the courage
of people who dare to think. It is the timidity of those
who fear and hate whenever conventions are questioned.*

"The First Amendment Is An Absolute"

Alexander Meiklejohn

Teacher of Freedom

*a collection of his educational,
philosophical, and legal writings,
along with a biographical study and
introductions to the selections*

edited by Cynthia Stokes Brown

series editor Ann Fagan Ginger

MEIKLEJOHN CIVIL LIBERTIES INSTITUTE
STUDIES IN LAW AND SOCIAL CHANGE NO. 2

MEIKLEJOHN INSTITUTE, P.O. BOX 673, BERKELEY, CA 94701

Meiklejohn Civil Liberties Institute is a California nonprofit corporation. Donations of research materials are welcome; monetary contributions are essential to the Institute's continued operation; all are tax deductible.

Meiklejohn Civil Liberties Institute
P.O. Box 673
Berkeley, CA 94701
(415) 848-0599

Library of Congress
Catalog Card No.: 81:81355

    Brown, Cynthia Stokes
      Alexander Meiklejohn: Teacher of Freedom
    Berkeley, CA: Meiklejohn Civil Liberties Institute
    281 p.
    8109   810327

ISBN 0-913876-16-x (cloth)
ISBN 0-913876-17-8 (paper)

Production: David Christiano
Design: Zipporah Collins
Printing and binding: Maple-Vail Book Manufacturing Group
Photo reproduction: Art Graphics

Recent Publications by Meiklejohn Civil Liberties Institute

The Ford Hunger March
(Studies in Law and Social Change No. 1)

Human Rights Organizations and Periodicals Directory

Human Rights Docket US 1979

The Legal Struggle to Abolish the House Committee on Un-American Activities: The Papers of Jeremiah Gutman
(Meiklejohn Institute Inventory No. 1)

The National Lawyers Guild: Guide to Records (1937-1974) and Index to Periodicals (1937-1979)
(Meiklejohn Institute Inventory No. 2)

Angela Davis Case Procedural Guide and Index
(Meiklejohn Institute Case Collection No. 1)

Pentagon Papers Case Procedural Guide and Index
(Meiklejohn Institute Case Collection No. 2)

Contents

Credits

Articles

The editor wishes to thank these publishers and persons for permission to reprint from the following works by Alexander Meiklejohn:

Specified material from pp. 45-58, 61-66, 377-379, 410-412, 315-318 in *The Experimental College* by Alexander Meiklejohn. Copyright 1932 by Harper & Row, Publishers, Inc.; renewed 1960 by Alexander Meiklejohn. Reprinted by permission of the publisher.

Specified material from pp. 277-291 in *Education Between Two Worlds* by Alexander Meiklejohn. Copyright 1942 by Harper & Row, Publishers, Inc.; renewed 1970 by Helen E. Meiklejohn. Reprinted by permission of the publisher.

Specified material from pp.107-124 in *Political Freedom* by Alexander Meiklejohn. Copyright © 1960, 1948 by Harper & Row, Publishers, Inc. Reprinted by permission of the publisher.

"The Machine City," reprinted by permission of Hawthorn Properties (Elsevier-Dutton Publishing Co., Inc.) from the book *Freedom and the College* by Alexander Meiklejohn. Copyright 1923 by The Century Company; 1951 by Alexander Meiklejohn. Reprinted by Books for Libraries Press, 1970. Distributed by Arno Press Inc.

W. W. Norton & Company, Inc. for *What Does America Mean?* Copyright 1935 by W. W. Norton & Company, Inc., renewed 1963 by Donald Meiklejohn.

The State Historical Society of Wisconsin for permission to quote from "I'm An American" (NBC interview, August, 1941) and to print Meiklejohn's letter to the Federal Bureau of Investigation, December, 1951.

American Library Association for *Philosophy*. Copyright 1926 by the American Library Association.

Brown Alumni Monthly for "Under the Elms" (July 1953).

The New Republic, Inc., for "Adult Education: A Fresh Start" (August 15, 1934).

Helen E. Meiklejohn for "Teachers and Controversial Questions," *Harper's Magazine* (June 1938). Copyright by Alexander Meiklejohn.

The New York Times Company for "Should Communists Be Allowed to Teach?" March 27, 1949. © 1949 by The New York Times Company. Reprinted by permission.

The University of Chicago Press for "The First Amendment Is An Absolute." Reprinted from *The Supreme Court Review 1961,* edited by Philip B. Kurland, by permission of the University of Chicago Press. Copyright by the University of Chicago Press.

Photographs

Page iii: From the collection of the University of Wisconsin—Madison Archives

Page 3: Aylsworth's Photographic Studio, Apponaug, Rhode Island

Page 6: Evans, the University Art Gallery, Ithaca, New York

Page 11: Courtesy of Amherst College Archives

Page 18: Underwood & Underwood

Page 50: Carol Baldwin

Cover; Page 52: Theodore Benner

Page 55: Carol Baldwin

Page 77: Courtesy of Amherst College Archives

Page 108: M. E. Warren

Page 209: Russell Leake

Page 228: Johann Hagenmeyer

Page 258: Arthur Swoger

Introduction

Ann Fagan Ginger

About This Book

Alexander Meiklejohn was an educator, first and foremost. He was a believer in the idea that the people should run the government, above all else. He found these views in perfect harmony, as he found a continuum between the first decades of his life as a teacher and school administrator, and the later decades as an expert on the First Amendment whose writings were highly regarded by several justices of the U.S. Supreme Court.

Many of us who knew Meiklejohn in one capacity did not know of his work in the other. The Institute named after Meiklejohn is pleased that this book will introduce students of Meiklejohn the educator to Meiklejohn the civil libertarian, while colleagues of Meiklejohn the First Amendment man will meet Meiklejohn the educational experimenter.

Each of us privileged to know Meiklejohn the man, even for a short time, remembers where we met and what he said. I went to visit Alex and Helen Meiklejohn at their home on La Loma Avenue in Berkeley after I moved there in 1959. Like many before and after me, I had a problem on which I thought Meiklejohn could be of some assistance. My brother-in-law, Edward Yellin, had refused, under the First Amendment, to answer questions about his political beliefs and affiliations while working in a steel mill. He and most of the other subpoenaed Steelworkers Union members maintained that the House Committee on Un-American Activities did not have the authority to question them on these subjects since Congress could not pass any laws in this area.

I was looking to Meiklejohn for some specific new ideas about how to explain and use the First Amendment in the Yellin trial. I got what I came for. But more than that, I got a feeling of confidence that somehow the First Amendment would survive and prosper. I talked to many educators, lawyers, and journalists about the Yellin case during that period, seeking to understand better how our country could be moving so far away from its democratic moorings, and to find effective ways to fight back. My afternoon with Alexander Meiklejohn stands out as if I had taken a photograph of his book-lined room, with Alex and Helen sitting on the couch. I remember best the mood of serenity not present in my own crammed and busy office, and the confidence Alex exuded that we would find the time, place, and manner for preserving and extending the First Amendment.

Although we followed Meiklejohn's advice in the trial, the federal judge convicted Ed Yellin, and the University of Illinois, where he had become a graduate student, suspended him. When I went back to La Loma Avenue, Alex agreed to write a letter to the administration. This time we won; the University reinstated Ed after a hearing. And in 1963 we won the Yellin case in the U.S. Supreme Court (5-4), on the due process ground that the Committee had violated its own rules in denying Yellin a hearing in executive session. Still, the First Amendment issue had been raised clearly, and not decided against us.

Every time I talked with him after that, Alexander Meiklejohn said something new and surprising about a subject I thought I had explored quite fully, from the role of private religious schools to the responsibility of professors to show intellectual leadership. In 1963 he agreed to the use of his name on a unique civil liberties research center we were planning, and as soon as we got the building up, Alex Meiklejohn came down to see our new institution, and to talk to the press about it. I was very busy at the time and said, with a sigh, that we *must* have a large celebration on opening day. Alex surprised me again by asking "Why?" Without his question, I would not have been able to conscientiously postpone doing what I had no strength for at the moment. Later, during the Free Speech Movement struggles in 1964 at the Berkeley campus of the University of California, he said that in every classroom there must be two generations. Since I have become a teacher, I have found many occasions when this comment seemed appropriate.

Now the Meiklejohn Civil Liberties Institute is proud to publish this collection of the basic writings of Alexander Meiklejohn, and a short biography of his thought and work by Cynthia Stokes Brown. While the subject grew up in England and New England, the biographer was reared in the American South. After earning a B.A. from

"I have always been greatly interested in freedom, and I like getting the word around," said Alexander Meiklejohn at a press conference with Ann Fagan Ginger at the new Meiklejohn Civil Liberties Library, April 14, 1964.

Duke University, she went on to Johns Hopkins on a fellowship from the American Association of University Women and an honorary Woodrow Wilson Fellowship. Her Ph.D. in the history of education led her into high school history teaching in Baltimore and on to co-directing a credential program for elementary teachers at the University Without Walls in Berkeley. Her Preface describes how she became acquainted with Alexander Meiklejohn's work. Ms. Brown is now teaching at Antioch University—San Francisco and serving as a director of the Coastal Ridge Research and Education Center in Point Arena, California.

We all hope this book will find its way into the hands of the current generations of college students studying the liberal arts, reentry students enrolled in adult education programs, as well as law

students and lawyers studying the First Amendment. Alex Meiklejohn believed passionately in the education of these groups. We
believe as passionately that his writings are essential to that process.

About This Series of Studies on Law and Social Change

Alexander Meiklejohn turned very naturally to the law in trying to
find one discipline that would raise, for students, the key questions
with which he thought every educated person must grapple. Like
many other philosophers, educators, and nonlawyers, Meiklejohn's
own readings and experience had taught him the importance of law in
understanding society and in changing society.

The law, to Meiklejohn, was the ideas of law, the theory of government, the law as spelled out by the founding fathers in the Constitution and the Bill of Rights, and as set forth by the U.S. Supreme
Court. He was not concerned with the law as practiced by lawyers to
earn a living by representing private commercial interests or with the
law as meted out by trial court judges following precedent.

This book by and about Alexander Meiklejohn could have been a
traditional study of two cases on academic freedom, if Meiklejohn had
chosen that path in his life. Once he lost his position as president of a
college and once an experiment he headed was ended. The reason in
both cases was the same: his theories of education, his style of life
and teaching, his principles did not conform to those of his employers.
A strong supporter of academic freedom, he chose to take his lumps
and move on to the next educational adventure rather than to sue to
retain or regain his college presidency or leadership of an experimental
college.

As a result, this book is a study in law and social change in the
broad sense that its central figure believed that social change is necessary. He worked to bring it about first as an educator, using law as
the focus for teaching about society, and later as a full-bodied proponent of the law guaranteeing freedom of expression. This volume
is the second in a series of studies on law and social change that began
with a book by labor lawyer Maurice Sugar about one of his cases in
Detroit. The unusual feature of *The Ford Hunger March* is that the
lawyer's goal was to forestall a trial of the innocent rather than to conduct a courtroom defense. One of Sugar's master strokes was to get
the grand jurors to subpoena a famous educator, Scott Nearing, so he

could teach them some of the economics they had not learned in school and could explain the confrontation that left four young workers dead in Dearborn.

As it has developed, the first two books in this series have involved a lawyer acting, in part, as a teacher and a teacher acting, in part, as a lawyer. Both authors combined theory and practice, using tactics appropriate to their differing philosophies. Later books will present other studies of law and social change, from the viewpoints of the client, the legal defense committee, defense counsel, prosecutor, judge, legislator, administrator, or juror. The subject is so vast and essential that we look forward to filling a long bookshelf in the coming years.

Ann Fagan Ginger
President, Meiklejohn Civil Liberties Institute

Preface

Who was "Mr. Free Speech"? Students in Berkeley, if asked that question now, would not be likely to find a ready answer. Berkeley's middle-aged citizens, however, are likely to answer: "Mario Savio of the Free Speech Movement of 1964." But the answer of civil libertarians, lawyers and theorists, in Berkeley and elsewhere in the nation, would almost surely be: "Alexander Meiklejohn."

Meiklejohn lived in Berkeley thirty-two years, from 1932 until his death at age ninety-two in December 1964, not long after demonstrations demanding free speech had erupted on the campus of the University of California. By then he had spent sixty-five years teaching, speaking, and writing about the meaning and role of free speech in a self-governing society.

No lawyer, Meiklejohn began his adult career as a teacher of philosophy. His early students may not have foreseen that he would emerge as the preeminent theorist of free speech, but in retrospect, the pattern of his life can be seen as richly consistent. Coming from a Scotch Presbyterian, working-class background, he strove as a beginning teacher at Brown University to teach his students how to govern themselves. Governing required thinking; thinking required fearless consideration of all possible positions; and thereby was he set on his life's course.

Thousands of people remember Alexander Meiklejohn, many with great devotion—students and teachers from Brown University, Amherst College and the University of Wisconsin, colleagues and students at the San Francisco School for Social Studies, university presidents, citizens from the American Civil Liberties Union, lawyers and judges, and countless friends of every variety. Even those who heard him give only a single speech can hardly forget him, he made such a vivid impression. Nor can those who disagreed with Meiklejohn easily put from their minds the gentle, courteous, immovable adversary who suffered an occasional amendment but never budged an inch.

Those who knew Meiklejohn during one aspect or another of his career, however, do not always grasp the whole of him. Remembering him as president of Amherst College, they may not know that much later he founded a school attended by blue-collar workers and other adults in San Francisco. Many who knew him as chairman of the Experimental College at the University of Wisconsin may not realize that he later served as chairman of the National Committee to Abolish the House Un-American Activities Committee. Lawyers who read his analysis in legal journals of cases pertaining to the First Amendment may have no idea that he once was dismissed by the trustees of Amherst. Even those acquainted with the whole range of his varied activities may not realize the consistency of conviction that undergirded all his work.

No biography has yet been written to weave together the strands of Meiklejohn's life. I have chosen to write a short account of his life and ideas that would provide a framework for understanding him, and then to let him speak for himself. Only a few of his books are still in print, in expensive library editions, and much of his output was given as speeches or published in articles not readily accessible. From his entire production I have selected samples that display the whole range of his thinking.

We need the ideas of Alexander Meiklejohn now because he believed in the capacity of "We, the People" to govern and because he was able to analyze with lucidity the problems that such a belief entails. No one who listens to his distinction between happiness and excellence, or between liberty and freedom, can ever again use those words loosely. His commitment to the rights of all humanity never faltered; he wrote in 1961:

> . . . the adoption of the principle of self-government by "The People" of this nation set loose upon us and upon the world at large an idea which is still transforming men's conceptions of what they are and how they may best be governed. Wherever it goes, that idea is demanding— and slowly securing—a recognition that, with respect to human dignity, women have the same status as men, that people of all races and colors and creeds must be treated as equals, that the poor are at least the equals of the rich.

Meiklejohn was a critic who saw ahead of his time. He was in the minority all his life on most issues that concerned him. An independent agent operating without a continuous base and stream of students such as his contemporary John Dewey had at Columbia University, Meiklejohn opposed pragmatism, capitalism, and self-centered individualism. People in power were only too glad to keep him at the fringes as much as possible. Now that Protestant-capitalist civilization has further disintegrated, more people may be able to follow his argument.

As a philosopher, Meiklejohn formulated four basic positions. He framed a moral, rather than economic or religious, critique of Protestant-capitalist society. He built a curriculum whose contents could teach critical thinking at the college and adult level. He created a general theory of education whose content and method derived from the political purpose that it served. Finally, he propounded a general theory of democracy that interpreted the U.S. Constitution as requiring self-government as the basic political form, but not requiring capitalism as the essential economic arrangement.

Friends and enemies alike agreed that Meiklejohn had encompassed this range in his thinking, but they disagreed passionately about whether his assertions were valid. Controversy boiled about him wherever he went—just what he intended. My task has been to present Meiklejohn's ideas clearly, not to argue their merit. To clarify the context of his polemics, my notes indicate who was arguing with whom, what the issues were at the time, what Meiklejohn's argument grew out of, and to whom it was addressed. But I have not appraised Meiklejohn's argument. If this book manages to present his ideas in one place as he marshalled and defended them, then I trust they will generate their own evaluation. The first step must be a clear presentation.

My impetus for assembling this book arose from my desire to fill in some serious gaps in my own education. Through my mother I felt linked to the tradition of progressive education, especially the Dewey-ite, midwestern branch of it, even though I grew up in a small, segregated, southern town. But no one ever mentioned that Dewey was a socialist. That word was not pronounced in the late 1950s and early 1960s when I emerged into adulthood. As I began to learn, through my own teaching in Baltimore and Berkeley, the connection between education and politics, my need to understand the progressive educators of the 1930s became overwhelming. After meeting Helen Meiklejohn and reading "Liberty or Freedom," I pounced on the life of Alexander Meiklejohn as a way to clear for myself a path through the obfuscations. I was richly rewarded and hope this book will bring to others some measure of the satisfaction I found.

Now, after more than four years' work, I am thoroughly indebted to a host of Meiklejohn's associates. The bibliography contains a formal list of my interviews and correspondence, but no list can convey my pleasure in finding Meiklejohn's spirit alive in his friends, colleagues, students, wife, and children. I am especially grateful to teachers and students from the Experimental College, who welcomed me to their fiftieth anniversary reunion and encouraged me in every possible way, among them the late Walter Raymond Agard and John Beecher, and R. Freeman Butts, Wilbur Cohen, DeLisle Crawford, Kenneth Decker, Alvin Gordon, Robert Havighurst, Emanuel Lerner, Leonard Michels, John Powell, and Michael Sapir. Marge Frantz has been of inestimable assistance.

This book would never have been published without the generosity of many people willing to write checks to preserve the ideas of Alexander Meiklejohn, including many members of the Experimental College, W. H. Ferry, and the late Charles Hogan.

My family has contributed in myriad, marvelous ways. My parents, Louise and Stanley Stokes, studied at the University of Wisconsin while Meiklejohn was there and made his name a household word for me. My aunt, Cynthia L. Stokes, shared her scrapbook of her student days at Wisconsin, 1925-29. My husband, James R. Brown, supported me while I wrote, and my sons, Erik and Ivor, made room for Meiklejohn in our lives.

I want to thank the members of the Meiklejohn Civil Liberties Institute for bravely and cheerfully assuming this task, especially Ann Fagan Ginger, David Christiano, Frances Herring, Jennifer Terry, and Amy Bank. Amy L. Einsohn and Nelda Cassuto did the proofreading, and Joel Kies provided the computer programming to typeset the manuscript. Working with Zipporah Collins, who designed this book, has been a great pleasure.

Finally, I am indebted most of all to Helen Everett Meiklejohn, wife of Alexander, with whom I have worked closely. Through her love and intelligence Helen understood Alex, and she has been completely generous in sharing that understanding. All of us involved with creating this book want to acknowledge her assistance and inspiration.

Cynthia Stokes Brown

Alexander Meiklejohn
Teacher of Freedom

Cynthia Stokes Brown

Alexander Meiklejohn was Scottish to the core, but he was born in England. His seven older brothers teased him because he alone in the family had not been born in Scotland. He longed to be a Scot so much that he finally devised an argument to meet his brothers' challenge: "Jesus was born in a stable," he said, "but that didn't make him a horse." This was his first conscious effort at logical argument.

Alexander's parents, James and Elizabeth (France) Meiklejohn, had moved from Dunipace, Scotland, to Rochdale, England, shortly before the birth of their eighth son on February 3, 1872. James Meiklejohn was a textile worker, and he needed to be close to the technological advances in that industry.

One of the first things Alex remembered was standing beside his mother as she washed the family's dirty socks. She maintained a high quality of housekeeping by washing the socks first on the outside, then turning them inside out to wash the inside. She allowed Alex to turn the socks as she washed, and he felt the happiness of being useful and helping keep up the family's high standards. He also remembered his family reading and discussing the Bible and the poetry of Robert Burns as he was growing up, and these books refreshed him all his life.

Another lifelong influence on Meiklejohn began in Rochdale, his home town. He early learned that Rochdale was famous for being the place where the consumer cooperative movement began. In 1844 twenty-eight poor weavers had pooled a pound each (about five dollars) to open a tiny grocery store. This store and its capital had greatly expanded on the basis of its unique business principles: membership shall be open to all, each member shall have only one vote no matter how many shares are owned, and any profit earned by the business shall be given back to the members in proportion to their shares. As a boy Meiklejohn learned these Rochdale Principles, and he believed in some form of cooperative ownership all his life.

The Meiklejohn family belonged to the Rochdale cooperative. What Alex noted and remembered was the way his parents held open house on Saturday mornings, and how the other workers came to air their grievances and discuss problems. His father's colleagues came to talk to him informally, but regularly. They respected him, not only as a skilled craftsman in color design, but as a man. There was never any question in Alexander's mind about where he and his family belonged. They belonged with the workers, sharing their struggles and living in daily cooperation with them.

The Meiklejohn boys also shared the sports of the children of the mills—soccer and cricket. Alexander especially loved to play cricket, and his cricket bat was one of his prized possessions.

After eight years in Rochdale, James Meiklejohn was sent by his employer to Pawtucket, Rhode Island, to set up improved color techniques there and to train other workers in his skills. When the family sailed for the United States on the first day of June 1880, what Alexander carried along was his cricket bat.

A steady stream of textile workers from England flowed into Pawtucket during these years, and the Meiklejohn residence often sheltered a new family until it could find a place of its own. Eventually James Meiklejohn became superintendent of the color department at the U.S. Finishing Company's plant at Pawtucket. He served for some years as a member of the town's School Commmittee and became a member of the Union Lodge of Freemasons in Pawtucket. He was also a chief of the Clan Fraser of the city and always took a deep interest in the Scottish organizations there.

But his new loyalties forced his son, Alexander, into more complex thinking. His father had been devoted to Queen Victoria, and it seemed incomprehensible that he could have forsworn her. Yet, of course, he had to be loyal to his new country. In some way, somehow, President Garfield had replaced the queen. How was this possible? Looking back at this early dilemma, Alex Meiklejohn wrote when he was eighty:

> Nine years after our arrival, my father renounced his political allegiance to the realm of Queen Victoria and was naturalized under the laws of the United States. By that action of his, I too became a citizen. But that act also brought me into contact with the first paradox or dilemma which I faced. As I look back over the course of my life, that doubleness of loyalty seems to me

Meiklejohn as a boy of about ten in Pawtucket, Rhode Island.

one of its most influential and exciting features. In a boyish way
I soon discovered that the taking on the character of being
American did not imply the losing of the character of being
Scottish. In fact, in one actual situation, the two loyalties sup-
ported and enriched each other.[1]

Alex attended public school in Pawtucket. A high school teacher
recognized his unusual talent and gave him elocution lessons for three
years. His family was too poor to be able to send eight sons to college
so, following the custom in a Scottish family, they all worked and
saved to enable at least the youngest to pursue his studies. After all
the saving, Alex postponed going to college for one year because his
brother Harry died of epilepsy.

Meiklejohn lived at home and attended Brown University, only
four miles away at Providence, Rhode Island. Brown was a private
university run by trustees who included John D. Rockefeller, with a
long line of Baptist ministers as presidents. Brown's president from
1889 to 1897 was Benjamin Andrews, a man who made an extraordinary impression on Meiklejohn. The year Meiklejohn arrived as a
freshman Andrews was inaugurated as president—a scholar in history,
philosophy, and economics. For him books were weapons for one
overriding purpose—to make men of character. All learning had a
moral aim. He gave people the feeling that a college like Brown had
mighty work to do and that, under Andrews, it was doing it. Andrews'
grip on living caught everyone around him and made them want to
join in his work. In 1923 Meiklejohn wrote: "More than anyone else
whom I have known in academic life, Andrews gave to me the dream
of having freedom, of being free and yet in action."[2]

Meiklejohn was an outstanding student at Brown. He made Phi
Beta Kappa in his junior year, which was the first he had heard of the
honor. He was also an exceptional athlete, skilled in soccer, cricket,
squash and tennis, and a member of the first collegiate ice polo team
in the country. When that team went to Canada, Meiklejohn brought
back the rubber puck instead of a ball, transforming ice polo into ice
hockey.

Before his graduation, Meiklejohn asked President Andrews' advice
about his future. "Benny" Andrews observed, "Well, Meiklejohn,
you're a Scotchman; so far as I can see, you're not very strong on
whiskey; so I guess you must be long on philosophy. You'd better stay

here awhile and study with this man Seth; he's as good as they make 'em, Meiklejohn, you won't regret it. Good day, sir.''[3]

So Meiklejohn took his master's degree in philosophy at Brown under James Seth, a Scotch philosopher who left Brown for Cornell in 1896. Meiklejohn followed him there in order to take his Ph.D. under Seth. It seemed perfectly natural to support himself with a hockey scholarship while writing his dissertation on Kant's theory of substance, and he managed to get back to Providence to play with the Wanderers in the soccer play-offs.

1. Learning the Score at Brown

Meiklejohn returned to Brown in the fall of 1897 to join the faculty as an instructor in philosophy. During the prior summer a struggle in academic freedom had begun at Brown. The university's enrollment had rapidly expanded under President Andrews, and the need for buildings and equipment had become acute. The endowment had not been increased during those years, and retrenchment was necessary to avoid continued deficits. President Andrews sought rest in Europe for the year 1896-97.

While Andrews was abroad, the presidential election of 1896 heated up. Republican McKinley, with the backing of moneyed interests who supported the gold standard, barely defeated Democrat William Jennings Bryan, who advocated the coinage of silver at the ratio of sixteen silver to one gold. Andrews was known to have supported Bryan and international bimetalism, though being in Europe he took no active part in the campaign. While he was away, and without his consent, some of his private letters were published, in which he advocated that the United States begin coining silver at sixteen to one without waiting for other countries. After McKinley's election, when the trustees met in June 1897, one of them, who was also chairman of the U.S. House Committee on Banking and Currency, suggested that Andrews' ideas were preventing donations to the university. For example, John D. Rockefeller had made no gift, even though his son was in the graduating class of 1897. The trustees voted to confer with Andrews on his return.

When Andrews returned, the trustees asked him not to change his views, but to keep them to himself. Andrews resigned instead, feeling that being asked not to advocate his views was an intolerable

Meiklejohn as a graduate student of philosophy at Cornell University, 1896-97.

infringement on his, or any university president's, freedom of speech.

President Eliot of Harvard leaped to Andrews' defense. So did Gilman of Johns Hopkins, Dewey of Chicago, and many other leading administrators and teachers.

The trustees soon asked Andrews to withdraw his resignation, which he did. He remained at Brown one more year, while William Harper, president of the University of Chicago, arrranged for him to become superintendent of Chicago's public schools in the fall of 1898.

(Rockefeller had given $1,600,000 to the University of Chicago when it opened in 1892.)

Meiklejohn's first year of teaching at Brown was the final year of Andrews' term as president. During these early years Meiklejohn took his teaching with such seriousness and anxiety that he regularly vomited before addressing his first morning class in logic. He was struggling to learn how to think as a philosopher as well as how to teach that kind of thinking. He soon found his stride and advanced steadily up the academic ladder, becoming full professor of logic and metaphysics in 1906, after nine years at Brown.

Students found Meiklejohn an inspiring teacher, with many of the characteristics of his hero, Benjamin Andrews. Both men challenged students to be men in the highest sense. Meiklejohn's ability to think and at the same time to be kind irresistibly drew students to him. His course in logic was not primarily devoted to the syllogisms of formal debate. It was rather a vigorous debate on "What is Truth?" Meiklejohn, a master of giving lectures, preferred the give-and-take of discussion because he believed it to be the only method that could teach critical thinking. At Brown he was able to organize and stimulate a class of as many as a hundred students so that every member became a vigorous participant. A student later remembered:

> The class was divided up and I was picked with a few others to propound and defend the thesis of the Sophists, which we did with utmost vigor. Before we finished, our position was torn to shreds by the class. In the process we learned to think, hard and sharply. This was Alexander Meiklejohn's great contribution to our generation, that he compelled people really to think.[4]

As a speaker Meiklejohn had certain handicaps—a high voice and a height of five feet, seven inches. His was not the graceful and effortless eloquence of ornamental speakers, but he could bring out the issue with startling clarity and drive home his remarks with such unexpected quickness of repartee and merciless logic that even the most unresponsive freshmen were aroused.

In his logic course (Philosophy 19) Meiklejohn wanted students to learn to defend a position. He taught them how to justify a contention and how to refute a statement, and then he let them practice on questions of their own choosing: Is it a duty to report a cribber (a man who cheats on an exam)? Is it right to engage in political combinations or deals? Is a promise always to be fulfilled? Are Sunday excursions justifiable? Is it right for a college ball player to accept any consideration for his service? Is the ambition to make Phi Beta Kappa laudable? Is capital punishment justifiable? This course came to be known as "Rag-Chewing 19," and students who could never finish their arguments in class formed the Sphinx Club in which to continue them.

Meiklejohn was learning while he was teaching, and later he said that his own philosophy was forged at Brown on his daily walks with the chairman of the philosophy department, Walter Goodnow Everett. Since both men had classes from nine to ten and from eleven to twelve three days a week, they walked together on these days from ten to eleven. On these walks Everett defended philosophical naturalism and Meiklejohn philosophical idealism. Both enjoyed the clarification that resulted from their clashes.

When Benjamin Andrews left in 1898, Brown acquired as its new president W. H. P. Faunce, who had been rector of the Fifth Avenue Baptist Church in New York where John D. Rockefeller was president of the Board of Trustees. President Faunce was experienced in raising money and in dealing with an institution's external relations, but he needed a dean who understood students and could handle discipline, class absences, sports, fraternities, and all the daily problems that affect the general morale. In 1901 Meiklejohn was appointed dean; after 1903 he served as undergraduate dean while another professor dealt with graduate affairs. Meiklejohn turned out to be just the complement that Faunce needed; their relationship was close and cordial even after Meiklejohn left Brown.

The qualities that made Meiklejohn an inspiring teacher made him a powerful dean. For him, philosophy was not simply an academic exercise but a way of thinking about the basic question people must face: "What shall we do?" Even as dean he forced students to think, as when he met around the table with representatives of the fraternities and insisted that they justify their manner of life.

Control of athletics became the central issue that engaged Dean Meiklejohn. He maintained that students should govern their own sports, that they could be relied on to curb any abuses that occurred in sports. A specific problem arose over the fact that some men who played baseball in the summer for money also played on the college teams. The colleges, including Brown, had ruled that these men must

*At **Brown**, Dean Meiklejohn continued to play cricket, one of his favorite sports.*

be disqualified from college baseball. Other colleges began overlooking this rule.

What should Brown do? Meiklejohn persuaded his school to stand by its agreement, even though it meant disqualifying its championship team. Some of the alumni were furious, but the faculty supported Meiklejohn and turned sports over to the students. They repaid his faith by establishing amateur sports and fair conduct. This incident confirmed Meiklejohn's belief that freedom could not be taught by compulsion. He had desperately wanted collegiate boys to learn to be free men and had set the conditions in which they could achieve that goal. They had not abused the freedom given them.

2. Making Minds at Amherst

Alexander Meiklejohn met Nannine La Villa while they were graduate students at Cornell, where she was studying art history. She came from an Italian family living in Orange, New Jersey. They were married in 1902, and during their years in Providence had three sons—Kenneth Alexander, born in 1907, Donald, born in 1909, and Gordon, born in 1911.

Five weeks after Gordon's birth, Amherst College asked Meiklejohn to become its president.

Standards at Amherst had declined during the two decades from 1890 to 1911. Alumni of the class of 1885 published an address to the trustees in 1910 complaining of low entrance standards, low salaries for the faculty, and failure to regulate extracurricular activities. They called for a return to the classics and an end to the Bachelor of Science degree. In 1911 the dispute over goals was waged in the *Amherst Graduates' Quarterly*. Religious leaders called for a return to piety; the faculty called for better scholarship. When a vacancy occurred in the presidency, the faculty made it known that their choice for president was George Olds, Amherst professor of mathematics.

The trustees ignored the faculty's plea. They wanted an exceptional man to lead Amherst into the modern world, someone who could bring it to life again and adapt it to the newly emerging goals of higher education. They inquired about Meiklejohn at Brown. Everyone there agreed he was an exceptional man who could promote both moral and intellectual development.

Some of Meiklejohn's friends advised him not to accept—Amherst

was a small town of only 5,000 people. The college was too conservative and narrow-minded. But Meiklejohn, having forged his ideas at
Brown and found them workable, wanted a chance to lead a whole
college. He was forty years old, and he was ready for the challenge.

Amherst had been founded to make preachers. This aim had
evolved into the more general one of making men. The new goal of
twentieth century higher education would be to make knowledge, but
Meiklejohn's own goal was to make minds. The difference between
making knowledge and making minds was not at all clear to the
Amherst trustees in 1912. Meiklejohn would teach them the

*Meiklejohn at his inauguration as president of Amherst College on
October 16, 1912.*

difference during his tenure, bringing more life to the school than the trustees had imagined, or could endure.

Meiklejohn believed that in college men should learn to think and that thinking means applying knowledge to the problems of living. He opposed an elective curriculum, since students could hardly be expected to make sense of discrete bits of knowledge stuck together in any fashion. He held the faculty responsible for devising a required curriculum that had some chance of leading students to understand the whole human situation. Meiklejohn instituted a freshman class called "Social and Economic Institutions" to get freshmen started thinking in the right direction. He wanted this class to study law because he thought law would reveal the full scope and complexity of conflicts and values in the United States. But no one on the faculty was ready to present law in terms of liberal understanding, so the course had to build on materials from politics and economics.

Throughout his presidency Meiklejohn kept proposing possible required curriculums, modifying them with electives in the upper years as a compromise with his opponents. He brought in stimulating new teachers; by 1922-23, when fourteen of the faculty were new and thirteen old, the new ones were attracting 1,110 of the 1,700 students. Meiklejohn also invited outstanding people from outside the college— William Butler Yeats, Charles Beard, Harold J. Laski, and Ernest Barker—to spend several weeks on campus stirring up controversies among the students.

Celebrated guests had been featured at many other colleges, but at Amherst Meiklejohn tried something no college had tried before. In collaboration with labor unions, he set up classes for workers in the mills at Holyoke and Springfield. Both faculty and students were encouraged to teach these classes in economics, history, government, reading and writing.

To help with this project Meiklejohn brought to Amherst a man who had pioneered in workers' education in England—R. H. Tawney. By 1920 Tawney had been on the executive board of the Workers Educational Association for fifteen years. During these years he had lectured to workers and had held tutorial classes through university extension departments. His first tutorial had been with thirty workers from Meiklejohn's home town of Rochdale. Tawney had become a legend with his students, who had taught him economic history and made him a socialist.

During his three months at Amherst in the spring of 1920 Tawney lectured in the medieval history course, gave a seminar on "The Control of Social Development," and gave four public lectures on industrial education in Britain. Meiklejohn came to count Tawney an "adored friend" and in 1964 still felt that "no other Englishman I have met has seemed to me so enlightened and so powerful."[5] Tawney returned to the London School of Economics and in the next decade published his major books: *The Acquisitive Society* (1921), *Religion and the Rise of Capitalism* (1926) and *Equality* (1931).

Perhaps most important for the liveliness of the campus, Meiklejohn himself continued to teach. In the classroom he was without rival. Here is one account of the Amherst years:

> No one who took his sophomore course in logic can forget its thrills. A hundred or more of us sat on benches in the dingy chemistry lecture hall where the periodic table of the elements on the chart before us was soon forgotten (along with the smells from the laboratory) as we watched and listened while Prexy held forth. He would begin with a selection from the *Euthyphro* or perhaps the *Phaedrus*. Then, eyes flashing, and voice trembling from excitement, he would carry the battle to us, testing our comprehension of what had been said, summoning us to debate, challenging us to criticize his thought and our own. There was nothing namby-pamby about his use of the discussion method—no easy-going "What do you think, Mr. Smith?" or "How do you feel, Mr. Jones?" Instead it was: "How should you think? What ought you to feel? What conclusion have you reached and why?" The effect of the sword-play was both devastating and stimulating in the extreme. Meiklejohn had that asset possessed only by the great teacher of a sense for the dramatic unity of the teaching hour. On occasions, before the closing bell, a kind of incandescence would descend on us, and the embers of the argument, so to speak, would burst into blazing flame. Afterward we would realize that the experience had touched us where we lived.[6]

In 1923 Roscoe Pound, the dean of the Harvard Law School, told a friend that "Amherst has sent us regularly, for the past five or six years, a little group of men who have stood absolutely at the head of the Law School. Their prominence has been out of all proportion to their numbers. How the miracle has been wrought I don't know," Pound said, "but they are sending us men who know how to think," testifying to the effectiveness of Meiklejohn and his faculty as teachers.[7]

3. Getting Fired at Amherst

Critical thinking is not comfortable to those who are criticized. "One of the awkward results of the . . . years of liberal thought in Amherst College was that it frequently made the sons of upper and middle class families zealous to liberate those whom their fathers exploited," a reporter noted.[8] President Meiklejohn's reforms had touched one group after another in vulnerable spots.

The classes in the factories touched parents, alumni, and trustees. They owned and ran the factories, and they expected their sons to follow them. Here was Amherst, to which they had sent their boys for safekeeping, encouraging them to sympathize with the workers and to question the foundations of capitalism.

Since Meiklejohn valued training the mind, he emphasized sports as a wholesome way to keep fit and to generate spirit and cooperation. To the annoyance of many alumni, he stressed intramural rather than intercollegiate games and urged amateur rather than professional coaching. Ironically, Meiklejohn was himself a better competitive athlete than those who found fault. He was still in demand for cricket games; he defeated students on the varsity team at tennis; and in squash, he remained New England champion, playing seldom but winning when he did.

In 1915 the alumni began asking for permanent baseball and football coaches; Meiklejohn steadfastly refused. They blamed him for Amherst's athletic decline, and at the Alumni Council meeting in November 1922, they presented a written request that he answer the question: How are we to measure the worth of Amherst if not in the generally recognized currency of athletic prowess?

Meiklejohn answered characteristically:

> When you look at our team on the field you will see college students playing football, not football players attending college in order to play. . . . The victory must take care of itself. If you win, you win. If you don't win, somebody else does. I don't know what more can be said.[9]

Meiklejohn clashed with Amherst tradition in other ways. He doubted whether World War I was necessary, and he was in no hurry to send the boys off. Before the United States entered the war, he opposed preparedness training on campus. In 1916 when Lt. Governor Calvin Coolidge (Amherst '95) presided over a preparedness meeting, Meiklejohn insisted that the views of those who opposed the war be represented. Meiklejohn counseled students to remain at Amherst as long as possible, for study was a reasonable form of patriotism, but he conceded that when they were drafted they must go.

Parents and alumni were upset by reports of some little details that seemed significant to them. Meiklejohn loved the Bible and the poetry of Robert Burns above all other literature. But when he noticed that students were taking the Bible for granted during chapel services, he dropped it as a regular feature and substituted readings from Robert Burns, from the Greek slave Epictetus, another of his favorites, and from *The New Republic*. No Bolshevik was on the faculty at Amherst, but Meiklejohn let it be known that he would be glad to have one, as long as he was a good teacher.

Meiklejohn and his family did not fit completely into the small-town, Congregational culture that prevailed in Amherst. Meiklejohn gave little thought to some social niceties; he did not always return letters or calls. He failed to attend town meetings because his attention was thoroughly on the college. His wife smoked and did not belong to the Ladies Aid or to the Congregational Church. She was busy with her three sons and a daughter, Ann, who was born in 1916, and her aged mother, who lived with them. She also continued her interests in art, music and literature. She traveled to Italy, brought back objects of art, which the college did not appreciate, and wrote a children's book called *A Cart of Many Colors*. These divergences from the local code provided grist for the rumor mill operated by Meiklejohn's opponents.

Meanwhile, real conflicts developed within the faculty. The group in control in 1912 consisted mostly of Amherst men comfortably settled in that charming town with a great deal of affection for the college. These department heads chose subordinates who were socially and intellectually compatible. Some took an instant dislike to Meiklejohn, who moved without delay or compromise to find the staff he wanted. After five years the faculty of twenty-seven consisted of half new men and half old ones. There was no adequate pension system, and since Meiklejohn could not fire without cause, he had to wait for the older men to reach retirement age. Some of them felt threatened and useless, while the younger men were eager and assertive. Bitter things were said and repeated.

For several years three factions existed in the faculty: pro Meiklejohn, anti Meiklejohn, and fence sitters. As support from the trustees cooled, the opposition within the faculty came out in the open. By the winter of 1922-23 the neutrals had taken sides. On any issue, the vote was two to one against Meiklejohn; the deadlock was complete.

The trustees gradually withdrew the support they had given Meiklejohn unanimously and enthusiastically in 1912. George A. Plimpton, president of Ginn and Company Publishers in Boston, was chairman of the Board of Trustees throughout Meiklejohn's presidency. Several of Meiklejohn's chief supporters died or retired from the original board, and the men who replaced them represented the critical sentiment of the alumni, and several were tied by personal friendship to the opposition on the faculty. One trustee, Stanley King, appointed in 1921, later became president of Amherst, and two others, Frederick J. E. Woodbridge and Dwight Morrow, would probably have liked to. Morrow, a partner in the banking firm of J. P. Morgan & Company, became a trustee of Amherst in 1916, and the banking and investment business of the college was consolidated in the hands of that company.

According to some of Meiklejohn's supporters, it was his questioning of the social order that the trustees opposed. Since they did not dare to dismiss him on the ground of his ideas, they alleged administrative incompetence. Under Meiklejohn, Amherst operated with an annual deficit, as it had the last year of his predecessor's tenure. Just how much was the deficit? This could not be ascertained, because in 1920 trustee Morrow had initiated a comprehensive study of Amherst's finances, and no treasurer's reports were issued between 1920 and 1924. When the study was finally released, it was favorable to Meiklejohn. Under his presidency the endowment had increased by 139 percent, more than twice the rate in the previous decade. The deficit was lower than had been supposed, for items that were capital improvements had been improperly charged as expenses. Although the market value of investments had seriously declined, that was the responsibility of the trustees, not of Meiklejohn.

But none of these facts were available in 1923. Besides, the trustees made it known that for several years the Meiklejohn household had not lived within its income and had been bailed out by individual trustees. In addition, they pointed out that Meiklejohn could not keep peace in his faculty and charged that this demonstrated incompetence.

Throughout these differences Meiklejohn continued his friendships with some of his opponents. He played tennis almost daily with one of the most conservative members of the opposition to his educational policies, Professor "Crock" Thompson. Meiklejohn's friend George Plimpton, chairman of the Board of Trustees, told him in 1921 that he had lost the confidence of the trustees. "That is unfortunate," replied Meiklejohn, "but under the circumstances it might be a good idea for the trustees to resign."[10]

The New Republic, in an open letter to trustee Dwight Morrow, challenged him to explain the real reasons for wanting Meiklejohn's dismissal and noted: "If the victories Meiklejohn was winning were your victories, you would have advised all other colleges to find presidents who neglected their personal finances."[11]

Amherst celebrated its hundredth anniversary in 1921. At the 100th commencement, while everyone else spoke of Amherst's history, Meiklejohn concluded with "What Does Amherst Hope To Be in the Next Hundred Years?" Afterward he sailed to Europe for a year of rest, while alumni and trustees got busy raising a centennial gift of $3,000,000.

Meiklejohn returned in the fall of 1922, and by commencement time in 1923 matters had come to a head. On Tuesday, June 19, the chairman of the Board of Trustees transmitted to Meiklejohn the Board's opinion that it was not advisable for him to continue as administrative head of the college, though they desired him to continue as professor of logic and metaphysics.

Within hours Meiklejohn resigned both as president and as professor. The trustees promptly accepted his resignation. Meiklejohn went to the baseball game and sat through it all next to his friend George Plimpton who, as chairman of the trustees, had announced Meiklejohn's resignation just an hour earlier.

The next day was commencement, and emotions ran high. In his final speech Meiklejohn said simply: "I don't know where I am to go, but I know that I am to do the same thing again in the same way."

In June, 1923, at age fifty-one, Meiklejohn faces the future deter-
mined to carry on his work.

Twelve seniors refused their diplomas. Eight members of the faculty resigned. Many juniors felt as if the gates of life had been slammed shut. At the alumni lunch that day, Meiklejohn concluded: "I differ from you on most of the issues of life, and I shall keep it up."

The trustees appointed as president George Olds, then seventy years old, and Amherst College returned to its quiet tradition of accepting the social order.

Meiklejohn returned to his quest. Through the publicity surrounding his dismissal from Amherst, he gained a national audience who saw him as a defender of principle against entrenched interests. Like Andrews at Brown and Woodrow Wilson at Princeton, he became a shining symbol. Liberals flocked to his banner. He received a flood of letters from supporters all over the country. He needed time for making a decision on his future course, so in the summer of 1923 he moved his family to New York City as a base from which to write and lecture. His wife, ill with an undiagnosed condition, left with her mother and daughter for a year's rest in Italy.

Meiklejohn quickly put together a collection of Amherst speeches and essays that were published under the title *Freedom and the College* (New York: The Century Company, 1923). In the introduction he included a tribute to Benjamin Andrews, whom the trustees of Brown had dismissed while Meiklejohn was a student there. He recalled one aspect of Andrews that his own recent experience had made particularly vivid:

> More than any other man whom I have known in college office, Andrews mastered administration, made it his servant, kept it in its place. . . . I sometimes think that no man should be allowed to have administration in his charge unless he loathes it, unless he wishes to be doing something else. I dare not trust the willing middlemen of life, the men who like arranging other men and their affairs, who find manipulation satisfying to their souls. These men if they can have their way will make of life a smooth, well-lubricated meaninglessness. Andrews was not like that. He was a scholar and teacher. He knew that colleges exist for teaching and study, and what he cared for was that study and teaching should be done. He was a maker of men because he had a mad, impetuous vision of what a man may be. He wanted something done, something accomplished in the spirit of

man. For him administration was Idea guiding and controlling circumstance. It was not, as many men demand it should be made, mere circumstances slipping smoothly past each other in the flow of time.

On the lecture circuit Meiklejohn's most popular speech was called "Democracy and Excellence." He never wrote it down, each time depending on his audience to draw it from him. He gave it repeatedly to enthusiastic listeners, 3,000 people at Carnegie Hall, New York City, on October 21, 1923, for instance. His slight build belied his ability to hold throngs without a microphone. He talked about the conflict between the moral imperative to be sensitive to life, to keep it high in quality—excellence—and the moral imperative to share whatever is excellent, to be sure all people have a chance at it—democracy. In the United States, said Meiklejohn, people are overwhelmed with opportunity and possessions, but life is not good because we do not understand the difference between good and bad. Some fear that excellence, when given to the crowd, will be pulled down. But the United States has ventured to unite both excellence and democracy; whether we can succeed or will break down under the fundamental conflict is not yet known. But we must make a good try at it. We must start by facing the fact that we do not yet have even the beginnings of the educational system required for this task.

4. Building the Experimental College

From 1923 to 1925 Meiklejohn wrote articles for popular magazines— *Harper's, The Saturday Review,* and *The Century Magazine.* Glenn Frank, the editor of *Century,* became so interested in Meiklejohn's description of what a liberal college ought to be that he set up a committee in New York to study the question of establishing a new college. In January 1925, *Century* published Meiklejohn's article "A New College, Notes on the Next Step in Higher Education." When Roscoe Pound, dean of the School of Law at Harvard, declined to become Wisconsin's new president, the committee, without consulting the Wisconsin faculty, offered Glenn Frank the job. He accepted, and before he assumed office, offered Meiklejohn a professorship.

Meiklejohn did not accept immediately. His wife, Nannine, had just died of cancer in February 1925, after twenty-two years of marriage, leaving Meiklejohn with four children not yet fully raised—Kenneth, seventeen, Donald, fifteen, Gordon, thirteen, and Ann, eight. Moving to Madison at the age of fifty-three would require him to set up a whole new life.

Six months later, in January 1926, Frank wrote Meiklejohn again. He said he had found a way to create and sustain an experimental college within the university if Meiklejohn would agree to run it. Meiklejohn accepted, assuming the post of professor of philosophy in March 1926, teaching one course, and planning the Experimental College.

In June 1926, Meiklejohn married Helen Everett, whom he had met first when he was a student at Brown and she was two years old. Helen's father, Walter Goodnow Everett, had started out as Meiklejohn's teacher. Later he became Meiklejohn's colleague and closest friend at Brown. Helen had graduated from Bryn Mawr, then had earned a master's degree from Radcliffe and a Ph.D. from the Brookings Graduate School of Economics and Government in Washington, D.C. She had taught economics at Vassar, then worked with the Brookings Institute of Economics. She was busy writing a book with Isador Lubin, *The British Coal Dilemma* (New York: Macmillan, 1929) when she married Meiklejohn. Helen was not able to take a place on the faculty of the University of Wisconsin, since regulations there prohibited both husband and wife from holding positions above the level of instructor.

During the early fall of 1926, Meiklejohn addressed the National Student Federation in Ann Arbor, Michigan. In this speech he gave one of his clearest descriptions of the paradox of freedom as it applies to college students:

> Students so often say that what they would like to have in college is freedom, to be themselves, to do as they choose, each to go his own way, freedom from interest, from requirements, individual freedom.
>
> I'm as much committed to freedom as anyone, and yet I am quite sure that no college or other institution can be organized on the basis of freedom in this negative sense. There are very definite limitations under which freedom can be given to the membership of a social group. It is possible only where the freedom which each man takes is of such character that it contributes to the freedom of every other member of the community.

Freedom is possible in a community only when all the members of the community are so disposed in mind and so equipped in intelligence that the action they will take when free shall be such, not only that it will not interfere with another, but will contribute to the freedom of every other; when every member has the same purpose in mind.

Separate freedom is possible in a group of people only when that group of people has something which dominates every member of the group, every member of the community has a sameness of obligation, only when the whole thing is dominated, controlled, obliged, ruled by some central purpose; and that is true of a college as well as any other institution.

I would like to see every member of a college community free only by finding a certain compelling, dominant, central motive, which every member of the community receives and takes as his own. The college must find a purpose, common to all its members, accepted by all its members, before every member can be set free to further that purpose in his own way. If then we presuppose that an American college becomes a community of intelligence, it means that all the members of the community accept the same gospel of intellect as their guide in life.[12]

The Experimental College opened in the fall of 1927 as a two-year course with a freshman class of 119 and a faculty of eleven chosen by Meiklejohn. Its goals were to get students to think about human problems, without being restricted by academic disciplines, and to get them to construct a scheme of reference, which they could use to make sense of specialized knowledge as they acquired it later in their last two years in the regular university classrooms.

To achieve cohesion and identity, Meiklejohn wanted the Experimental College to be residential, with staff and students living and working together. This proved impossible, however, because the university did not have at its disposal a building suitable for such arrangements. The Experimental College had to be accommodated within an existing dormitory, which it shared with regular students. Offices for the staff and a room for the college's library were included in the dormitory, but since it was a men's dorm, women had to be excluded from the college. Meiklejohn regretted this, but if he had insisted on co-ed dormitories, the college would never have opened, since such arrangements were unheard of at that time. If he had given up united living arrangements, he would have given up an essential principle, that the most important learning takes place in the informal life outside the classroom.

The Experimental College could be a radical departure from traditional curriculum and teaching methods because the faculty of the College of Letters and Science approved it with almost no restrictions. They stipulated that there had to be a grade for the two years' work and that students had to be permitted to take one course in the regular university during each of the experimental years, because certain degree programs required languages taken during the first two years. No other restrictions were placed. Whatever work was done in the Experimental College would be given the usual number of credits and considered by Letters and Science as fulfilling the usual requirements of the first two years.

What did Meiklejohn and his staff do with their freedom? First they abandoned all courses and subjects. Instead they planned a curriculum with one central theme for each of the two years. The first was to be devoted to the study of Athenian civilization in the fifth century B.C., from Pericles to Plato. The second year the students would become immersed in the civilization of the United States in the nineteenth and twentieth centuries. The contrast between these two civilizations was intended to bring into focus the common underlying problems of human living in Western societies. To bring these problems home, each student would be required to conduct a regional study, an investigation of his own home region, modeled on the recent study by Robert and Helen Lynd, *Middletown*. Students would conduct this investigation during the summer vacation betweeen their two years at the college and would submit it by January of their second year.

When put into effect, the curriculum of the first year fell into three parts—1) a general survey of fifth-century Athens, 2) a study of eight aspects of Greek life: economics, politics, art, literature, law, religion, science and philosophy, and 3) a specialized study of one of these aspects on a topic chosen by each student. The specific assignments changed slightly from year to year.

What comprised a weekly assignment during the freshman year? This is one, assigned on October 20, 1930:

In our study of Greek society we find men holding conflicting opinions in regard to matters of public policy. Both parties to a controversy are observed to claim "right" or "justice" in suppport of their views. A question naturally arises as to the meaning and validity of these terms. The reading and discussion during the coming week will be concerned mainly with this question.

Reading:
Otto, M.C., *Things and Ideals,* pp. 57-155
McGilvary, E. B., *Warfare of Moral Ideals*
Plato, *The Republic,* Bk.I and Bk.II to p. 368
Thucydides' *History of the Peloponnesian War,* Plataean
    Episode, pp. 146-152, 183-187, 204-217; Melian Episode,
    pp. 392-401; Mitylenian Episode, pp. 187-204

Paper, due October 27:
The student is requested to take one of the above episodes and examine it in the light of the week's reading and discussion. Is there a "right" involved in the situation? If not, give the basis for your judgment. If so, how do you justify your opinion?

Talks:
Tuesday, October 21, Professor McGilvary of the University Department of Philosophy.
Thursday, Occtober 23, Professor Otto of the University Department of Philosophy.
Friday, October 24, Mr. Boegholt will lead the discussion.
Saturday, October 25, Mr. Boegholt will lead the discusssion.

The curriculm for the second year fell into four parts: physical science (six weeks), nineteenth-century U.S. democracy (eight weeks), contemporary U.S. literature (twelve weeks), and contemporary philosophy (four weeks). The two weeks following the study of physical science were devoted to organizing the regional study since students were not accustomed to social investigations and needed direction. Some of the books featured during this second year were *Middletown* by Robert and Helen Lynd; *Other People's Money and How the Banks Use It* by Louis Brandeis, then sitting on the Supreme Court; *The*

Acquisitive Society by Meiklejohn's friend R. H. Tawney; and *The Education of Henry Adams.*

By Meiklejohn's definition, liberal studies could be carried out successfully only on the basis of common goals and materials—a required curriculum. Yet the same principle of liberal studies when applied to methods expressed itself in freedom of action, not in requirement. Students themselves must assume responsibilty for the commitment they had made. Once committed to a specific course of study, they must be able to pursue that work in ways that expressed their inner individualities. Teachers must not say either, "Do as you please," or "I cannot help." Rather they must say, convincingly: "The time has come for your freedom; you must make it for yourself."

The faculty of the Experimental College, three of whom had been with Meiklejohn at Amherst, agreed to be called advisers rather than professors or teachers. To carry out the principle of freedom, they abolished all compulsion connected with the daily work. To help a student get through his assignments, three kinds of meetings were arranged: 1) class meetings, three or four times a week, attended by the class as a whole and by the advisers; 2) personal conferences of an adviser and a student once a week; and 3) meetings of groups of about twelve students under the direction of an adviser, once a week. In addition, the college as a whole met once a week to try to accomplish in a secular way the purpose of the college chapel of older days.

To give students the opportunity to decide whether they were capable of self-direction, advisers removed all external rewards and penalties. Because the customs of the larger university required that they assign a letter grade, they did so, but only to the regional study and the final study made at the end of the sophomore year. These two grades together formed the final grade for two years' work. The daily meetings and conferences had no external rewards or penalties attached—only the satisfaction of getting on with the craft of reading, writing, and thinking. Each full-time adviser was assigned by lot twelve students, who rotated to a new adviser every six weeks. At the end of each six-week period, the advisers wrote estimates of the progress of each of their students. These estimates were kept on file, and, together with the reports written by the students, provided a permanent record of how things went.

How did things go? For the advisers it was a killing task—being tutors, speakers, counselors, and curriculum committees

simultaneously. They could not hide within the bounds of their own
fields. They had to learn to talk without lecturing. They had to teach
while at the same time devising a scheme for teaching. All of them
except Meiklejohn had joint appointments in regular departments of
the College of Letters and Science with a teaching load there of one-
third time. Some of them had to cope with the criticism and hostility
of the regular staff. But the advisers had been chosen for their capacity and eagerness for this sort of work. Their exhilaration was as
intense as their burden, as students came to intellectual life in their
care.

Meiklejohn assembled an extraordinary group of young advisers—
men who proved deeply congenial with one another and who continued after the Experimental College to have distinguished and produc-
tive careers. In the brief years of the experiment they broadened their
interests, learned in spirited company materials never before considered by them, and confronted the social and economic issues of
their time. Nothing of academic hierarchy tainted the college. Meiklejohn as chairman led the staff as a cohort of equals, and the young
advisers shared in decision-making as they had never previously been
allowed to do. For many, the experience of the college determined the
fundamental direction of their subsequent lives and careers. A few of
the more prominent names may suggest the range and quality of the
staff: John Beecher, teacher and poet; Robert Havighurst, physicist
turned educator; Walter Agard, chairman of the Classics department
at the University of Wisconsin; Lucien Koch, director of Commonwealth College; Malcolm Sharp, School of Law, University of
Chicago.

The methods devised at the beginning of the Experimental College
changed very little, but the content of the curriculum was always
under discussion and revision. The staff used Greek material because
it was more fully developed than any other comparative material at
the time. By the later years of the college, advisers enjoyed playing the
game of substituting civilizations: "If we compared _____ to _____,
what materials would we use? But they kept to the general
Athens/America theme, and controversy centered on what books to
read. After several years of experimentation, Plato's *Republic* and *The
Education of Henry Adams* came to be the central book of each year
respectively. Some advisers felt that more time should be given to
Jefferson and the Constitution than to Henry Adams, but they did not

prevail. A few students strongly disliked *The Education of Henry Adams,* but in general students responded to it with excellent papers. The regional study proved to be the most effective and stimulating part of the curriculum. Students had to learn how to interview people, how to grasp the complexities of their own communities. The staff observed the students practicing exactly what the teachers wanted them to learn.

Student activities flourished at the Experimental College. Given freedom, students created in the first year alone the Players, the Workshop, the Philosophy Club, the Forum, the Law Group, the Music Group, and the Dancers. The Book Group produced an annual, *The First Year of the Experimental College,* and the literary students published a miscellany of their writing. The Players produced several plays of excellent quality, including Aristophanes' *The Clouds,* Euripedes' *Electra,* and an expurgated, raucous production of *Lysistrata.* In succeeding years the Players produced *Antigone* in a translation done by one of their members. This raised some eyebrows in the departments of Greek and drama; after all, the student who made the translation had studied Greek with "Doc" Agard for only one year. "The Hill," as the guinea pigs called the regular university, was not accustomed to such uninhibited zest for thought and for action.

What kind of students did the Experimental College attract? Were they significantly different from the usual students at Wisconsin? Both President Frank and Chairman Meiklejohn hoped they would be a regular cross-section, so that the results of the experiment would fully apply to regular instruction. For Meiklejohn's purposes, this condition was essential. Writing in 1927 for the Wisconsin magazine, *Survey Graphic,* he described his intentions:

> We wish to experiment on the general run of students. It seems to me that the vital social question in American education today is not, How well can we do with specially qualified groups of students? but rather, Can our young people as a whole be liberally educated? Must we accept the aristocratic division of people into two classes, one of which can be trained to understand while the other is doomed by its own incapacity to remain forever outside the field of intelligence? . . . For the present our primary task is that of taking all types of young people and discovering their powers.[13]

The first year, before the college had a reputation, some students were drawn by Meiklejohn's reputation at Amherst. Some freshmen were sent by high school principals who said, "We think this is a hopeless student; you try." One was sent by a football coach in the belief that all his time would be free for practice, and one came because his father, a farmer, mistook the Experimental College for the Agricultural Experiment Station. The Experimental College made no selection; it welcomed warmly all applicants.

Meiklejohn is surrounded by the staff and students of the Experimental College, 1927-28.

Of the initial 119 students, only one came from Madison (Meiklejohn's son Gordon), and only forty-three came from other parts of Wisconsin (thirty-seven percent). Thirty-nine (thirty-three percent) came from other midwestern states, and twenty-seven (twenty-three percent) came from eastern states. The second freshman class again had thirty-seven percent from Wisconsin; this compared with seventy-four percent of the university's general enrollment coming from state residents. Of this class, thirty percent were from

large cities (over one million) and twenty-six percent from small
towns (under 10,000).

On the Scholastic Aptitude Test the scores of the Experimental
College freshmen (average: 80.3 percentile) surpassed those of regular
UW freshmen (average: 57.6 percentile). The percentage of Jewish
students in the Experimental College was found to range from about
twenty percent in the class of 1927-28 to forty percent in the class of
1930-31. The portion of Jewish students in the regular university was
estimated as ten-fifteen percent of the entire enrollment.

So the Experimental College was not a representative sample of the
University of Wisconsin. It attracted a larger portion of students from
outside the state, from large cities, and from Jewish backgrounds than
did the regular university, and its students did significantly better on
their entering SAT than did regular students.

The Bureau of Guidance and Research compiled this information
in a report it made on the Experimental College in 1932. This was a
period of pervasive quotas limiting Jewish students in graduate
schools and of close scrutiny of the percentage of Jewish undergraduates. Few black students enrolled in the Experimental College,
although the Bureau of Guidance and Records did not record this
information. Apparently one black student, the national collegiate
champion in forensics, was enrolled in the regular university during
this time; this, too, went unrecorded in university documents.

Behind these cold facts lay some complex realities. When the
Experimental College welcomed its first class in 1927, most of the
United States was still enjoying postwar prosperity. Republican Calvin
Coolidge was president, and in the national election the following year
Republican Herbert Hoover, carrying all but eight states, defeated the
Catholic Democrat Alfred E. Smith. A straw vote among students at
the Experimental College in October 1928 showed that seventy-nine
favored Hoover, fifty-eight were for Smith, and forty-two were for
Norman Thomas of the Socialist Party.

A year later, in October 1929, the stock market crashed and the
Depression set in. In 1930 the University doubled its tuition. Many
students had to delay or quit their studies. The Experimental College
had planned to take a class of 125 each year, and the number of
freshmen in the first year, 1927-28, was 119. But the number dropped
to ninety-two in 1928-29. Only seventy-nine registered in 1929-30,
and seventy-four in 1930-31. Many of these suffered constant

financial uncertainty. Meiklejohn set up a loan fund to help students stay in school, appealing to the students from higher-income families to contribute money to help their fellows. Distribution of wealth was no abstract intellectual problem. Some students could not purchase the Experimental College's blazer for $7.50, while a few could squander large amounts for weekend amusements.

The state of Wisconsin had both a socialist and a progressive tradition. In 1911 the Socialists elected the mayor of Milwaukee, Daniel W. Hoan, and the representative to Congress, Victor Berger. The Socialist Party stayed in power in Milwaukee for twenty years. The Progressives, a wing of the Republican Party, elected Robert La Follette governor three times and in 1906 sent him to the U.S. Senate for the next nineteen years. La Follette ran for president of the United States on a third-party ticket in 1924, a year before his death. In 1930 his sons controlled Wisconsin politics— Phillip La Follette as governor and Robert La Follette, Jr., as U.S. senator. In 1931 the Wisconsin legislature was the first in the country to pass an unemployment insurance act, drafted in part by Paul Raushenbush, an adviser at the Experimental College. The Progressives wanted to regulate capitalism rather than replace it.

These social and economic issues had to be dealt with by the Experimental College. But how? At Amherst, Meiklejohn had labored to raise these issues, but by the time he got to Wisconsin, the Depression had thrown them into urgent perspective. In public speeches Meiklejohn had persistently criticized the competitiveness and materialistic values of capitalism, but he had never joined the Socialist Party, or any other political party. He believed in some kind of cooperative socialism, and he voted regularly for Norman Thomas. In 1927 he became a national vice-president of the League for Industrial Democracy, a national group founded in 1905 to promote the study of socialism, especially in colleges and universities. He never gave up this position.

Chairman Meiklejohn chose some advisers with socialist connections. Walter Raymond Agard had been president of the Amherst chapter of the League for Industrial Democracy, while it was still called the Intercollegiate Socialist Society. Lucien Koch came from (and returned to) Commonwealth College in rural Arkansas, a socialist college established to train working-class people as political leaders. Percy Dawson was the representative from Wisconsin to the national

committee of the League for Industrial Democracy in 1925-26. Delos
Otis and John Powell ran for local office in Madison on the Socialist
ticket.

The advisers did not try to keep their interests and struggles outside the classroom. They made Wisconsin's legislative proposals and
enactments required reading. They took students to attend legislative
hearings and debates. They took sides on public issues and defended
their positions; they asked students to do likewise.

Meiklejohn set the example. He welcomed polemics as a good way
to clarify and understand a problem. Argument was, for him, a
mutual search for truth, not a device for humiliating an opponent. His
students never forgot him, standing firm and erect, breathing fire
through thin white nostrils, but never more than a word away from a
generous thought and a smile. Most students came to feel at ease with
him, even in disagreement, as he taught them to question, to criticize,
to think—and then to decide and commit themselves to a position.

The students staked out as many positions as they could reasonably
defend. A minority of the Experimental College students was radical,
but it was a larger minority than at the regular university. The communist group of perhaps half a dozen was vocal, and the state press
exaggerated any incident they could uncover. They had a field day
when one of the Experimental College students was arrested in
Milwaukee for participating in a demonstration allegedly led by Communists. The same student ran for state governor on the Communist
Party ticket as a resident of the House of Correction, to which he had
been sentenced.

Another much publicized incident occurred in February 1928,
when Dora Russell came to Madison to speak about the school she
ran in England with Bertrand Russell. No group in Madison, including
the university, would permit her to speak because she had publicly
advocated sexual intercourse before marriage. Some members of the
Experimental College formed a Free Speech Club and located a place
for her to speak at a Unitarian church. Bertrand Russell had stayed
with the Meiklejohns the previous year, and Dora was their guest on
this visit, a fact that the local press made certain everyone knew.
Some women made a point of crossing the street to avoid meeting
Mrs. Helen Meiklejohn on the sidewalk.

The Depression was not the only cause of declining enrollment in
the Experimental College. Unsympathetic accounts in the newspapers

caused rural parents to be anxious about the cultural and political environment of the college. They worried that their sons would not acquire there the knowledge they would need in order to specialize in their final years and prepare for jobs on the depressed market. The success of the college in attracting Jewish students repelled some people. Others were deterred by persistent rumors spread by resentful students, faculty, and administrators from the regular university that the experiment would soon be abandoned.

5. Losing the Experimental College

By Christmas vacation, 1930, the problems of declining enrollment and hostile public opinion had become so acute that a delegation from the Experimental College called on George Clark Sellery, Dean of the College of Letters and Science and professor of history. They appealed to him to speak up for the college. He agreed to do so only if the college would introduce final exams for each year of the course. The delegation rejected this condition, and aggravations continued between the Experimental College and the College of Letters and Science.

The administration of the Experimental College both was and was not autonomous, and this internal contradiction caused many problems. Teachers in the Experimental College were considered regular members of their respective departments in the College of Letters and Science. But they were chosen by Meiklejohn, not by the regular departments, and several of them came from Amherst and other institutions; only a few had been selected from the staff already at Wisconsin. All except Meiklejohn gave one-third of their time to the regular program and received one-third of their salary from their regular departments.

The budget for the Experimental College came directly from President Glenn Frank, who reserved certain special bequests for this purpose. Meiklejohn had complete power to determine salaries in the Experimental College, and these he often set higher than comparable ones in the regular departments. Jealousies arose. The dean of the College of Letters and Science, who viewed Meiklejohn as an upstart challenging his own jurisdiction, was not a man known for magnanimity.

Each year the advisers of the Experimental College reported to the faculty of the College of Letters and Science. In their report of

February 1931, they asked that no freshmen be admitted to the class of 1931-32, so that the fifth year could be used to take stock and consider future policy. This decision was reached after internal disagreement about strategy. For Meiklejohn it was a matter of principle that the Experimental College be the University of Wisconsin experimenting. If the university did not wish to experiment, then for him the Experimental College had lost its reason for being. He persuaded the advisers to seek reaffirmation from the College of Letters and Science, although it seemed unlikely that such approval would be given.

In January 1932, Meiklejohn presented on behalf of the advisers a comprehensive report on their five-year experimentation. (This report was published as Alexander Meiklejohn, *The Experimental College,* New York: Harper & Brothers, 1932, reprinted by Arno Press, 1971.) This "big report" evaluated the gains and losses, the achievements and difficulties as seen by the advisers. It concluded that the university should continue the experimentation it had begun.

The report made two recommendations as to how the experiment should proceed. 1) There should be four experimental units instead of one for freshman/sophomore instruction—one for men in a dorm, one for women in a dorm, one for men without dorm arrangements, and one co-ed without dorm arrangements. 2) There should be an experimental unit working on problems of instruction in the junior and senior years.

The faculty of Letters and Science established a committee of five to consider this "big report," and in April 1932, presented its response. Four test units would require the enrollment of a larger fraction of the incoming freshman class and of the faculty "than past experience gives the assurance would voluntarily take advantage of such opportunity, and this uncertainty as to the attitude of students and faculty towards the project would tend to demoralize the plans of the university for 1933-34." Instead, the committee recommended a single test unit, coeducational and nonresidential, with two hundred freshmen who would take half integrated courses and half regular courses during their first two years.

The advisers of the Experimental College found this proposal unsatisfactory. They offered amendments, namely, that the number of freshmen not exceed one hundred, that the course of study apply to all four years, and that a maximum of five credits a semester be courses in the regular university.

During this debate, President Glenn Frank was present, but he did not speak up for the Experimental College. He realized that he had not established a base of support within the university. (Five years later the trustees were able to remove him without due process, and with no protest from the faculty.)

The faculty of Letters and Science never voted on the advisers' proposals; they were referred to a new committee to be appointed by Dean Sellery. The dean did not make the appointments. In November 1932, he asked the faculty if they really wanted such a committee, in view of the economic depression that had caused waivers and cuts of staff salaries the previous July. The faculty voted to postpone the committee until the economic crisis had passed, and the committee was never appointed.

The Experimental College of the University of Wisconsin closed its doors in June 1932. It had enrolled only 327 students. But its effect on many of them proved extraordinary, and its influence lived on. The solidarity of the "guinea pigs" and their sense that something special had happened to them were expressed repeatedly at reunions in 1942, 1962, and 1977. The idea of the college persisted and found expression in other experiments, among them the Integrated Liberal Studies program at the University of Wisconsin from 1948 to 1980, the Experimental Program at the University of California-Berkeley from 1965 to 1969, and the Evergreen State College at Olympia, Washington.

Alexander Meiklejohn, now sixty, might have been discouraged at having his program discontinued once again. But he was not. He believed that to go down with an idea is to make it live. His values and beliefs had not been defeated or invalidated; they had been overcome momentarily by the circumstances. He retained his exuberance at having been able to engage real problems, however briefly. The opposition he had aroused served to confirm that he had identified correctly the essential issues.

The University of Wisconsin and Meiklejohn arranged that he would stay on part-time as professor of philosophy. Since he needed to be in Madison only during the fall semester, the Meiklejohns moved to Berkeley, California, in the summer of 1932 to give him the quiet he needed for writing. Helen had spent a year in Berkeley years before, helping her father with his book, *Moral Values* (1918), so Berkeley to her seemed the ideal place for writing. They also had many friends in Berkeley and San Francisco.

6. Stirring Up Adults in San Francisco

Even before moving to Berkeley, Meiklejohn had been contacted by
people in San Francisco who wanted him to found a school for adults.
Meiklejohn had long been eager to teach adults. He knew that the
ability to think critically could not be stamped into people by four
years of college, even with the best education—and that did not prevail. Besides, many able adults had never been to college. After
Amherst, Meiklejohn had been asked to join the staff of the New
School for Social Research in New York. He had gone to Wisconsin
instead, but he admired their work. Here was a chance to establish a
similar school on the West Coast.

At the San Francisco School for Social Studies, Meiklejohn aimed
to arouse all kinds of people to think critically and systematically
about social problems. Democracy required serious thinking from its
functioning adults, and not nearly enough was being done to promote
it, he believed. Being open-minded was not sufficient. Adults had to
make decisions, to take sides, and to bear the consequences. Thinking
meant focusing on controversy, and Meiklejohn was prepared to do
just that.

From the beginning the San Francisco School for Social Studies
was a small private agency, independent of the public school system
and any university, funded by private subscriptions raised by a board
of leading citizens. One early benefactor who made it possible for the
school to start was Andrew Welch. He had become a millionaire in the
sugar industry and gave to please his daughter. She had met Meiklejohn through her teacher, one of his students at Brown. Leon and
Dorothy Liebes gave office space in their building, which housed a
famous fur shop on the ground level and a library of metaphysical
books on the top floor. The budget for the opening year was less than
$4,000.

The school got underway in January 1934. The faculty for the first
year consisted of four permanent staff: Alexander and Helen Meiklejohn; John Powell, from the Experimental College; and Charles
Hogan, from the philosophy department of the University of
California-Berkeley. Three temporary faculty also helped the first
year, including Walter Goodnow Everett, Helen Meiklejohn's father.

Three hundred students signed up. They were selected by interview
with no weight given to ability to pay or to previous education, but

rather on the basis of seriousness of purpose. No fees were charged. Students had to agree to attend regularly, to read assignments, and to participate in the discussions. Twenty groups of fifteen students each were organized. One group led by Alexander Meiklejohn was from the Bakery Wagon Drivers; one led by Helen Meiklejohn was from the International Ladies' Garment Workers' Union.

The staff of the San Francisco School for Social Studies was experimenting in adult education. They did not know in advance what the content, source materials or method of a curriculum for adults should be, but they agreed on two hypotheses. People learn best when they can see and imitate the best possible model of what they want to learn. Teachers teach best when they invite students to share what they enjoy doing most.

The staff decided that the content of the curriculum would be the ideas of the finest social thinkers as developed by the thinkers themselves, not as someone else described them. This meant that great books, not textbooks or other secondary materials, would be used. The method would be discussion, since no other method could provide a means for adults to take an active part in the practice of thinking.

The books chosen were ones the staff enjoyed most and thought most likely to generate controversy and argument. In the first year different groups started with Plato, *The Republic;* Strachey, *The Coming Struggle for Power;* Dewey, *Individualism, Old and New;* and Rugg, *Culture and Education in America.* They moved on to Tawney, *The Acquisitive Society;* Veblen, *The Vested Interests;* and Ortega y Gasset, *Revolt of the Masses.* The second year successful sequences of books began to emerge—Adam Smith, Karl Marx, and Thorstein Veblen, or *The Republic* along with Dewey's *Human Nature and Conduct.*

After the first semester, Helen Meiklejohn reviewed the purpose of the school in an interview for *The Christian Science Monitor* (July 18, 1934). She stated that "the San Francisco School for Social Studies is dedicated to the task of enabling people to understand and control the social order in which they live." The school proceeds, she explained, on the premise that all is not right with the capitalist system, that that is a matter of fact not opinion, and that maldistribution of income and unbridled profit have resulted in serious abuse. The first object is to rectify these abuses—a political task. The second aim is to enable people to exercise intelligently the increased control they will be asked to exert—a social problem. "In every respect," she concluded, "the school is an ally of democracy. It will teach and teach until the nation has constructed such a backlog of intelligence that the fire of democracy would never burn out, even under the deluge of Fascist and Communist propaganda."

Mrs. Meiklejohn gave this interview in the midst of the San Francisco general strike that closed down the city completely for four days in July 1934. The longshoremen had already closed the port for sixty-eight days, demanding a fair system for hiring dock workers, not revolution as some wealthy citizens feared. In the tense city, the School for Social Studies tried to deal with the educational needs of the total community. The school made clear that it advocated no political or economic doctrines. As a result it was under fire from all the parties seeking control of the community.

John Powell later described how these tensions affected the school:

> Every partisan group either wanted the School to serve its purposes, or feared it was lent to the service of the opposing group. Some saw its curriculum as too radical; others saw its sponsors as too respectable. The School's task was to get both those parties into its study-groups and make them talk together. One section of people resented the School's offering further education to people who had already been to college; another was suspicious of the School's work with labor unions. But the School was trying to show both the dressmaker and the doctor of philosophy that intelligence has other functions than the garnering of credits. Committed to a policy of keeping the study-groups open to all without cost, so as to keep the range of membership as wide as possible, the School was refused money because the students were not asked to pay their own way, and also because the small voluntary registration fee was asserted to be keeping people out of the groups.[14]

By the end of the 1935-36 academic year the school was firmly on its feet. It had a teaching faculty of five permanent and four associate staff. John Powell had become its director, a position he held until 1942; Alexander Meiklejohn continued to teach but dropped administrative duties for time to write. Some of San Francisco's most influential citizens served on the board of directors: businessman Mortimer Fleishhacker, Jr., James K. Moffitt, attorney Bartley A.

Crum, Mrs. Edward Macauley, Bishop Edward L. Parsons, Rabbi Irving Reichert, and Robert Gordon Sproul, president of the University of California. The school had received small grants from the Workers' Education Bureau and from the Elmhurst Fund to expand its program with working people.

However, the finances of the school were never secure; its staff could never see more than a year ahead. For the year 1937-38 the Carnegie Corporation provided a grant through the American Foundation for Adult Education to expand the program. In January 1939, the Rosenberg Foundation of San Francisco provided a two-year grant of $10,000 a year to set up a branch program in Sonoma County to test whether the methods of the school were applicable to rural communities.

Between 1934 and 1942 the school enrolled 1,400 students formed into 120 groups in San Francisco and over 300 students in thirty groups in Sonoma County. Sixty percent of the students were women. Eleven percent were in manual crafts and trades, seventeen percent were clerical workers, seventeen percent were nonpaid married women, and forty percent were in professional occupations. A dozen labor unions were represented by nearly a hundred members. Seventy percent of the students had some schooling beyond high school; twenty-two percent had graduate training. But the college graduates were never alone in their groups: the vitality of the school stemmed from the mixture of its members. In political terms, the students ranged from a mild right-wing to an energetic left-liberal orientation. The students who persisted and who signed up repeatedly tended to be the leaders of whatever group they represented. Many women emerged to become influential civic leaders in San Francisco.

World War II killed the school. Time for reflection and money were no longer available. The school closed in 1942 with most of the staff convinced that adult education should be supported by some public agency—municipal libraries or state universities.

7. *Writing It All Down*

Meiklejohn felt that the School for Social Studies was the most
significant work he had done. At the same time, he had to make time
to write. He called the first book he wrote in Berkeley *What Does
America Mean?* In it he rewrote the lectures he had given in 1924 at
Northwestern University, which he had felt keenly, but which were
not clearly formulated. What have Americans been doing? What have
they intended to do? Have they succeeded or failed? What does
America mean, viewed as a human enterprise? These questions
pressed him for answers.

During the Depression Meiklejohn had pulled his ideas together.
Although in Madison he had been immersed in the everyday concerns
of setting limits, arousing students, writing parents, consulting staff,
and working with committees, he had seen that every teaching problem was embedded in the aims and process of the whole society. He
had become increasingly conscious of the essential incoherence of the
social order in which he worked, and of the way in which his struggle
to teach constituted a battle with an entire society. He had said so in
1932 in his report to Wisconsin's faculty:

> This closeness of connection between the character of a
> society and the character of its education cannot be too strongly
> stressed. Schools and colleges are not something apart from the
> social order to which they belong. They are that order trying to
> prepare its youth for participation in its own activities. And a
> society can teach only the hopes, the knowledge, the values, the
> beliefs which it has. If knowledge is broken to pieces, if beliefs
> are shaken, if values become uncertain, then inevitably teaching
> loses its grip, falls into hesitations and incoherence.[15]

During 1934 Meiklejohn wrote his analysis of the U.S. experience.
This is the argument he laid out in *What Does America Mean?*:

> The most striking feature of the modern mind is the loss of the
> term "spirit."
> But man is a paradoxical creature; he is two opposing things
> (body and spirit) at once. Present U.S. culture considers only
> the external side of human life—body, desires, external pur-
> poses, and happiness. We ought to consider the internal side—
> spirit, ideals, obligations, and excellence.

America's ideal is liberty or freedom. [Meiklejohn uses these words interchangeably in this book.] We value liberty, even when we destroy it; our sense of guilt reveals our ideal.
Freedom is not for property but for people—freedom of worship, of thought, of expression, of assembly, and for universal suffrage and universal education. These freedoms have been betrayed by our insistence, given frontier conditions, on the unlimited freedom to own property and to make money.
Our external independence has been won and has created the illusion that we are free. But our inner freedom has yet to be won.
External activities, i.e., amassing wealth, should not be free from regulation. Only internal activities, i.e., creating intelligence, must be free from interference.

To the question of what we should do to create our inner freedom, Meiklejohn made four suggestions:

1. The national program of education should be radically transformed and extended.

2. Newspapers should be financially supported by public money to free editors and reporters from the constraints of selling so they can create the fair and genuine news that a self-governing people must have.

3. Capitalism must be radically transformed or wholly abandoned because the competitive economic order is incompatible with the purposes of democracy.

4. Social change should come, not by class warfare which is ineffectual and self-defeating, but by democratic processes.

This book was as near a confession of faith as Meiklejohn ever made. He had always been outspoken and blunt in his educational and philosophical convictions, but about his political and economic beliefs he had been prudent outside his classroom. He wanted to keep the influence he had, and he was not an economist by training. As president of a college and later as chairman of an experimental college within a large state university, he had been required to deal with older faculty, trustees, alumni who influenced with their money, and parents who wanted their boys to be successful. He could hardly begin his speeches to them with the words, "The essential defeat of the capitalist order is, in my opinion, that it is revolting as a form of human behavior. It makes the men who engage in it ashamed of themselves".[16]

People were not outraged by *What Does America Mean?* They hardly noticed it. The Sunday *New York Times* gave it a rave review, but sales were low. In 1935 one-third of the nation was ill housed, ill clothed, and ill fed. People were driven to find short-range solutions. They permitted President Roosevelt and his "Brain Trust" to patch up capitalism rather than to replace it. Inner freedom was not as much on their minds as where their next meal was coming from. (The book was long out of print until Norton and Company reissued it in paperback in 1972.)

After publication of this book, Meiklejohn was busy teaching alternate semesters at Wisconsin and at the San Francisco School for Social Studies. His work in San Francisco kept focusing on the problem of how to educate adults to govern themselves. He had long wanted to teach from legal materials, and at the School for Social Studies he had the chance to use the U.S. Constitution as the basis for discussion with a group of Bakery Wagon Drivers.

The Constitution proved to be excellent teaching material, but the opinions of the Supreme Court were not. Adults could not read them. One of the teachers at the School for Social Studies, Myer Cohen, had studied law under Walton Hale Hamilton at Yale. Earlier Hamilton had taught under Meiklejohn at Amherst the freshman course on "Social and Economic Institutions" that Meiklejohn had hoped could be based on the study of law and the courts. At that time Hamilton could not base his course on legal materials, but he spent the next twenty years interpreting the law as a form of social understanding. It was appropriate that his student, Myer Cohen, was able to prepare for the School for Social Studies a selection of readings from decisions of the Supreme Court in a form that made them accessible to ordinary adults. Eventually the U.S. Constitution, along with these selected decisions of the Supreme Court, served as the unifying document of the School of Social Studies.

By 1938 Meiklejohn had fully retired from Wisconsin and turned over the directorship of the School for Social Studies. He was sixty-six years old and still had not formulated a general theory of education. In *What Does America Mean?* he had set out the inner failure of Americans to achieve democracy, but he had not discussed the relationship of education to democracy, the connection of intelligence to freedom. In the months during which the United States was being inextricably drawn into World War II to defend democracy against totalitarianism, Meiklejohn developed a general theory of education. He was seventy years old when it was published as *Education Between Two Worlds.*

In it Meiklejohn begins by asserting that what he calls capitalist-Protestant civilization has disintegrated and its education along with it. His title emphasizes this conviction; it is taken from Matthew Arnold's poem, "The Grande Chartreuse":

> Wandering between two worlds, one dead,
> The other powerless to be born,
> With nowhere yet to rest my head,
> Like these, on earth I wait forlorn.

Abandoning his strictly philosophical method for a few chapters, Meiklejohn calls up some figures from the past to testify to the disintegration of education. Three hundred years ago control of education passed from the church to the state. How did this revolution occur? What did the state intend to achieve by means of its teaching? As Meiklejohn follows this line of questioning, he analyzes the conceptions of the origin of the state prevalent in England in the seventeenth century when the agent of education changed from church to state.

If only the ideas of the Czech bishop, John Amos Comenius (1592-1679) had prevailed with England's parliament, Meiklejohn laments. Instead, the notions of John Locke (1632-1704) won acceptance. Locke reasoned that while governments are made by people, individual rights are given by God. Therefore, in any conflict between them, individual rights can claim higher sanction than can communal obligations. This imbalance justified capitalists in developing laissez-faire economics without restriction, since it justified the state in not curbing individuals in their pursuit of unlimited wealth. This pursuit was considered part of their individual liberty. From this, it easily followed that the purpose of education was to prepare individuals to pursue their self-interest. Locke, however, devised a dual system of education, one for upper classes and another for lower classes, who would not be free to pursue their self-interest.

This internal contradiction set Western civilization on the course to disintegration, Meiklejohn finds. He calls as eloquent witness Matthew Arnold, who was for thirty-four years the contemporary in London of

Karl Marx. Meiklejohn believes these two men came to the same conclusion, Marx in economic terms and Arnold in literary and pedagogical terms.

The person who first suggested the way out of disintegration, in Meiklejohn's opinion, was Jean Jacques Rousseau (1712-1778). Rousseau maintained that government and individual rights alike are created by people. God does not give authority to either. Individual rights have no divine sanction; they have only the protection given by the state. The scale is evenly balanced. Since both Locke and Rousseau influenced the writers of the Declaration of Independence, much confusion was caused by the incompatibility of their theories. Meiklejohn argues that the Declaration of Independence and the Constitution must be given a Rousseauvian interpretation if a way out of the dilemma is to be found.

Before constructing a theory of education based on the social contract, Meiklejohn pauses to examine pragmatism and its chief proponent in education, John Dewey. Meiklejohn holds that pragmatists could not reconstruct society; they were still committed to the chaotic individualism of Protestant-capitalist society. Meiklejohn finds that Dewey had a passion for democracy but no theory of democracy that could provide for more than a medley of pressure groups in conflict with one another. He failed to see that "the theories of democracy and of laissez-faire are flatly contradictory of each other. We will not make a free society by letting each man separately fight for his own freedom."[17]

The problems in education arise from the fact that teachers serve two masters—customs and intelligence, says Meiklejohn. Reconstruction can only take place when the two become one. He believes that the basis for reconstruction is the belief that men are brothers and that all activities we term "intelligence" are expressions of that kinship. Only brothers can reason together. Government is human reasonableness in action. The human race, by virtue of its intelligence and kindness, is a world-state in the making. A democratic state is the cooperative enterprise of a group of individuals who regard dignity and freedom as the supreme values of their education.

From this a general theory of education can follow. Education is properly a function of the state, and its ruling purpose is initiation into the human fellowship of reasonableness. Education is the fitting of people, young and old, for the responsibilities and opportunities of being citizens of the world. In addition to vocational training, all human beings should have the same essential education in order to learn to share, as far as possible, in the common enterprise of self-government.

It is a bit dizzying to try to follow these assertions as if they were descriptions about the world as it is. Meiklejohn knew they were not. But for him they are descriptions, not only of what the world ought to be, but also of what real people, deep inside at their best moments, want the world to be and what they are willing to struggle toward.

By the end of World War II, how many people believed that such a world could ever be? Meiklejohn did not know, but he stood with them. Hitler had been defeated, and the world stood waiting to be rebuilt. Meiklejohn served as a delegate from the United States to the convention charged with setting up the educational branch of the United Nations. Three hundred delegates met in London in November 1945 to draft the charter for what they named the United Nations Educational, Scientific, and Cultural Organization, UNESCO. Meiklejohn returned discouraged about how little people understood the magnitude of the problem.

8. Defending the First Amendment

After 1945 Meiklejohn focused on defending freedom of speech, which was coming under intensified attack. In 1938 the House of Representatives voted 191 to 41 to create a special Committee on Un-American Activities to investigate persons with "dangerous ideas." In 1945, by a vote of 208 to 186, the House made permanent this committee (HUAC). Following the congressional election of 1946 the national administration undertook a comprehensive "loyalty-security" program; President Truman issued his Loyalty Order in March 1947. The Department of Justice listed seventy-eight organizations in 1947 whose members might be considered "disloyal" to the United States, and the Attorney General restricted the freedom of speech of foreign visitors.

Meiklejohn could not remain silent in the face of such duplicity. The self-respect of U.S. citizens required that they practice what they preach and preach only what they practice. He asked, "Does the First Amendment mean that dangerous ideas shall be suppressed or does it mean that no ideas shall be suppressed?"

He published his answer in 1948 as *Free Speech and Its Relation to Self-Government.* There are two kinds of civil liberties, he said, even though we use no term to distinguish them. One kind is unlimited and cannot be abridged in any way. An example is the liberty of religious belief. The other kind of civil liberty can be limited for the public welfare. An example is the liberty to own and use property. The reason the Constitution prohibits any limitation of liberty of belief, while insisting on some limitation of liberty of property, is that the public welfare requires both actions. Liberty of belief must not be limited, since in a government where each person governs, each person must have access to every possible argument for and against every issue in order to make wise decisions. Liberty of property must be limited so that the government can obtain income to promote the general welfare. We speak of freedom of belief and freedom of property as if, in the Constitution, the word "freedom" always has the same meaning. Because of this confusion we are in danger of giving to man's possessions the same dignity and status that we give to man himself.

Meiklejohn continued his argument by maintaining that in regard to the first kind of civil liberty, the liberty of belief and speech, the Constitution has been wrongly interpreted by the Supreme Court ever since 1919, when Justice Oliver Wendell Holmes ruled that freedom of speech may constitutionally be abridged by legislative action in times of clear and present danger (in this case, World War I). This interpretation is incorrect, Meiklejohn says, because the Constitution provides for unlimited freedom of speech and belief, so that those who govern—the people—can reach wise decisions. Since the purpose of free speech is wise government, the need for free speech is greater in times of clear and present danger, not less, and the protection offered by the First Amendment is absolute: no idea shall be suppressed. No danger can be so great as the suppression of ideas. The unabridged freedom of discussion is the rock on which the U.S. government stands.

Armed with this argument the spare, tenacious, seventy-five-year-old retired professor of philosophy stepped up to challenge the mighty giants of the Supreme Court, themselves the reputed bearers of the liberal standard. A citizen might have to abide by the Supreme Court's interpretations, thought Meiklejohn, but he certainly did not have to agree with them. Justice Felix Frankfurter could not suppress the suggestion that their common interests might be better served if

Meiklejohn would spend three years in a good law school. Undaunted, Meiklejohn responded merrily that he would be glad to do so, if he could know that the Justice would spend the same three years in a school of philosophy.

Meiklejohn's defense of free speech was never limited to writing. In 1927 he had been elected to the National Committee of the American Civil Liberties Union, and in 1934 he had helped found the Northern California chapter of the ACLU. He held responsible positions in both these organizations until his death. In November 1955, he testified on the meaning of the First Amendment before the Hennings Sub-Committee on Constitutional Rights of the Senate Judiciary Committee. In 1957 he petitioned the House of Representatives for a redress of a grievance—the grievance being the violation of the Constitution done by the establishment of the House Committee on Un-American Activities. In 1962, at age ninety, he became the honorary and active chairman of the National Committee to Abolish the House Un-American Activities Committee.

In all this activity words were his weapons, words designed to influence the course of events, not to fill up libraries. Meiklejohn published in every forum available to him. Law schools at Indiana, Duke, and Chicago published his legal arguments in their journals. He continued to write for the magazines and audiences that had always been eager for his ideas— *Harper's, The Nation, The New York Times Magazine, The Progressive.* In all these articles Meiklejohn submitted his interpretation of how the Constitution applies to the practical situations that the courts and universities were facing.

In every case Meiklejohn argued that while there are circumstances in which the expression of ideas can be temporarily suspended, the ideas themselves must be permitted expression at a more prudent time, because the holding and expression of any belief whatever cannot constitutionally be abridged. The limit of the Constitution's protection, argued Meiklejohn, is reached only when people take overt violent action against the government or incite such action. Incitement implies immediate action. The Constitution offers no protection for overt action or for incitement to it, but it does protect *advocating* the violent overthrow of the existing form of government. Advocacy and incitement, Meiklejohn urged, must always be distinguished.

Meiklejohn saw politics and education as two sides of the same coin, freedom. He had plunged into the interpretation of the First

Amendment in his search for a political basis for the educational process. He could see no better reason for enduring the rigors of learning how to think well, and of teaching others to think well, than to be able to conduct one's life in common with all people. If the people are to be able to govern, then the people had better be able to think well. Freedom of speech is necessary to effective thinking, and thinking is necessary to self-government. To sum up this apparent paradox, Meiklejohn often quoted one of his favorite heroes, the Greek slave Epictetus, who said: "The rulers of the state say that only free men shall be educated. But Wisdom has said that only educated men shall be free."

Another of Meiklejohn's heroes was Immanuel Kant. Meiklejohn held Kant to be the most significant philosopher of the modern world because he dealt with the basic problem of our civilization—governing ourselves. Kant's grandfather, it is said, was a Scot; and for Kant, as for Meiklejohn, the moral quality of his parents was the beginning and end of all his thinking. Meiklejohn recognized this kinship. When he lectured about Kant to philosophy students at UC-Berkeley in 1947, he recounted Kant's recollection of his parents:

> I still remember how a quarrel once broke out between the harness makers and the saddlers. [Kant's father was a saddle maker.] My father suffered considerably; nevertheless, even in conversation among his own family he spoke about this quarrel with such forbearance and love toward his opponents, and with such firm trust in Providence, that, although I was then only a boy, I shall never forget it.

Meiklejohn begged his audience to see that every word of the *Metaphysics of Morals* is an attempt to understand the quality of behavior which so honorably distinguished Kant's parents. Meiklejohn closed his talk by quoting Kant as he reflected on his career as a student and teacher of philosophy:

> I am an investigator by inclination. I feel a great thirst for knowledge and impatient eagerness to advance, also satisfaction at each progressive step. There was a time when I thought that all this could constitute the honor of humanity, and I despised the mob which knows nothing about it. Rousseau set me straight. This dazzling excellence vanishes. I learn to honor men, and would consider myself much less useful than common

laborers if I did not believe that this purpose could give all others a value—to establish the rights of humanity.[18]

To establish the rights of humanity, Meiklejohn concurred, is the
chief thing worth thinking about, the only thing worth teaching about.
He had come to see that for himself ethics takes precedence over logic
and metaphysics.

During his years of retirement Meiklejohn expressed his passion
for teaching by serving as a consultant to St. John's College in Annapolis, Maryland. A new liberal arts program was introduced there in the
summer of 1937 by Stringfellow Barr and Scott Buchanan, who based
their program on a required curriculum of great books, small sem-
inars, and dormitory life. Scott Buchanan, a former student and great
friend of Meiklejohn, arranged for him to spend a month each year at
St. John's to talk and to criticize what he saw.

Many aspects of St. John's were different from the Experimental
College. The number of books to be studied was much larger, and
there was less emphasis on the raising of questions about current
society and more emphasis on mathematics and laboratory study of
science. Robert Hutchins, president of the University of Chicago
which also used a great books curriculum, expressed the opinion that
Meiklejohn did not fully qualify as a critic because he had not himself
read all the books on the list. Meiklejohn agreed he had not, and
would not, since they were not all useful to him. The years of association with St. John's were lively, happy ones for him, keeping him in
touch with young people.

As an educator and father Meiklejohn took pride in the careers of
his own children. Kenneth, a lawyer, worked for the U.S. government
and was legislative counsel for the AFL-CIO. Donald taught philosophy and social science, principally at the University of Chicago and
Syracuse University. Gordon, a physician, specialized in virology and
internal medicine, headed the Department of Medicine at the University of Colorado, and worked through the World Health Organization
to eradicate smallpox. Ann, with a Ph.D. in psychology, worked as a
psychological counselor at the University of California-Berkeley. All
had developed some branch of their father's interests and concerns.

To the end of his life Meiklejohn kept clear about what he held to
be the ideal of education. At the same time he acknowledged the dis-
tance between his ideal and the reality around him. During his last

years he recognized that the thinking power of people in the United States had slipped disastrously in his lifetime, and he faced the likelihood of the outright failure of the U.S. experiment. He wrote for himself:

What is the matter with our national education? Throughout the country there is an uneasy and desperate sense that our teaching in schools and colleges, as well as out of them, fails to do what we want it to do. . . . We must face the possibility that, without realizing it, we have assigned to our teachers a task which, under the present conditions of our national life, neither they nor anyone else can perform with a reasonable prospect of success. As measured by what we expect of it, our education is threatened by fundamental failure. And as that failure comes upon us, it means that our "Way of Life" does not work. If we cannot teach freedom we cannot have it. It may be that the "Great Experiment" upon which the American people entered nearly two centuries ago is ending with the discovery that, under

Helen and Alexander Meiklejohn about 1954.

present conditions at home and abroad, the brave attempt to create and maintain a Free Society has run its course.[19]

During the years after World War II many kinds of recognition came to Meiklejohn. He received the Teachers Union for Defense of Constitutional Liberties Award in 1953, a Pacific Coast Unitarian Council Award in 1958, the Susan Colver Rosenberger Medal of Brown University in 1959, and the Franklin D. Roosevelt Award of the National Lawyers Guild in 1960. In 1957 the alumni and former faculty of the Experimental College established a fund which they turned over to the American Association of University Professors for a periodic Alexander Meiklejohn Award to a college or university administrator or trustee of a governing board who had made an outstanding contribution to academic freedom. Both Brown University and the University of Wisconsin established lectureships in Meiklejohn's name. In 1963 President Kennedy chose him to receive the Medal of Freedom, which President Johnson presented to him. In 1964 he agreed to the use of his name on a civil liberties library opened in Berkeley, which expanded its function later to become the Meiklejohn Civil Liberties Institute.

Mciklcjohn's eighty-fifth birthday was the occasion of a celebration held by the Northern California chapter of the American Civil Liberties Union. On October 29, 1957, several hundred people gathered at the Sheraton-Palace in San Francisco to honor their champion. James C. Caldwell, professor of English at UC-Berkeley, had the audience reeling with laughter by choosing to analyze Meiklejohn's defects rather than his virtues on the assumption that this would take less time:

> I think perhaps that in activities such as these [his legal work] we can find most clearly compounded and concentrated all of those disturbing traits of which I have been speaking. In these he speaks beyond his generation, in the bold disregard of vested authority with an unsettling penetration. And in all, obviously he is exceeding by far the usual limits of the field of philosophy and the field of education. I suppose this kind of thing must be fraught with the most serious consequences for the stability and comfort of the academic world.[20]

*Meiklejohn seated in the backyard of his house in the hills of
Berkeley, three blocks north of University of California-Berkeley*

Meiklejohn responded by proposing a semantic reform that could clear up the prevailing confusion over the two kinds of civil liberties, i.e., those that cannot be constitutionally abridged and those that can be. He suggested that the first kind, freedom of speech, belief, and expression, should be called freedoms, and those of the second kind, freedom of property and the pursuit of wealth, should be called liberties. This reform never took root; an immediate, though minor, difficulty was the name of the Civil Liberties Union itself. A more serious difficulty was the radical nature of the concept.

Meiklejohn never really knew old age. He stayed in training all his life and kept fit as long as he lived. He and Helen established a routine for their days in Berkeley. After breakfast Meiklejohn entered his study, a sunny southern room, to write until 12:15. He emerged for a forty-five-minute walk with Helen along a regular route through their neighborhood in the Berkeley hills, where the children called them "Adam and Eve." After lunch Meiklejohn returned to his study for revisions of his morning's work and for correspondence. A longer walk with Helen followed, and sometimes, through his ninety-first year, a game of tennis. Usually two evenings a week were social; the others provided time for reading the stacks of books always waiting.

Once on their regular walks the Meiklejohns encountered a gentleman, an engineer from Europe, who told them that he walked twice a day and had kept his strength by being on a healthy diet that included blackstrap molasses. He held them for some time detailing his living habits. Then he turned to Mrs. Meiklejohn and said, "I am telling you all this, madam, so that you can take such good care of your husband that at seventy-nine he will be as strong as I am."

Meiklejohn was then ninety-one, but no twinge of rebuke crossed his face, and he replied with a charming smile, "This is very kind of you."

During his last years Meiklejohn derived much satisfaction from his participation in the Center for the Study of Democractic Institutions in Santa Barbara, California. Founded by Robert Hutchins, this center invited scholars to discuss the most difficult questions in a free society. During the summer of 1964 the Meiklejohns stayed in Santa Barbara for four weeks, while Meiklejohn informally presided over an ambitious attempt to formulate a general theory of the First Amendment. Others in the group that summer included Scott Buchanan, Joseph Tussman, Robert Hutchins, and Harry Kalven. They divided sharply over whether the First Amendment should be given a positive reading or a negative one. They reached no agreement.

During the last Saturday night of the arguments Meiklejohn leapt from his bed and jotted down this amendment to the Constitution that would follow from a positive interpretation of the First Amendment:

> In view of the intellectual and cultural responsibilities laid upon the citizens of a free society by the political institutions of self-government, the Congress, acting in cooperation with the several States and with non-governmental organizations serving the same general purpose, shall have power to provide for the intellectual and cultural education of all citizens of the United States.

In early December 1964, Meiklejohn developed a cold. Upright in bed, he planned a letter he wanted to write to the Regents of the University of California. The students had just conducted a massive sit-in at Sproul Hall, and Meiklejohn wanted to tell the Regents that the uprising could be partially traced to the impersonality of university organization, to the failure of the curriculum to be relevant to students' interests, to the archaic method of teaching, and to the lack of a significant relationship between students and faculty. Meiklejohn's cold became pneumonia, and on December 16, seated at home in a chair between his wife and his doctor, he died.

Three memorial services were held, in Berkeley, in Washington, D.C., and in New York City, so that his friends, students, and admirers from all parts of the country could celebrate his life. A great many words were assembled to define his essence. A student of his at St. John's College, Peter Weiss, composed this sentence, later to be inscribed on a bronze tablet at St. John's College:

> Here passed Alexander Meiklejohn, with a twinkle in his eye, the truth by his side, freedom in his bones, conviction in his heart, and scorn for no man.

Footnotes

1. Personal notes by Meiklejohn, kept by Helen Meiklejohn.
2. Alexander Meiklejohn, *Freedom and the College* (New York: Century Co., 1923), p. xiv.
3. Letter from Meiklejohn to Fred Ladd, *Providence* (R.I.) *Journal*, November 9, 1904.
4. W. Randolph Burgess, "What Is Truth?" *Rights* XII (February 1965): 29.
5. Letter from Meiklejohn to Gladys Boone, professor at Sweetbriar College, of February 25, 1964, quoted by Ross Terrill, *R. H. Tawney and His Times: Socialism as Fellowship* (London: Andre Deutsch, 1973), p. 57.

6. J. Seelye Bixler, "Alexander Meiklejohn and the Making of the Amherst Mind," *Amherst: The College and Its Alumni* (Spring 1973), p. 2.

7. Quoted by Willard L. Sperry in a letter to Meiklejohn, July 2, 1923, State Historical Society of Wisconsin.

8. Lucien Price, *Prophet Unawares: The Romance of An Idea* (New York: Century Co., 1924), pp. 35-36.

9. Alexander Meiklejohn, "The Measure of a College," *Amherst Graduates Quarterly* 12 (February 1923): 85-92.

10. Donald Ramsey, "Old Amherst Sells Its Soul," *Labor,* from an excerpt in the Meiklejohn Papers, State Historical Society of Wisconsin.

11. *The New Republic* (July 25, 1923), p. 222. Financial statements are from Stanley King, *A History of the Endowment of Amherst College* (Amherst, Mass.: Amherst College, 1950) and Charles J. Cooper, "Alexander Meiklejohn: Absolutes of Intelligence in Political and Constitutional Theory" (Ph.D. dissertation, Bryn Mawr, 1967).

12. Alexander Meiklejohn, *Education for a Free Society: Selected Papers,* two vols. (Mimeographed: The Fund for Adult Education, 1957), II: 195-196.

13. "Wisconsin's Experimental College," *Survey Graphic* (June 1927), p. 269.

14. John Powell, *Education for Maturity* (New York: Hermitage House, 1949), p. 80.

15. *The Experimental College,* p. xi.

16. *What Does America Mean?,* p. 242

17. *Education Between Two Worlds,* p. 94.

18. Alexander Meiklejohn, "Inclinations and Obligations," Howison Lecture, 1947, *University of California Publications in Philosophy* 16 (October 1948): 209, 222-223.

19. Undated manuscript, State Historical Society of Wisconsin, Box 65, Folder 7.

20. James Caldwell, "Tribute to Dr. Meiklejohn," *ACLU News* (December 1957), p. 1.

Selections from Meiklejohn

Alexander Meiklejohn realized in his late years, as he considered writing about his life, that he had spent most of his time on earth talking or writing. Written and spoken words—he had struggled all his life to cultivate and refine them, so that they could say what he meant. He had published eight books, 115 or more articles and speeches, fourteen book reviews, and twelve tributes and memorial speeches. In addition to these published materials there are sixty-nine boxes of his correspondence, reprints and unpublished writings at the State Historical Society of Wisconsin in Madison, and another seventy boxes of documents relating to the Experimental College in the archives of the University of Wisconsin in Madison.

Selecting and arranging from this record have been made easier by the fact that Meiklejohn's life and thinking revolve consistently around a few major themes. These grew out of his concrete experience and led to new experience and new themes in a remarkably coherent manner. This has made it possible, with few exceptions, to arrange the selections that follow in a natural order that is both chronologic and thematic, without having to choose between them. The thematic arrangement is chronologic in an overall sense, but within each theme the selections may range over many years.

The earliest theme to absorb Meiklejohn in adult life was the question: "What should a liberal college be?" This engrossed him throughout the thirty-five years from 1897 until 1932—at Brown, Amherst, and Wisconsin—as he tried to construct such a liberal college. His new vision, of course, involved him in criticism of colleges as he found them.

At least by the time he reached Amherst he had realized how deeply the purposes and methods of education are formed by the culture in which it is rooted, and his criticism of educational institutions led him to a critical examination of "Protestant-captialist society" in the United States. This critique was sometimes implicit, as if one could assume that it was commonly accepted that capitalism was breaking down. But at other times he thoroughly examined this assumption. Hence the second group of selections is arranged under the title "Critique of Protestant-Capitalist Society."

Meiklejohn usually stated questions in terms of what something should be. Values were more real to him than any other aspect of the world. In this he differed from many of his contemporaries, for whom scientific thinking meant excluding all talk about values. They avoided speaking of ideals, excellence, obligations, or aspirations. Not Meiklejohn. He saw the world primarily in terms of these realities. The third group of selections is therefore arranged under the title "The Reality of Values."

After retiring from Wisconsin, Meiklejohn refined the two consuming themes of his life—freedom and education. He constructed a general theory of democracy to support his general theory of education, and he related these general theories to the major events of his time. The fourth section, "Education for a Free World," suggests what Meiklejohn's theory of education would imply for the reconstruction of the world after World War II. The fifth section, "Liberty and Freedom," shows how Meiklejohn understood academic freedom and how he interpreted the First Amendment as he applied it to legal cases arising from the suppression of free speech during the McCarthy era and the Cold War.

In choosing what to include I have intended, first, to show Meiklejohn's ideas clearly and, second, to display the range and virtuosity of his skill in adapting his presentation to his audience. The brief note preceding each selection places it in the framework of Meiklejohn's life, while the longer notes preceding each section set Meiklejohn's work in the context of his time. Most of his writing was polemic or occasional, so it is important to know how the issues were being defined and what position he was attacking.

The Liberal College

For most of his life Alexander Meiklejohn worked within a college. A true philosopher, he could never suppress questions about his own activity. "What are we doing here?" he asked. What is a liberal college? What is a liberal education? How is it different from professional or vocational education? In a democracy, who should have it? What is its content? Is there some common set of books or information or problems that every college student should deal with? If so, what are they? Who should decide?

During Meiklejohn's fifteen years at Brown (1897-1911), liberal colleges were facing many challenges. It was a time of confusion. The pattern of the old-time classical liberal college was giving way to that of the modern university, but the goals and meaning of the new institution were not yet clear. Whatever else the modern university was going to mean, somehow it had to encompass vast areas of new knowledge—biology, chemistry, anatomy, anthropology, economics, modern languages and cultures, and psychology. Students were going to Europe in search of this knowledge, and they returned wanting to teach and extend it.

One basic question was whether the curriculum should be elective. Harvard University had become the model for answering that question as its president, Charles William Eliot, instituted the view that the curriculum should be totally elective. When Eliot assumed the presidency in 1869, the faculty of Arts and Sciences at Harvard consisted of twenty-three members and students had no choice of courses, except as seniors when they could choose two or three electives. In 1870-71 their "studies" became "courses," each labeled with an Arabic number. Every year after 1872-73 some of the required courses became electives, and every new course automatically became an elective. By 1886 the faculty of Arts and Sciences numbered sixty-one; they gave 163 full courses and sixty-one half-courses. Students could earn a bachelor's degree by passing eighteen courses, no two of which needed to be related. The unified classical curriculum common to every educated person had vanished at Harvard within seventeen years.

The introduction of electives at Brown, where Meiklejohn both studied and taught, had actually preceded Harvard. President Wayland had established a limited elective system back in 1850. Brown needed more students to sustain itself, and Wayland saw that the traditional classical curriculum was attracting a diminishing number of students, limited to the wealthier classes. He believed that by offering more scientific courses Brown would attract the larger range of students necesssary to its survival, and on his recommendation a partially elective curriculum was agreed on as just, expedient, and necessary.

While Meiklejohn was a student at Brown (1889-93), the university underwent rapid expansion. Between 1888 and 1896 the number of teachers increased from twenty-two to sixty-eight, the number of departments from seventeen to twenty-five, and the hours of instruction given from 135 to 460. Of a student's course work, seventy-two percent was required in 1889; by 1896 only forty-one percent of their course work was required.

As Meiklejohn began his teaching at Brown in 1897, the younger faculty felt a thrill of excitement as they welcomed the broadening and deepening that the new forms of investigation promised to bring to their teaching. They spoke proudly of their newly devised "university college," which they hoped would fuse the pursuit of knowledge and the pursuit of understanding on a higher intellectual plane. But by the end of his teaching at Brown, Meiklejohn had come to believe that the elective system was "a thing of shreds and patches with little pretension to any unity of design or purpose." ("Logic in the College Curriculum," a paper given in 1911 to the Religious Education Association, in *The Liberal College* [Boston: Marshall Jones Co., 1920], p. 113.)

When Meiklejohn assumed the presidency of Amherst in 1912, the curriculum there was two-thirds elective. In his inaugural address Meiklejohn announced his opposition to unlimited electives and his determination to make Amherst a place of unified understanding rather than specialized knoweldge. By 1918 he reported to the trustees:

> The longer one attempts to devise a liberal training by the additions and combinations of courses, the more one becomes convinced that addition is an illusion and that courses are the chimeras of an imagination perverted by the categories of mechanics. Twenty courses do not make a college education any more than twenty legs make a man, or twenty heads, or even ten hearts, two legs and eight fingers. And in the same way

three courses do not make an intellectual interest, an experience of the actual process of the working mind. Something is wrong with the terms, something is radically wrong with the process of combining them. ["President's Report to the Trustees", in *The Liberal College,* p. 149.]

Meiklejohn proceeded to defend a required curriculum—not a classical one, but a modern one. He believed that every student should think about the problems basic to human living, should think about how to think about them, and about which mode of thinking is appropriate to each problem. For him, using one's mind is the activity that defines a liberal college (selection 1).

As chairman of the Experimental College at the University of Wisconsin, Meiklejohn was able to try the newer ways of teaching of which he had dreamed. He could assemble a faculty who wanted to experiment with an integrated curriculum. They created a two-year study of basic human problems, with the first year focused on fifth-century Greece, the second year on the 19th- and 20th-century United States, and the summer vacation on a study by each student of his own region. This curriculum included classical material, but it was as different from a classical curriculum as Margaret Mead from Cotton Mather. The comparison of civilizations, the integration of the material, and the examination of current problems were radically new (selection 2).

In defending a required curriculum, Meiklejohn took a traditional position, but the curriculum itself was progressive in focusing on current problems and in using knowledge for social action. On other pedagogic issues Meiklejohn took an explicitly progressive position. He respected students and did not blame them for defects in the outcome of education. He insisted that students run all the non-classroom activities—sports, politics, drama—to which he attached much importance. In methods he stood squarely against recitations and lectures, although he himself was considered a great orator. He believed in discussion. It was his form of learning by doing. Since good thinking necessarily involved give and take, he believed the best way to learn it was by practicing with people skilled at it. He avoided textbooks on the ground that they are not usually examples of thought developed by fine minds.

Thus Meiklejohn pioneered "progressive" goals and methods before the word became popular in educational circles. During the 1920s Meiklejohn considered himself, and was considered by others, a progressive educator. He spoke to local chapters of the Progressive Education Association and on February 21, 1929, gave the keynote address at the ninth national meeting of that association in St. Louis. The theme of the conference was "Education: An Active Process," and Meiklejohn's address was billed as "The Function of Activities in Education." Instead, he took as his topic "What Next in Progressive Education?" He hailed John Dewey as the leader of the movement, then characteristically sailed into the difficulties in Dewey's presentation of the progressive position. Meiklejohn believed Dewey and other progressive educators were unclear about their goals and too wrapped up in considerations of method. Dewey, in his address the prior year, had called on teachers "to intellectually organize their work." Meiklejohn found that while Dewey had shown the need for coherence and order in the curriculum, he had not shown along what lines it should be sought. Meiklejohn argued that the question determining how the whole content of the curriculum can be organized is "How can the quality of human life be exalted—not here or there, not merely in this favored place or in that center of my affections, but wherever men may achieve or fail to achieve the qualities of growth and freedom." (*Progressive Education Journal* VI [April-June 1929]: 108.)

Meiklejohn continued to support the progressive education movement at the same time that he criticized its statement of its goals. During the 1930s and 1940s some of Meiklejohn's friends and ex-students (Robert Hutchins, Scott Buchanan) became well-known advocates of a return to tradition in education. They called for classical studies, a required curriculum, and knowledge for its own sake. By his association with them, as students and friends, Meiklejohn was mistakenly seen by some during this period as a traditionalist. This became evident in another debate with Dewey, published in the pages of *Fortune* magazine, that was thoroughly unsatisfactory to both parties. Dewey attributed to Meiklejohn beliefs that were Hutchins', not Meiklejohn's. Meiklejohn in fact agreed with Hutchins and Buchanan on the need for a required curriculum, but he disagreed about the reasons why the curriculum should be required and about the purpose it should serve, as well as about other pedagogic questions.

After World War II several leading universities returned to some required core of courses. The University of Wisconsin created the Integrated Liberal Studies, a small program within the total university. Teachers at Amherst produced a core course on American civilization involving all departments and undergraduates. In 1945 Harvard issued a book, *General Education in a Free Society,* that argued that there exists a body of ideas and content that should form the foundation of a liberal education and that students should not be entirely free to choose their own curriculum. Known as "The Redbook," this plan was implemented only half-heartedly at Harvard and with more enthusiasm elsewhere.

These postwar attempts to recapture the core of Western civilization were charged with feelings about World War II. The war had seemed a very close brush. Teachers felt that a different outcome would have meant the end of western civilization as they understood and valued it. But what did they value in it? Precisely this question they were unsure about but had to answer before they could design a core curriculum. To this discussion Meiklejohn contributed the important distinction between knowledge and understanding, a distinction that he believed to be at the root of the conflict he had seen going on in colleges during all of his sixty years in them (selection 3).

The defeat of fascism was followed almost immediately by the McCarthy era, when many basic questions could not be raised for discussion, and college teachers drifted back to their specialized studies. The 1960s, the decade of Meiklejohn's death, saw the abolition in most colleges of the few remaining required subjects. Yet even during this period some "experimental" programs kept alive the old idea of a common curriculum; see the account by Gerald Grant and David Riesman, *The Perpetual Dream: Reform and Experiments in the American College* (Chicago: University of Chicago Press, 1978.)

Whenever undergraduate curriculum committees feel the need for more coherence in the curriculum, whenever students ask faculties to look up from their research and assume more responsibility for what students learn, the record of Meiklejohn's deeds and ideas is pertinent. The problem is one that he struggled with for sixty years. He saw it with clarity by 1911 and maintained all those years a sense of urgency about it that most other teachers felt only at times of utter crisis. Meiklejohn found that ethics provides the unifying foundation of the curriculum, for the core is not a body of knowledge, but a body of proper questions about human living. He found, too, that teachers could not teach what they could not do; they must themselves be able to think about human living in a unified way.

1
_____

What the Liberal College Is

*Alexander Meiklejohn gave the following speech as his
inaugural address when, at the age of forty, he was
invested as president of Amherst College on the crisp, sunny
morning of October 16, 1912. When Amherst approached
its centennial in 1921, it published a collection of
Meiklejohn's speeches and essays, including this one, under
the title* The Liberal College *(Boston: Marshall Jones,
1920). This speech was reprinted in 1961 as a statement
of the traditional ideal of liberal collegiate education in*
American Higher Education: A Documentary History,
*vol. II, edited by Richard Hofstadter and Wilson Smith
(Chicago: University of Chicago Press, 1961).*

*It should be mentioned that Amherst College in 1912
was a men's college, staffed by men teaching young men.
When Meiklejohn used "he" for teacher and "boy" or
"young man" for students, he was not using masculine
terms to include women. He was referring only to men,
since women were not present in the college.*

In the discussions concerning college education there is one voice which is all too seldom raised and all too often disregarded. It is the voice of the teacher and the scholar, of the member of the college faculty. It is my purpose to devote this address to a consideration of the ideals of the teacher, of the problems of instruction as they present themselves to the men who are giving the instruction. And I do this not because I believe that just now the teachers are wiser than others who are dealing with the same questions, but rather as an expression of a definite conviction with regard to the place of the teacher in our educational scheme.

It is, I believe, the function of the teacher to stand before his pupils and before the community at large as the intellectual leader of his time. If he is not able to take this leadership, he is not worthy of his calling. If the leadership is taken from him and given to others, then the very foundations of the scheme of instruction are shaken. He who in matters of teaching must be led by others is not the one to lead the imitative undergraduate, not the one to inspire the confidence and loyalty and discipleship on which all true teaching depends. If there are others who can do these things better than the college teacher of today, then we must bring them within the college walls. But if the teacher is to be deemed worthy of his task, then he must be recognized as the teacher of us all, and we must listen to his words as he speaks of the matters entrusted to his charge.

In the consideration of the educational creed of the teacher I will try to give, first, a brief statement of his belief; second, a defense of it against other views of the function of the college; third, an interpretation of its meaning and significance; fourth, a criticism of what seem to me misunderstandings of their own meaning prevalent among the teachers of our day; and finally, a suggestion of certain changes in policy which must follow if the belief of the teacher is clearly understood and applied in our educational procedure.

First, then, What do our teachers believe to be the aim of college instruction? Wherever their opinions and convictions find expression there is one contention which is always in the foreground, namely, that to be liberal a college must be essentially intellectual. It is a place, the teachers tell us, in which a boy, forgetting all things else, may set forth on the enterprise of learning. It is a time when a young man may come to awareness of the thinking of his people, may perceive what knowledge is and has been and is to be. Whatever light-hearted undergraduates may say, whatever the opinions of solicitous parents, of ambitious friends, of employers in search of workmen, of leaders in church or state or business,—whatever may be the beliefs and desires and demands of outsiders,—the teacher within the college, knowing his mission as no one else can know it, proclaims that mission to be the leading of his pupil into the life intellectual. The college is primarily not a place of the body, nor of the feelings, nor even of the will; it is, first of all, a place of the mind.

Against this intellectual interpretation of the college our teachers find two sets of hostile forces constantly at work. Outside the walls there are the practical demands of a busy commercial and social scheme; within the college there are the trivial and sentimental and irrational misunderstandings of its own friends. Upon each of these our college teachers are wont to descend as Samson upon the Philistines, and when they have had their will, there is little left for another to accomplish.

As against the immediate practical demands from without, the issue is clear and decisive. College teachers know that the world must have trained workmen, skilled operatives, clever buyers and sellers, efficient directors, resourceful manufacturers, able lawyers, ministers, physicians and teachers. But it is equally true that in order to do its own work, the liberal college must leave the special and technical training for these trades and professions to be done in other schools and by other methods. In a word, the liberal college does not pretend to give all the kinds of teaching which a young man of college age may profitably receive; it does not even claim to give all the kinds of intellectual training which are worth giving. It is committed to intellectual training of the liberal type, whatever that may mean, and to that mission it must be faithful. One may safely say, then, on behalf of our college teachers, that their instruction is intended to be radically different from that given in the technical school or even in the professional school. Both these institutions are practical in a sense in which the college, as an intellectual institution, is not.

In the technical school the pupil is taught how to do some one of the mechanical operations which contribute to human welfare. He is trained to print, to weave, to farm, to build; and for the most part he is trained to do these things by practice rather than by theory. His possession when he leaves the school is not a stock of ideas, of scientific principles, but a measure of skill, a collection of rules of thumb. His primary function as a tradesman is not to understand but to do, and in doing what is needed he is following directions which have first been thought out by others and are now practised by him. The technical school intends to furnish training which, in the sense in which we use the term, is not intellectual but practical.

In a corresponding way the work of the professional school differs from that of the liberal college. In the teaching of engineering, medicine, or law we are or may be beyond the realm of mere skill and within the realm of ideas and principles. But the selection and the relating of these ideas is dominated by an immediate practical interest which cuts them off from the intellectual point of view of the scholar. If an undergraduate should take away from his studies of chemistry, biology and psychology only those parts which have immediate practical application in the field of medicine, the college teachers would feel that they had failed to give the boy the kind of instruction demanded of a college. It is not their purpose to furnish applied knowledge in this sense. They are not willing to cut up their sciences into segments and to allow the student to select those segments which may be of service in the practice of an art or a profession. In one way or another the teacher feels a kinship with the scientist and the scholar which forbids him to submit to this domination of his instruction by the demands of an immediate practical interest. Whatever it may mean, he intends to hold the intellectual point of view and to keep his students with him if he can. In response, then, to demands for technical and professional training our college teachers tell us that such training may be obtained in other schools; it is not to be had in a college of liberal culture.

In the conflict with the forces within the college our teachers find themselves fighting essentially the same battle as against the foes without. In a hundred different ways the friends of the college, students, graduates, trustees and even colleagues, seem to them so to misunderstand its mission as to minimize or to falsify its intellectual ideals. The college is a good place for making friends; it gives excellent experience in getting on with men; it has exceptional advantages as an athletic club; it is a relatively safe place for a boy when he first leaves home; on the whole it may improve a student's manners; it gives acquaintance with lofty ideals of character, preaches the doctrine of social service, exalts the virtues and duties of citizenship. All these conceptions seem to the teacher to hide or to obscure the fact that the college is fundamentally a place of the mind, a time for thinking, an opportunity for knowing. And perhaps in proportion to their own loftiness of purpose and motive they are the more dangerous as tending all the more powerfully to replace or to nullify the underlying principle upon which they all depend. . . .

How then shall we justify the faith of the teacher? What reason can we give for our exaltation of intellectual training and activity? To this question two answers are possible. First, knowledge and thinking are good in themselves. Secondly, they help us in the attainment of other values in life which without them would be impossible. Both these answers may be given and are given by college teachers. Within them must be found whatever can be said by way of explanation and justification of the work of the liberal college. . . .

In a word, men know with regard to thinking, as with regard to every other content of human experience, that it cannot be valued merely in terms of itself. It must be measured in terms of its relation to other contents and to human experience as a whole. Thinking is good in itself, —but what does it cost of other things, what does it bring of other values? Place it amid all the varied contents of our individual and social experience, measure it in terms of what it implies, fix it by means of its relations, and then you will know its worth not simply in itself but in that deeper sense which comes when human desires are rationalized and human lives are known in their entirety, as well as they can be known by those who are engaged in living them.

In this consideration we find the second answer of the teacher to the demand for justification of the work of the college. Knowledge is good, he tells us, not only in itself, but in its enrichment and enhancement of the other values of our experience. In the deepest and fullest sense of the words, knowledge pays. This statement rests upon the classification of human actions into two groups, those of the instinctive type and those of the intellectual type. By far the greater part of our human acts are carried on without any clear idea of what we are going to do or how we are going to do it. For the most part our responses to our situations are the immediate responses of feeling, of perception, of custom, of tradition. But slowly and painfully, as the mind has developed, action after action has been translated from the feeling to the ideational type; in wider and wider fields men have become aware of their own modes of action, more and more they have come to understanding, to knowledge of themselves and of their needs. And the principle underlying all our educational procedure is that on the whole, actions become more successful as they pass from the sphere of feeling to that of understanding. Our educational belief is that in the long run if men know what they are going to do and how they are going to do it, and what is the nature of the situation with which they are dealing, their response to that situation will be better adjusted and more beneficial than are the responses of the feeling type in like situations.

It is all too obvious that there are limits to the validity of this principle. If men are to investigate, to consider, to decide, then action must be delayed and we must pay the penalty of waiting. If men are to endeavor to understand and know their situations, then we must be prepared to see them make mistakes in their thinking, lose their certainty of touch, wander off into pitfalls and illusions and fallacies of thought, and in consequence secure for the time results far lower in value than those of the instinctive response which they seek to replace. The delays and mistakes and uncertainties of our thinking are a heavy price to pay, but it is the conviction of the teacher that the price is as nothing when compared with the goods which it buys. You may point out to him the loss when old methods of procedure give way before the criticism of understanding, you may remind him of the pain and suffering when old habits of thought and action are replaced, you may reprove him for all the blunders of the past; but in spite of it all he knows and you know that in human lives taken separately and in human life as a whole men's greatest lack is the lack of understanding, their greatest hope to know themselves and the world in which they live.

Within the limits of this general educational principle the place of the liberal college may easily be fixed. In the technical school pupils are prepared for a specific work and are kept for the most part on the plane of perceptual action, doing work which others understand. In the professional school, students are properly within the realm of ideas and principles, but they are still limited to a specific human interest with which alone their understanding is concerned. But the college is called liberal as against both of these because the instruction is dominated by no special interest, is limited to no single human task, but is intended to take human activity as a whole, to understand human endeavors not in their isolation but in their relations to one another and to the total experience which we call the life of our people. And just as we believe that the building of ships has become more successful as men have come to a knowledge of the principles involved in their construction; just as the practice of medicine has become more successful as we have come to a knowledge of the human body, of the conditions within it and the influences without;—just so the teacher in the liberal college believes that life as a total enterprise, life as it presents itself to each one of us in his career as an individual,—human living,—will be more successful in so far as men come to understand it and to know it as they attempt to carry it on. To give boys an intellectual grasp on human experience—this, it seems to me, is the teacher's conception of the chief function of the liberal college. May I call attention to the fact that this second answer of the teacher defines the aim of the college as avowedly and frankly practical? Knowledge is to be sought chiefly for the sake of its contribution to the other activities of human living. But on the other hand, it is as definitely declared that in method the college is fully and unreservedly intellectual. If we can see that these two demands are not in conflict but that they stand together in the harmonious relation of means and ends, of instrument and achievement, of method and result, we may escape many a needless conflict and keep our educational policy in singleness of aim and action. To do this we must show that the college is intellectual, not as opposed to practical interests and purposes, but as opposed to unpractical and unwise methods of work. The issue is not between practical and intellectual aims but between the immediate and the remote aim, between the hasty and the measured procedure, between the demand for results at once and the willingness to wait for the best results. The intellectual road to success is longer and more roundabout than any other, but they who are strong and willing for the climbing are brought to higher levels of achievement than they could possibly have attained had they gone straight forward in the pathway of quick returns. If this were not true the liberal college would have no proper place in our life at all. In so far as it is true the college has a right to claim the best of our young men to give them its preparation for the living they are to do.

But now that we have attempted to interpret the intellectual mission of the college, it may be fair to ask, "Are the teachers and scholars of our day always faithful to that mission? Do their statements and their practice always ring in accord with the principle which has been stated?" It seems to me that at two points they are constantly off the key, constantly at variance with the reasons by which alone their teaching can be justified.

In the first place, it often appears as if our teachers and scholars were deliberately in league to mystify and befog the popular mind

Meiklejohn walking in the processional at his inauguration as president of Amherst College.

regarding this practical value of intellectual work. They seem not to wish too much said about the results and benefits. Their desire is to keep aloft the intellectual banner, to proclaim the intellectual gospel, to demand of student and public alike adherence to the faith. And in general when they are questioned as to results they give little satisfaction except to those who are already pledged to unwavering confidence in their *ipse dixits.* And largely as a result of this attitude the American people seem to me to have little understanding of the intellectual work of the college. Our citizens and patrons can see the value of games and physical exercises; they readily perceive the importance of the social give and take of a college democracy; they can appreciate the value of studies which prepare a young man for his profession and so anticipate or replace the professional school; they can even believe that if a boy is kept at some sort of thinking for four years his mind may become more acute, more systematic, more accurate, and hence more useful than it was before. But as for the content of a college course, as for the value of knowledge, what a boy gains by knowing Greek or economics, philosophy or literature, history or biology, except as they are regarded as having professional usefulness, I think our friends are in the dark and are likely to remain so until we turn on the light.

When our teachers say, as they sometimes do say, that the effect of knowledge upon the character and life of the student must always be for the college an accident, a circumstance which has no essential connection with its real aim or function, then it seems to me that our educational policy is wholly out of joint. If there be no essential connection between instruction and life, then there is no reason for giving instruction except in so far as it is pleasant in itself, and we have no educational policy at all. As against this hesitancy, this absence of a conviction, we men of the college should declare in clear and unmistakable terms our creed—the creed that knowledge is justified by its results. We should say to our people so plainly that they cannot misunderstand, "Give us your boys, give us the means we need, and we will so train and inform the minds of those boys that their own lives and the lives of the men about them shall be more successful than they could be without our training. Give us our chance and we will show your boys what human living is, for we are convinced that they can live better in knowledge than they can in ignorance."

There is a second wandering from the faith which is so common among investigators that it may fairly be called the "fallacy of the scholar." It is the belief that all knowledge is so good that all parts of knowledge are equally good. Ask many of our scholars and teachers what subjects a boy should study in order that he may gain insight for human living, and they will say, "It makes no difference in what department of knowledge he studies; let him go into Sanskrit or bacteriology, into mathematics or history; if only he goes where men are actually dealing with intellectual problems, and if only he learns how to deal with problems himself, the aim of education is achieved, he has entered into intellectual activity." This point of view, running through all the varieties of the elective system, seems to me hopelessly at variance with any sound educational doctrine. It represents the scholar of the day at his worst both as a thinker and as a teacher. In so far as it dominates a group of college teachers it seems to me to render them unfit to determine and to administer a college curriculum. It is an announcement that they have no guiding principles in their educational practice, no principles of selection in their arrangement of studies, no genuine grasp on the relationship between knowledge and life. It is the concerted statement of a group of men each of whom is lost within the limits of his own special studies, and who as a group seem not to realize the organic relationships between them nor the common task which should bind them together.

In bringing this second criticism against our scholars I am not urging that the principle of election of college studies should be entirely discontinued. But I should like to inquire by what right and within what limits it is justified. The most familiar argument in its favor is that if a student is allowed to choose along the lines of his own intellectual or professional interest he will have enthusiasm, the eagerness which comes with the following of one's own bent. Now just so far as this result is achieved, just so far as the quality of scholarship is improved, the procedure is good and we may follow it if we do not thereby lose other results more valuable than our gain. But if the special interest comes into conflict with more fundamental ones, if what the student prefers is opposed to what he ought to prefer, then we of the college cannot leave the choice with him. We must say to him frankly, "If you do not care for liberal training you had better go elsewhere; we have a special and definite task assigned us which demands that we keep free from the domination of special or professional pursuits. So long as we are faithful to that task we cannot give you what you ask."

In my opinion, however, the fundamental motive of the elective system is not the one which has been mentioned. In the last resort our teachers allow students to choose their own studies not in order to appeal to intellectual or to professional interest, but because they themselves have no choice of their own in which they believe with sufficient intensity to impose it upon their pupils. And this lack of a dominating educational policy is in turn an expression of an intellectual attitude, a point of view, which marks the scholars of our time. In a word, it seems to me that our willingness to allow students to wander about in the college curriculum is one of the most characteristic expressions of a certain intellectual agnosticism, a kind of intellectual bankruptcy, into which, in spite of all our wealth of information, the spirit of the time has fallen. Let me explain my meaning.

The old classical curriculum was founded by men who had a theory of the world and of human life. They had taken all the available content of human knowledge and had wrought it together into a coherent whole. What they knew was, as judged by our standards, very little in amount. But upon that little content they had expended all the infinite pains of understanding and interpretation. They had taken the separate judgments of science, philosophy, history and the arts, and had so welded them together, so established their relationships with one another, so freed them from contradictions and ambiguities that, so far as might be in their day and generation, human life as a whole and the world about us were known, were understood, were rationalized. They had a knowledge of human experience by which they could live and which they could teach to others engaged in the activities of living.

But with the invention of methods of scientific investigation and discovery there came pouring into the mind of Europe great masses of intellectual material,—astronomy, physics, chemistry. This content for a time it could not understand, could not relate to what it already knew. The old boundary lines did not enclose the new fields, the old explanations and interpretations would not fit the new facts. Knowledge had not grown, it had simply been enlarged, and the two masses of content, the old and the new, stood facing each other with no common ground of understanding. Here was the intellectual task of the great leaders of the early modern thought of Europe: to reestablish the unity of knowledge, to discover the relationships between these apparently hostile bodies of judgments, to know the world again, but with all the added richness of the new insights and the new information. This was the work of Leibnitz and Spinoza, of Kant and Hegel, and those who labored with them. And in a very considerable measure the task had been accomplished, order had been restored. But again with the inrush of the newer discoveries, first in the field of biology and then later in the world of human relationships, the difficulties have returned, multiplied a thousand fold. Every day sees a new field of facts opened up, a new method of investigation invented, a new department of knowledge established. And in the rush of it all these new sciences come merely as additions, not to be understood but simply numbered, not to be interpreted but simply listed in the great collection of separate fields of knowledge. If you will examine the work of any scientist within one of these fields you will find him ordering, systematizing, reducing to principles, in a word, knowing every fact in terms of its relation to every other fact and to the whole field within which it falls. But at the same time these separate sciences, these separate groups of judgment, are left standing side by side with no intelligible connections, no establishment of relationships, no interpretation in the sense in which we insist upon it within each of the fields taken by itself. Is it not the characteristic statement of a scholar of our time to say, "I do not know what may be the ultimate significance of these facts and these principles; all that I know is that if you will follow my methods within my field you will find the facts coming into order, the principles coming into simple and coherent arrangement. With any problems apart from this order and this arrangement I have intellectually no concern."

It has become an axiom with us that the genuine student labors within his own field. And if the student ventures forth to examine the relations of his field to the surrounding country he very easily becomes a populariser, a litterateur, a speculator, and worst of all, unscientific. Now I do not object to a man's minding his own intellectual business if he chooses to do so, but when a man minds his own business because he does not know any other business, because he has no knowledge whatever of the relationships which justify his business and make it worth while, then I think one may say that though such a man minds his own affairs he does not know them, he does not understand them. Such a man, from the point of view of the demands of a liberal education, differs in no essential respect from the tradesman who does not understand his trade or the professional man who merely practices his profession. Just as truly as they, he is shut up within a special interest; just as truly as they he is making no intellectual attempt to understand his experience in its unity. And the pity of it is that more and more the chairs in our colleges are occupied by men who have only this special interest, this specialized information, and it is through them that we attempt to give our boys a liberal education, which the teachers themselves have not achieved.

I should not like to be misunderstood in making this railing accusation against our teachers and our time. If I say that our knowledge is at present a collection of scattered observations about the world rather than an understanding of it, fairness compels the admission that the failure is due to the inherent difficulties of the situation and to the novelty of the problems presented. If I cry out against the agnosticism of our people it is not as one who has escaped from it, nor as one who would point the way back to the older synthesis, but simply as one who believes that the time has come for a reconstruction, for a new synthesis. We have had time enough now to get some notion of our bearing, shocks enough to get over our nervousness and discomfiture when a new one comes along. It is the opportunity and the obligation of this generation to think through the content of our knowing once again, to understand it, so far as we can. And in such a battle as this, surely it is the part of the college to take the lead. Here is the mission of the college teacher as of no other member of our common life. Surely he should stand before his pupils and before all of us as a man who has achieved some understanding of this human situation of ours, but more than that, as one who is eager for the conflict with the powers of darkness and who can lead his pupils in enthusiastic devotion to the common cause of enlightment.

And now, finally, after these attacks upon the policies which other men have derived from their love of knowledge, may I suggest two matters of policy which seem to me to follow from the definition of education which we have taken? The first concerns the content of the college course; the second has to do with the method of its presentation to the undergraduate.

We have said that the system of free election is natural for those to whom knowledge is simply a number of separate departments. It is equally true that just in so far as knowledge attains unity, just so far as the relations of the various departments are perceived, freedom of election by the student must be limited. For it at once appears that on the one side there are vast ranges of information which have virtually no significance for the purposes of a liberal education, while on the other hand there are certain elements so fundamental and vital that without any one of them a liberal education is impossible.

I should like to indicate certain parts of human knowledge which seem to me so essential that no principle of election should ever be allowed to drive them out of the course of any college student.

First, a student should become acquainted with the fundamental motives and purposes and beliefs which, clearly or unclearly recognized, underlie all human experience and bind it together. He must perceive the moral strivings, the intellectual endeavors, the aesthetic experiences of his race, and closely linked with these, determining and determined by them, the beliefs about the world which have appeared in our systems of religion. To investigate this field, to bring it to such clearness of formulation as may be possible, is the task of philosophy—an essential element in any liberal education. Secondly, as in human living, our motives, purposes and beliefs have found expression in institutions,—those concerted modes of procedure by

Seated at his desk in Walker Hall in 1912, Meiklejohn begins to direct the work of Amherst College.

which we work together,—a student should be made acquainted with these. He should see and appreciate what is intended, what accomplished, and what left undone by such institutions as property, the courts, the family, the church, the mill. To know these as contributing and failing to contribute to human welfare is the work of our social or humanistic sciences, into which a boy must go on his way through the liberal college. Thirdly, in order to understand the motives and the institutions of human life one must know the conditions which surround it, the stage on which the game is played. To give this information is the business of astronomy, geology, physics, chemistry, biology and the other sciences of nature. These a boy must know, so far as they are significant and relevant to his purpose. Fourthly, as all three of these factors, the motives, the institutions, the natural processes have sprung from the past and have come to be what they are by change upon change in the process of time, the student of human life must try to learn the sequence of events from which the present has come. The development of human thoughts and attitude, the development of human institutions, the development of the world and of the beings about us—all these must be known, as throwing light upon present problems, present instrumentalities, present opportunities in the life of human endeavor. And in addition to these four studies which render human experience in terms of abstract ideas, a liberal education must take account of those concrete representations of life which are given in the arts, and especially in the art of literature. It is well that a boy should be acquainted with his world not simply as expressed by the principles of knowledge but also as depicted by the artist with all the vividness and definiteness which are possible in the portrayal of individual beings in individual relationships. These five elements, then, a young man must take from a college of liberal training, the contributions of philosophy, of humanistic science, of natural science, of history, and of literature. So far as knowledge is concerned, these at least he should have, welded together in some kind of interpretation of his own experience and of the world in which he lives.

My second suggestion is that our college curriculum should be so arranged and our instruction so devised that its vital connection with the living of men should be obvious even to an undergraduate. A little while ago I heard one of the most prominent citizens of this country speaking of his college days, and he said, "I remember so vividly those few occasions on which the professor would put aside the books and talk like a real man about real things." Oh, the bitterness of those words to the teacher! Our books are not dealing with the real things, and for the most part we are not real men either, but just old fogies and bookworms! And to be perfectly frank about the whole matter, I believe that in large measure our pupils are indifferent to their studies simply because they do not see that these are important.

But if we really have a vital course of study to present this difficulty can in large measure be overcome. It is possible to make a Freshman realize the need of translating his experience from the forms of feeling to those of ideas. He can and he ought to be shown that now, his days of mere tutelage being over, it is time for him to face the problems of his people, to begin to think about those problems for himself, to learn what other men have learned and thought before him, in a word, to get himself ready to take his place among those who are responsible for the guidance of our common life by ideas and principles and purposes. If this could be done, I think we should get from the reality-loving American boy something like an intellectual enthusiasm, something of the spirit that comes when he plays a game that seems to him really worth playing. But I do not believe that this result can be achieved without a radical reversal of the arrangement of the college curriculum. I should like to see every freshman at once plunged into the problems of philosophy, into the difficulties and perplexities about our institutions, into the scientific accounts of the world expecially as they bear on human life, into the portrayals of human experience which are given by the masters of literature. If this were done by proper teaching, it seems to me the boy's college course would at once take on significance for him; he would understand what he is about; and though he would be a sadly puzzled boy at the end of the first year, he would still have before him three good years of study, of investigation, of reflection, and of discipleship, in which to achieve, so far as may be, the task to which he has been set. Let him once feel the problems of the present, and his historical studies will become significant; let him know what other men have discovered and thought about his problems, and he will be ready to deal with them himself. But in any case, the whole college course will be unified and dominated by a single interest, a single purpose,—that of so understanding human life as to be ready and equipped for the practice of it. And this would mean for the college, not another seeking of the way of quick returns, but rather an escape from aimless wanderings in the mere by-paths of knowledge, a resolute climbing on the high road to a unified grasp upon human experience.

I have taken so much of your time this morning that an apology seems due for the things I have omitted to mention. I have said nothing of the organization of the college, nothing of the social life of the students, nothing of the relations with the alumni, nothing of the needs and qualifications of the teachers, and even within the consideration of the course of study, nothing of the value of specialization or of the disciplinary subjects or of the training in language and expression. And I have put these aside deliberately, for the sake of a cause which is greater than any of them—a cause which lies at the very heart of the liberal college. It is the cause of making clear to the American people the mission of the teacher, of convincing them of the value of knowledge: not the specialized knowledge which contributes to immediate practical aims, but the unified understanding which is Insight.

> *Editor's Note: Thirty years after Meiklejohn gave his Amherst inaugural he added the following footnote. Addressing a reunion of students from the Experimental College in May 1942, in Chicago, he divulged how he felt while delivering his inaugural speech.*

As I turn now to more detailed examination of the relation between "having knowledge" and "being wise," it will, I trust, be in keeping with the character of this occasion if, for a moment, I indulge in reminiscence. Thirty years ago, in the autumn of 1912, I too was young and fresh and making plans. Thirty years ago I delivered an Inaugural Address at Amherst College. And among all the exciting incidents of that exciting day one incident has lingered in my memory with a poignancy exceeding that of all the rest. I can still shudder at the shock, the disturbance of it. As I advanced, line by line, page by page, through the text of that address, I suddenly found myself reading words whose meaning I could not accept as true. I can still recall how near I came to stopping. What should one do in such a situation? To myself I was saying, "I don't think I believe that. Why did I write it down?" What I wanted was time to think of something else to put in its place. And yet I could not stop. Driven helplessly on by the imperatives of the ceremonial procedure, I discovered in that bitter moment the meaning of the dictum, "All college presidents are liars." My intellectual innocence was gone. And yet I was safe. My sin was known only to myself. And I have never confessed it until the writing of this paper, raising again the same issue by which I was then confronted, has brought it back to me.

The sentences which, at the very start of my career, carried me to the edge of disaster, were saying that scholarship refuses to submit to certain practical demands which are made upon it. And in the face of that conflict I was taking the side of scholarship. Men of knowledge, I said, "are not willing to cut up their sciences into segments and to allow the student to select these segments which may be of service in the practice of an art or of a profession." And what suddenly threw me back upon my heels was the realization that I was approving this "high-and-mightiness" of the scholar. I was lining up the teachers on the side of knowledge for its own sake as against knowledge for the benefit of mankind. "In one way or another," I said, "the teacher feels a kinship with the scientist and the scholar which forbids him to submit to this domination of his instruction by the demands of an immediate practical interest." "Whatever it may mean," I continued, "he intends to hold the intellectual point of view and to keep his students with him if he can."

"Scholars are not willing to cut up their sciences into segments and to allow the student to select those segments which may be of service in the practice of an art or of a profession." Why not? What is knowledge for? Presumably the arts and professions are conducive to human welfare. Why, then should not the sciences contribute to them in whatever ways they can?

And especially there is one art, the greatest and most inclusive of them all, in the presence of which all science, all knowledge, all scholarship, must bow down in submission and humility. It is the art of morality, of wise and good behavior. The dictates of that art are supreme in all human relations. They are final and incontrovertible in the field of education. If a person is reasonable and kind in his dealings with his fellow-men, whether or not he knows chemistry or metaphysics or economics or literary history, he is essentially well-educated. And, on the other hand, a person may be a master in the fields of knowledge of which I have spoken and may yet be utterly lacking in the rudiments of liberal learning.

Our colleges, as I have known them, have been largely dominated by uneducated scholars. If my statement seems too harsh, too unrestrained, I beg of you to remember that I am speaking words of repentance. I am making atonement for wrong-doing. Thirty years ago I bowed down my head before the Golden Calf of Scholarship which, in the name of Truth, has led our colleges astray, has made them false to that supreme object of their devotion. And now, having in your presence acknowledged one of the grievous sins of my youth, I take up again the development of my theme.

2

The Experimental College

Alexander Meiklejohn wrote this book as a report to the faculty of the College of Letters and Science of the University of Wisconsin on the five years' work done by the advisers in the Experimental College. In it he analyzed both the achievements and failures of the Experimental College. It was published as: Alexander Meiklejohn, The Experimental College *(New York: Harper and Brothers, 1932). In 1971 Arno Press reprinted the book.*

I have selected from three parts of the book, namely, most of chapter 5, "Understanding Is Integration"; a sample from Appendix IV of the weekly assignments given to students; and a passage from chapter 18, "Recommendations," that describes the most profound impression made on the advisers by their adventure in teaching.

The demand for integration is the demand that throughout a scheme of instruction there shall run a single and dominating "scheme of reference." It means that, logically considered, the course of study shall have unity, shall hang together from beginning to end. There shall not be a series of disconnected readings or separate topics whose relations are left undetermined. Fundamentally the course shall be the study of a single topic, and every separate subject within it shall be recognized as a special phase of the central inquiry. The effect of the principle is, it is obvious, the discarding of separate "subjects" as given in the usual college arrangements and the substituting for these of a single enterprise running through the two years of the course. Its psychological influence upon teachers and students appears in the suggestion that there is one definite thing which all of them should do.

This demand for integration, for unification, of the curriculum has immediate regard for that quality which Mr. [Abraham] Flexner calls "intelligence, capable of being applied in any field whatever." The phrase suggests a mind which is able to go about, anywhere in the world of human experience, with sureness of footing, with certainty of touch. And the teaching question is, How does one develop and cultivate that quality in a growing, plastic mind? In answer to this question, the principle of integration, as discussed by the Advisers, is very direct and simple in its teaching theory. It says that the student should go, in terms of ideas, into all the fields in which we wish him to be intelligent, that in each of these fields his mind should be given active work to do, and especially that these separate pieces of work should be such that they will run into one another, have intellectual relations with one another. The underlying purpose is that the student shall in this way develop a "scheme of reference" covering all the fields, within which each field shall find its proper place. And the result of this will be that any new experience within any field may then be seen in its place, in its relations, in the ways which we sum up under the terms, "with understanding" or "intelligently." From this point of view the "intelligent" mind is not one which can go safely into unfamiliar fields. No mind can do that. In so far as a field is unfamiliar no thinking about it can be secure and certain. An intelligent mind is one to which, in some essential sense, all fields of experience are familiar.

As so defined, the view is radically opposed to a well-known theory which has now fortunately become quite disreputable. This was the view that one could, by cultivating one's powers in a chosen field, develop there an "intelligence" which would guide him in other fields. So formerly it was believed that study in mathematics and the languages would make one keen and accurate and penetrating in any field whatever. So now it is sometimes held by the scientists who have ousted the ancient languages that "science" will make men accurate of mind even about matters to which the application of scientific technique is quite impossible. But the refutation of that theory was very easy and crushing when once the issue had been stated. No one who has seen the uncanny accuracy, not to mention the courage and industry, of a boy at play on a tennis court or a baseball field, and has then encountered his mind and will in a classroom, can long keep his faith in such a notion. And the achievements of metaphysicians in practical affairs are equally disconcerting, not to mention the fumbling, the confusion, the incoherence with which "practical men" mishandle the affairs of the human spirit. As against this view in all its forms, the view of integration with which we are concerned insists that, in some very real sense, the only way to become intelligent in any field is to go into that field, with your mind, and to use your mind within it *in such a way* that the connections of intelligence are established, that the field is "placed" in your scheme of understanding.

Now it is the phrase *"in such a way"* which, in this statement, quickly becomes the center of educational controversy. If it be admitted that the intellectual purpose is to link together all significant fields in a scheme of intelligible relationships, the question remains, What do you do in each field as you work within it; what kind of mental operation do you and your students carry on? And here the answer of the typical advocate of integration involves him at once in difficulties with his colleagues, if not also with his own other principles. He says, to put it very bluntly, that you will never establish relations either within a field or between fields so long as you are merely seeking specific information. It is only in terms of general problems and general ideas that different situations and different fields are ever understood. What then shall we do with our students as we send them in search of intelligence? By some means or other we must arouse in them an activity in general ideas, must get them possessed of a store of general questions, must teach them to universalize, to infer, to deduce, to connect. In a word, they must think, in each field, about the things which are logically significant in that field. They must attempt to understand it as a whole and as in relation to a larger whole.

When the demand for unification is stated in this uncompromising way there inevitably breaks out against it a counter demand of great force and significance. It flared up in the first meeting at which the Advisers considered the course of study. It has persisted throughout the four years of their discussions. The advocate of integration has said, The student must approach a situation with general ideas, general questions; he must interpret the situation, reason about it, discuss it, must infer, deduce, connect and separate the meanings which relate to it. And to this his opponent replies, Would it not be well for him to *learn* something about the situation before he begins to understand it? How can he interpret a set of facts about which he knows nothing? Do you mean to suggest that he will bring to the situation, prior to any knowledge of it, a set of general ideas, general questions, general theories which he will use in understanding it? Where will he get

Seated in his office at Adams Hill, Chairman Meiklejohn writes the report of the Experimental College to the faculty of the University of Wisconsin in the winter of 1931-32.

those ideas and questions? What assurance is there that they will have any relevance for this new set of circumstances into which he goes for the first time? If you proceed to teach a young man in that way, will you not make of him a "crank," a person who can solve all universal questions inside his head, but who knows nothing whatever of any actual, specific, objective "facts" or situations?

As one looks back upon discussions of the controversy so stated, the delight of them stirs again in one's veins. One can still feel the rising fury in one's spirit as he sees how ridiculous is the opposing point of view. And it is especially pleasant to recall that, as one's own fury rose, that of his opponent rose with equal intensity. Each, with equal clarity, could see how absurd and objectionable the opposing position was. Which is prior—the asking of questions or the collecting of information by means of which to answer them? One side asserts that it is nonsense to ask questions if you do not know about what you are inquiring. The other retorts that to collect information is quite meaningless unless you have in mind a question for the answering of which the information is needed. Which is right? With which of these general ideas shall we approach the strange and baffling incidents of education? Do chickens depend upon eggs or eggs upon chickens? Shall we teach boys to "think"? Or shall we "give" them some "facts" to think about?

Now it is evident that only confusion of mind could lead one to make, in *general,* the choice suggested by the questions just stated. If one is asked, in the abstract, to choose between "facts" and "the understanding of facts," one must, denying the implication of the question, choose both, since each is, without the other, meaningless. But fortunately, no immediate, practical situation calls for such general answers. Our working questions take the form, What, under these special conditions and for this special purpose, will be your choice? Will you, this morning, have chicken or eggs for breakfast? Will you, this evening, have eggs or chicken for dinner? And it is just such a specific question with which the Advisers have been concerned. As a boy seeks liberal education, as he comes out of the American school and the American home, as he enters upon the last formal stages of his training for self-direction, which will you stress more strongly, the gaining of specific information or the building up of a general scheme of reference?

Now no single statement could summarize the varied responses of individual Advisers to this question. In their decisions, however, one finds a general drift which may be defined by two statements. First, in the "lower college" years, under present teaching conditions, the "integration" demand is of primary importance. In the large, we may say that "information" is secondary; it is valuable, at this time and for these pupils, only as it contributes to the building up of one's "scheme of reference." And second, there is at this point an important, though not a radical, difference between the two years. Information about America is, for our teaching purpose, far more important than information about Athens. As a young man tries to bring into order the world of his values, beliefs, decisions, it makes very little difference, in the last resort, whether he knows what was going on in Athens twenty-four centuries ago. It is, however, essential that he know what is going on in the American world of today. Quite clearly the two years cannot then be simply subsumed under a blank generalization. They have a common aim, but they serve it in different ways. We must now try, by illustration, to make these statements more clear and perhaps more convincing. And to do this we must at least indicate what is meant by a "scheme of reference."

In any organized understanding of contemporary life the distinction between riches and poverty must play an essential part. This cleavage in human societies is a vital element in any intelligent man's scheme of reference. How then shall we use studies in Athenian civilization of the fifth century B.C. for the teaching of freshmen about it? Now the answer to that question depends upon our judgment as to what the ordinary American boy needs first to have done to his mind with respect to the problem of riches and poverty. And the answer of the "scheme of reference" view is that he needs, to begin with, not primarily more information but a more active response to the information which he already has. If that response can be aroused, then one of its immediate effects will be a strenuous demand for further information which bears upon its question. For example, every boy who comes to college knows in his own immediate circle of acquaintance the tragic separation between the rich and the poor. One pupil comes to the university with a credit in the bank of two or three thousand dollars. Another comes with two or three hundred which he has earned during the summer. One is threatened by the dangers of wastefulness and folly. The other is uncertain whether or not he can "last the semester." Both boys are informed about this situation. Do they understand it? Do they regard it as something to be "understood," or do they simply accept it as matter of fact? If they do the latter they are, in so far, uneducated and failing in the essential process of getting an education.

Now at this point we may use the experience of Athens for teaching purposes. Athens had always much to do with the problem of the rich and the poor. It is recorded that in one of the earlier centuries, as a result of changing social and external conditions which no one seemed to understand, the division between the two classes became desperately serious. The ownership of land was drifting into the hands of a few. More and more the many were losing their freeholds, were becoming serfs, were selling their bodies to pay their debts. And as revolution threatened, all classes called upon Solon, who seemed both wise and honest, to take the city into his hands and to do with debts and ownership whatever he might think best. And so there came about the reforms of Solon. How shall this incident be used for teaching purposes?

It is clear that one might ask the student to learn, so far as he can, all that is known about the situation in Athens and about Solon's dealing with it. In very many excellent textbooks this material has been gathered, and so arranged that it can be memorized even by the most inactive of minds. And it would be easy, too, for the teacher, in this case, to tell whether or not the pupil has done his learning faithfully and well. He can be tested and marked on his mastery of facts. But the trouble is that by assigning a task in this form we give to the student a wholly false suggestion as to what his mind should be doing. For a young American, of eighteen or nineteen, in the present state of American society, to spend his powers in simply learning what was going on in the Athens of Solon would be an egregious waste of time, a sin against himself and against his approaching responsibilities.

The Advisers have, therefore, with much misgiving and with many hesitations, contrived a different policy. They have said to the student, "Look into the situation with which Solon was dealing; put yourself into his place; try to imagine what was going on in his mind; write a paper and tell what you would have done had you faced his responsibilities." And at this point there has occurred a curious reversal of teaching relationships. Having said to the students, "You must study Athens in order to understand America," we find ourselves constantly saying to them, "You must bring your knowledge of modern America to help you in interpreting ancient Athens." When the freshmen were reading the Greek dramas we urged them to read also Ibsen and O'Neill; when they were studying Plato's *Republic* we assigned the story of the Russian experiment in Communism in Hindus' *Humanity Uprooted.* And the same procedure has been followed in matters of art, religion, politics, philosophy, and science. And the belief underlying this method is very simple. It is that the essential difficulty with which the education of young Americans has to deal is that they do not think about the information which they already have.

We too have an economic and social crisis similar to that of Solon's time. With us, too, as a result of conditions which no one seems able to understand, the great bulk of the property tends to fall into the hands of a few; with us, too, the lower economic class is in terrible fear and distress; in America, as in Athens, unguided forces take from men their independence, make them the slaves of their fellows. And the primary task of liberal education is to make it impossible that boys or men should be in such a situation without attempting to understand and control it. The young man who can blithely and unthinkingly waste a thousand dollars in frivolity and dissipation, while the fellow in the next room is being forced to leave college because he cannot pay for his board, simply cannot be made to understand either Solon or the situation with which Solon dealt. He may learn words and facts and figures, but he will never understand them. The using of Solon is then not an end in itself. It is simply a device for stirring a young man to see that with which he is already acquainted, to think about what he knows. The chief task of the teacher as he deals with American college students is to get their minds active, to give them a sense of the urgency of human need, to establish in them the activity of seeing and solving problems. It is true that they are sadly in need of information, but it is far more true that they need the desire for information. We must set them to work at a task in relation to which information is the material to be used. If they will attempt to build up a "scheme of reference," then for them every new fact will take on significance, every new situation become an object of active inquiry.

We have cited the division between the rich and the poor as one of the matters about which a lower college student should learn to think. Now, from the point of view of the principle of integration, the problem of devising a course of study is that of listing and ordering all the problems of the class to which that of riches and poverty belongs. To put it quite simply, the task is that of stating in orderly arrangement and interrelation the essential problems with which human intelligence deals. One need hardly say that the Advisers do not think themselves to have accomplished this task. What they can say is that, in their attempt to make and use a course of study, they have worked at the task and have tried to enlist their students in the same endeavor. In so far as the college has been successful, both groups have been engaged in this never-accomplished but never-to-be-abandoned enterprise of the human spirit—the search for unified understanding. . . .

A course of study planned on the basis of [this search] would have as its critical question: What do men do as individuals and groups in the attempt to create and to conserve human values? It would naturally fall into three main divisions:

I. Appreciation of human activities in so far as they are immediately of value. In dealing with each civilization we should seek to become familiar with and to appreciate its literature and other arts; in addition to these, its forms of healthy activity, recreation, athletic games, dances, festivals, etc.,—in whatever ways individual or group seeks to express and to heighten the quality of living.

II. Understanding of human institutions as instrumentalities made and remade for the furthering of values. In studying these the student should see (1) the values to be served, (2) the limiting and determining conditions of which decisions must take account, and (3) the human planning, the consideration of ends and conditions which in each case have entered into the shaping of any given institution.

Under this heading a number of social arrangements are to be studied:

(a) The creation and distribution of property

Questions:

(1) How is property created; how can the methods be improved?
(2) By what forces or on what principles is property shared? Are better arrangements possible?

Contrast Capitalism, Socialism, and Communism.

Under the general heading, Riches and Poverty, we should study:

(1) Natural resources
(2) Technology
(3) Human labor and its reward
(4) Ownership and industry
(5) Commercial and financial organization
(6) Government and property
    (a) Class Conflict
    (b) Legislation
    (c) The growth of empire

(b) Group organization and control

General heading—Rulers and Ruled

(1) The Individual and the Group
What is the sphere and what the limits of control?
(2) The location of power
What are the forms and what the best form of control?
(Democracy, tyranny, etc.)
(3) Forms of political organization and administration
Comparison of constitutions
(4) Legal principles and procedure

(c) War and Peace—relations between groups

Theory and practice of states in relation to other states. By what forces and on what principles are these determined, should they be determined? (Nationalism, Internationalism, Imperialism)

(d) Status—accepted ratings of individuals and groups, in terms of standing and privilege

Democratic ideal *versus* others

(1) Class division
(2) Race division
(3) Slavery of various kinds
(4) Citizenship and exclusion from it
(5) Sex discrimination

(e) The rearing and training of children

Marriage and sex relations

III. The activities of thinking by which we describe the world of men and things as constituting the values and forces of which men must take account in their planning for the enhancement of value.

(a) Religious thinking—the attempt at interpretation of the world at large in terms of values. Are there such values? If so, what are they?

    (1) The origin and growth of religious ideas
    (2) The conflicts of these ideas
    (3) Modernism—the criticism of religious beliefs under changing social and intellectual conditions

(b) The sciences—the description of the world as a time-space process in which "facts" are accurately determined and verified.

    What do men find themselves and their world to be in terms of observation, experiment and inference based upon and verified by these?

    (1) What are the processes and forces of the inorganic world?
    (2) What are living processes aand their relations to the conditions which determine them?
    (3) What, as seen in the time-space series, are the processes of consciousness, value, and intelligence?

(c) Philosophy—the attempt at critical examination of intelligence and the world in relation to each other, at understanding of the total human situation so that the various studies may find their significance for each other and for human meaning as a whole.

    (1) What does control by intelligence mean? Is it an illusion? If not, what are its possiblities and limits?
    Freedom and Determinism
    (2) What are the values for the sake of which intelligence plans and directs action?
        (a) What is justice in social situations?
        (b) What is good, admirable, in individual living?
        (c) Are these values relative or absolute?
        Folkways *versus* principles
    (3) What is intelligence, especially in the form of conscious self-direction which we call thinking?
        (a) What is the aim of thinking—the difference between good and bad thinking or the absence of thinking?
        (b) What are the principles, the methods of thinking?

(c) What are the different fields of thinking?

(d) Is truth relative or absolute or both? How is it related to other values?

(4) What, in summary and in the best terms we can find, is the world and man's relation to it, his enterprise in dealing with it? What is human opportunity? What are human success and failure?

Note—This outline is not intended to suggest the order in which topics should be studied, nor that, if two civilizations are studied, that the same order of topics should be followed in the two cases.

In conclusion, it should be said again that neither this nor any other statement of a "scheme of reference" has been formally adopted or exactly followed by the Advisers. With regard to the problem here involved we have, whatever our differences, two strong convictions in common: first, it cannot be completely solved; second, it cannot be given up. It is the permanent problem of finding a "content" basis for a scheme of liberal education.

*   *   *

Freshman Assignments

November 1, 1930

Conflicts about Wealth

Reading:

Zimmern, *The Greek Commonwealth,* especially Pt. 2, Ch. 5.

See also:

Plutarch, *Life of Solon; Life of Pericles*

Aristophanes, Comedies

The Old Oligarch (in pamphlet form; and reprinted in Botsford and Sihler, *Hellenic Civilization*)

Croiset, *Aristophanes and the Political Parties in Athens*

Arisotle's *Politics,* Everyman edition, Bk. 5.

Compare any relevant modern material like *The Communist Manifesto;* R. H. Tawney, *The Acquisitive Society;* Andrew Carnegie's *Autobiography;* The writings of Henry Ford.

Paper, due November 10:

Describe the conflict about wealth with which Solon had to deal. What did Solon do about this conflict? Did any similar conflict face Pericles? Do you find any similar conflict today? If so, what is your opinion and your own attitude toward it?

Talks:

Tuesday, November 4, and Thursday, November 6, there will be opportunities for the class to discuss questions raised by the assignment, with Mr. Koch or Mr. Sharp or both.

November 10, 1930
Functions and Structure of Government

During this period, the situation in Athens should be compared particularly with the situation in Sparta, and still more particularly with the ideal scheme described in Plato's *Republic.* It seems likely that "democratic" Athens is being criticized, and "aristocratic" Sparta qualifiedly approved in the *Republic.* If we can develop a reasonably clear understanding of the government of both Athens and Sparta, we shall, among other things, be better prepared to understand and discuss Plato's philosophy of government.

We have now become acquainted with a good deal of the literature dealing with the economic and political life of Athens and Sparta; and it therefore seems unnecessary to set forth an extended list of readings.

Reading:

Zimmern, *The Greek Commonwealth,* especially Pt. II, Ch. 6.

See also:

Aristotle, *The Constitution of Athens;* Plutarch, *Life of Lycurgus;* Glotz, *The Greek City;* Greenidge, *Handbook of Greek Constitutional History;* Vinogradoff, *Historical Jurisprudence,* Vol. II; Calhoun, *The Growth of Criminal Law in Ancient Greece;* Bonner, *Lawyers and Litigants in Ancient Athens.*

A suggested modern book is A. P. Herring, *Group Representation Before Congress.*

Paper, due November 17:
What work did the governing bodies of Athens do, and how were they organized under Cleisthenes? Compare the constitution under Pericles. Compare the constitution of Sparta. Discuss the merits and defects of each constitution.

Talks:
There will be meetings of the class at nine o'clock on Tuesday and Thursday, November 11 and 13.

November 17—December 1, 1930
Democracy

During the next two weeks we shall have an opportunity to go over all the material which we have thus far been studying; and to organize and enrich our knowledge and understanding of the social, economic, and political life of Athens and the modern world. There will be an opportunity, for example, to consider the relationship of such institutions as the family, slavery, and the empire, to the other institutions and events which we have been studying. There will also be an opportunity for each of us to think further about any special phase of Athenian life which has interested him particularly, and to discuss the relationship of this phase of life to other aspects of Athens and the modern world. To prevent reading and discussion from becoming utterly formless there will be a two-weeks' paper on the rather large subject "Democracy."

Suggested Readings:
Herodotus' *History,* Vol. 1, pp. 250-253, Vol. 2. pp. 35, 40-45, 46, Vol. 1, pp. 86-87; Thucydides, *Peloponnesian War,* pp. 217-227, 276-278; 570-614; Xenophon, *Hellenica,* Bks. I and II; Plato, *Republic,* especially Bks. VIII and IX; Aristotle's *Politics,* translated by William Ellis, especially Bks. III to VI, inclusive; Sophocles, *Antiogne;* Euripides, *Alcestis, Medea, Trojan Women* (for the position of women); Savage, *The Athenian Family,* Zimmern, *Solon and Croesus* (essays on slavery), *Political Thought* (in *The Legacy of Greece*), *The Greek Commonwealth;* Jebb, *The Attic Orators.*

See also the books listed in previous assignments. Again compare books on contemporary conditions. Further suggested readings on conditions at other periods than the fifth century are:

> Rostovtzeff, *Social and Economic History of the Roman Empire;* G. B. Shaw, *The Intelligent Woman's Guide to Socialism and Capitalism;* Wallas, *The Great Society; Human Nature and Politics;* Santayana, *Character and Opinion in the United States;* Unemployment Conference Committee (Herbert Hoover, Chairman) *Recent Economic Changes in the United States;* Lippmann, *Public Opinion; The Phantom Public;* Frank Kent, *The Great Game of Politics.*

Paper, due December 1:

What do you mean by democracy—social, economic, political? Consider the social, economic, and political life of Athens, with reference to the question whether Athens was democratic in the sense in which you use the term.

Meetings:

There will be meetings on Tuesday and Thursday mornings at nine o'clock unless announcements to the contrary are made; and other meetings will probably be held, and announced on the bulletin board.

Sophomore Assignments
January 11—16, 1932

A brief paper dealing with some aspect of the "public control of business" will be due from each student by Monday noon, January 18, unless the student has previously made a substitute arrangement with his Adviser. (Several of the groups are taking special topics for group discussion and presenting individual papers in that connection.)

The following are suggested as possible topics for such papers:

The background, purposes and provisions of (one or more of) the three major antitrust laws; the work of the Federal Trade Commission as revealed in its annual reports (library document-room); specific unfair business practices; trade associations; industry planning, etc. (the Swope Plan and the Harriman Report); national planning (as discussed in testimony before Senator La Follette's Senate sub-committee—library document-room); conditions under which a business is so "affected with a public interest" that price regulation is economically and/or legally justified; present limits on the effective regulation of public utilities; the problems of administration involved in the public control of business; government competition as a means of control; any other topic growing fairly directly out of the week's general reading, subject to the Adviser's approval; or, alternatively, the economic facts and legal-economic issues in any *one* of the following legal cases:

(To locate any of these cases, in the Law School or the university library, see in the *Public Control of Business* its footnote reference to volume and page numbers of the U.S. Supreme Court decisions; for example, *251 U.S. 417* means Volume 251 at page 417, etc.)

The Standard Oil Company case (1911); the U.S. Steel Corporation case (1920); the earlier United Shoe Machinery case (1918); the Maple Flooring Association case (1925); the Duplex Printing Press Company case (1921); the Bedford Stone Company case (1927); the Wolff Packing Company case (1923); the Tyson and Brothers case (1927); the Ribnik case (1928); the State of Missouri ex rel. Southwestern Bell Telephone Co. case (1923); St. Louis and O'Fallon case (1929); Green v. Frazier (1920).

January 18—25, 1932

The book to be studied this week is *Other People's Money,* by Louis D. Brandeis.

College Meetings: 10 M T W Th F.

A brief paper dealing with some aspect of this book will be due from each student by 10 o'clock Monday morning, January 25, unless the student has previously made a substitute arrangement with his Adviser. (Suggested topics: The structure of the "money trust"; the importance of "interlocking directorates"; the function of the investment banker; the New Haven Railroad case; financing government borrowing by government agency;

the possible role of publicity; or any other related topic approved by your Adviser.)

January 25—30, 1932

The book to be studied by all the college will be *The Acquisitive Society,* by R. H. Tawney.

College Meetings: 10 M T W Th F, largely under the direction of Mr. Meiklejohn.

During this week, as will be further explained at Monday's meeting, each member of the college (including Advisers) will be asked to join one of three groups, respectively, for "capitalism," "socialism," or "communism." Each of these groups will meet, at hours to be arranged, for the purpose of working out and stating its position. Each group will then delegate representatives to explain and urge its point of view before the general college meetings the latter part of the week.

Over the present week-end, therefore, each student should try to define his own position, and should (by Monday morning) make up his mind which group to join for the week's discussions.

Every student should, during the week (before Saturday noon), write and hand in a brief paper either formulating his own present position or analyzing Tawney's conception of a "functional society."

*   *   *

. . . . Probably the most profound impression which has been made upon the Advisers by their adventure in the teaching of young Americans has been the sense of their own lack of adequate liberal education. This in not said by way of imitation of Henry Adams, the story of whose education, or lack of it, plays so dominating a part in the course of study of the second year of the college. It comes rather from a deeper and more lively realization of the possibilities and responsibilities of American education together with the sense of the obstacles and hindrances which stand in its way. As one studies the liberal teaching of our colleges, whatever their course of study, whatever their methods of teaching, the most appalling fact about them is the scantiness of their educational result, the poverty of their intellectual quality. And if one may speak only for himself, there can be no doubt that the deeper reason for this lies in the quality of the teacher himself. We do not teach liberal understanding well chiefly because we do not know what it is. We are very much at home in the field of scholarship. If a student will limit his interest to some field of intellectual abstraction, we can show him what the human mind has thus far done in that field, can build up in him the proper technique, can equip him, according to his ability, to take his place in the ranks of the craftsmen of that study. And along more practical lines, where scholarship is applied, without criticism, to the accomplishing of practical ends, where the human mind is used as the servant of its own lesser interests, we are again amazingly able, both in achieving results and in training younger men to create still greater ones.

But if the liberal question is asked, our skill and mastery vanish. If men inquire, "What should American life be; toward what ends should it be guided and inspired; in terms of what scheme of ideas and values should it be interpreted and controlled?", the characteristic attitude of many of our ablest scholars is one of despair and utter incapacity. We have many sciences but little wisdom. We have multifarious and accurate information, but we have lost hope of knowing what it means. And to say this is to say in the most unmistakable terms that we are ourselves, for the time, beaten in the struggle for liberal education and therefore unable to lead our students into its activities.

Far deeper, then, than any question of curriculum or teaching method or determining conditions is the problem of restoring the courage of Americans, academic or non-academic, for the facing of the essential issues of life. How can it be brought about that the teachers in our colleges and universities shall see themselves, not only as the servants of scholarship, but also, in a far deeper sense, as the creators of the national intelligence? If they lose courage in that endeavor, in whom may we expect to find it? Intelligence, wisdom, sensitiveness, generosity—these cannot be set aside from our planning, to be, as it were, by-products of the scholarly pursuits. They are the ends which all our scholarship and our teaching serve. If, then, one is set to inquire how American teaching can be better done, the most fundamental phases of the inquiry must concern themselves with the forces which create and fashion the attitude, the life, of the American teacher. The primary question concerning our academic system is not, "What is its effect upon the student?" but rather, "What is its effect upon our teachers?'' If we can get them rightly placed in relation to their work, nothing in the world can prevail against them.

3

The American College and American Freedom

After the closing of the Experimental College in 1932 its alumni, men who had been students or advisers on the college, held regular reunions—in Chicago in 1942, Annapolis in 1957, and Madison in 1962 and 1977.

These reunions were academic conclaves. They arose out of the desire of the alumni to think through again the meaning of the experiment and the questions it had raised in their lives. At their reunions the alumni held discussions in the Socratic mode that they had learned at the college. Meiklejohn used these occasions to learn from his former students. He presented his current ideas and challenged his audience to light into him, to reveal his flaws, and to raise questions he had neglected.

He gave the following address at the reunion on May 10, 1957, at St. John's College, Annapolis, Maryland. The occasion marked the 30th anniversary of the establishment of the Experimental College and the 85th anniversary of Meiklejohn's birth. The speech is a culmination of Meiklejohn's thought, the single document that best presents all his themes. It draws upon the twenty-five years he had spent after the closing of the Experimental College thinking about self-government, freedom of speech, and the First Amendment.

The speech was printed in the Congressional Record,
85th Congress, 1st Session, vol. 103, part 7 (June 7-20,
1957), pp. 8751-8755.

President Weigle, Dean Klein, the faculty and other members of the
St. John's community, we of the Experimental College come here, in
response to your very kind invitation, to celebrate the 30th anniversary of the birth of our own college. May I express to you our deep
appreciation of an act of courtesy which is, I think, unique in the
academic life of the United States. There are, as you know, many
differences in the method and the content of teaching of our two institutions. And yet, your invitation and our acceptance of it indicate, I
am sure, a fundamental kinship, an identity of purpose, between us.
Through many happy and exciting days and weeks and months on this
campus I have recognized the depth and the warmth of that kinship,
and have delighted in it. Coming here, we of the Experimental College find ourselves at home. . . .

The Committee in charge of our celebration has requested, or
directed, me to present my topic by posing a question or questions
and offering an answer or answers in such a way that throughout all
our meetings there may run a continuous effort of reflection and discussion concerning men and their minds, and especially concerning
the freedom of American minds. The plan seems to be that, so far as
we are capable of it, our reunion shall take on that mingling of gaiety
and seriousness, of belief and bewilderment, which the symposium of
Plato long ago established as the model of revelry and conversation
which are proper to reasonable beings.

As I say that, I am wondering if you recall as vividly as I do that
morning meeting of the college at which George Russell, whom his
readers knew as "AE," spoke to us about the symposium, telling us
that whatever he had won of human wisdom had its source in the say-
ings of the wise Diotima as she was quoted by Socrates in that beautiful and powerful platonic discussion of the nature of human love.

At this point, too, before the argument begins, I must pay my
respects to my two very good friends, Alan Barth and Harold Taylor,
who have been summoned by the committee to give my argument a
going over when I have got it stated. They are dangerous fellows both.
It may be that when they have had their say there will be nothing left
of my suggestions for you to talk about.

Shall we, however, summon our courage to try what the committee tells us to do? Shall we go Socratic to the limit for a day or two? If we do follow that program, then our celebration must find its fun in gay and fearless questioning of whatever we are, whatever we think, and whatever we care for. We must subject to critical assessment the truth or falsity of what we believe, must ponder ruefully over much that we have done and plan to do in a confusing and self-defeating contemporary world. The committee is, I am sure, right in thinking that these are the activities which our college would wish us to carry on and to enjoy in celebration of its birth. Can we enjoy them? If not, it is, I fear, all too clear that however much we celebrate, we are not celebrating a college.

Since we have been separated from one another for many years and have traveled many different paths, it will be wise, I think to make a slow beginning of our symposium. Let me then, in reminiscent mood, seek to reopen the lines of communication by referring to two features of the past which we have in common.

The Experimental College

First, then, I remind you that at the reunion of 1942, when we celebrated the college on the tenth anniversary of its ending, nine wise young members of the alumni group were called upon to answer on paper and by voice the question, "How do I fit in?" These men had worked in many occupations since leaving Madison and each of them spoke of his special work with deep concern. They were a lawyer, a doctor, an administrator of the Tennessee Valley Authority, an organizer for a labor union, a sculptor, a university teacher of history, a machinist, an employment supervisor, a writer of plays.

And yet, to my keen delight, they were also speaking as members of a college whose general interest, while referring to all their occupations, was wider and deeper than any one of them, than all of them together. As I listened to their words, I knew the recorded fact that Henry Adams had died thirty years before those papers were read and that Plato's writing had come to an end twenty-four centuries earlier than that. But still, on that happy morning I heard both Adams and Plato speaking. They were there in the words and phrases through which nine stories were told, in the questions and answers by which ten years of busy living in the United States were critically examined and interpreted. That was true, I am sure, in 1942. We had tried to make it true from 1927 to 1932.

I now suggest that it is still true in 1957. Since we are a college, Plato and Adams are here, waiting and eager to talk with any one, with any group, which seeks to find its way toward educated living. But so, too, are many others. John Dewey, whose gospel we often challenged, and who challenged ours, and Thorstein Veblen, Aristophanes, and Lincoln Steffens, Thucydides and Frederick Turner, the builders of the Parthenon, the builders of American railroads, Solon, and Thomas Jefferson—these and a host of other friends and teachers are always present where a genuine college is. They are now ready to talk with us here just as, three decades ago, they stirred and puzzled us and tried to make us think, in Adams Hall.

The road toward understanding of men and their world is often hard to travel; just now it is even hard to find; but it is not, for one who looks around him as he goes, a lonely road. To go to college, if one really goes to a college, is to be initiated into a fellowship of learning. It is that permanent fellowship which our impermanent little college now celebrates as, in these meetings, it celebrates itself.

And, second, it will perhaps stir old memories, and so reestablish old relations of controversial give and take, if we look once more at the curriculum, the course of study, which our college required of all its members. There were no separate subjects, so-called, in that curriculum. We made no carefully devised incursions into such special fields of investigation as economics or art, physics or logic, and the like.

We were seeking to learn, not how new knowledge may be won, but how knowledge already available to us may be so interpreted and reinterpreted as to be of use in the planning of human welfare.

To that end, we studied not subjects but civilizations—civilizations taken each in its entirety—and only civilizations. In the freshman year, advisers and pupils alike were thrown into the attempt to become acquainted with the city-state of Athens, in the age of Pericles and the decades which followed. After the fashion of critical observers just come to town, interested in the manner of life, the successes and failures, the joys and sorrows, the merits and defects, of a human enterprise, we read and considered together the records which that most self-expressive of civilizations has left of its daily experiences, its great achievements, its tragic blunders. So far as we could do it we shared in those experiences, those achievements and blunders, as if they were our own. And the study culminated in the endeavor to see and feel the city as Plato saw and felt it, to join with him, as pupils and critics, in the reflecting upon and planning of his Republic.

The second task was assigned to our pupils at the end of the freshman year. It was to be worked at during the summer vacation and continued, as a separate project, during the first half of the sophomore year. We called it a regional study of some American community which each of you chose as having special interest for him. Dealing with vastly different intellectual and cultural material, you were commissioned to write a critical examination of a nearby human enterprise just as you had tried to interpret that Grecian city, distant from us in time and space and circumstance, which still gives guidance and insight and warning to the Western World.

And, finally, as your third task, the main business of the sophomore year, you were asked, with the help of your advisers, to derive, from the records of the creative activities of the United States of America, the beginning of an understanding of this Nation of ours, what it cares for, what it does and fails to do, what it thinks about and fails to think about. As youthful Americans, you were to share, with mind and feeling and will, in the making and sustaining and transforming of the community of which you are members. And here again your success in the venture was assessed by your ability to read a book. You were asked to write a review of the account which Henry Adams gave of his own education. It seemed to the advisers that, insofar as you could see and interpret what Adams was saying about the United States and his attempt to understand it, could critically give assent or dissent to his assessment of our national career (our national destiny), you would have made a beginning in that process of education which the college wished you to suffer and enjoy.

Now, it is easy to see what was, and what was not, what is, and what is not, the purpose which animated that curriculum. When we asked you to size up, as a going, or not-going concern, some American village or city or district, when we cultivated and tested your ability and your eagerness to share with Plato and Adams the intellectual criticism and the emotional solicitude with which they planned for their respective communities, we were trying to initiate you into an art, the most difficult as well as the most important, the most practical as well as the most intellectual, activity in which the human mind can engage. It is the art of intelligent practical judgment, of understanding your life and that of the community of which you are a member, of so understanding them that you can share with your fellows in the making of those decisions which determine individual and social welfare. As I say this, I must remind you that the college which we celebrate made no provision for the teaching of the techniques of scholarly investigation, gave no training in the methods by which new knowledge is won. Other institutions should do that work. But we, as a college, had neither time nor interest for it. In our final report to the faculty of the University of Wisconsin, we said:

"To put the matter very bluntly, the college is as much and as little interested in the training of scholars as it is in the making of bankers, legislators, grocers, or the followers of any other specialized occupation or profession."

We imposed upon you and upon ourselves a required curriculum, with no elective, because we were convinced that standing apart from all special interest, from all specialized studies, there is a common interest, a common unspecialized form of study, which surpasses all of them in urgency and difficulty and significance. It is the need of understanding what we know. And that requires of us that we learn to use our minds in a way which, in content, in method, in presupposition, and in result, is radically different from any of the kinds of thinking by which scholarly research is done. To develop the power and zest for engaging in that creative inquiry is, in our opinion, the only legitimate purpose of an American college. . . .

I have talked long—I fear too long—and, perhaps, too sentimentally about what an American college is and, hence, what it ought to be. We must now discuss as briefly as we can, what American freedom is, and hence, ought to be. When that has been done we may be ready to try to determine the relation of each of these to the other.

Freedom and Liberty

. . . . I venture as a generalization which will run through the arguments which are to follow in this paper, the assertion that when we Americans talk about our Nation as free, we do not know very well what we are talking about, in fact we prefer, on the whole, not to know what we are talking about. In explanation and, I hope in support, of that accusation, I begin by offering two less general remarks.

First, throughout our history, but especially in recent decades, our Nation has had unequalled opportunities for the creation of external wealth and power. With a new world open before us for our conquest, we have seized upon those opportunities by the methods of what we call private or competitive business enterprise. The success of these methods has been so quick and so great that it has become a source of amazement, of envy, and of terror to the rest of the world. But the strains and stresses of that success, the preoccupation with material achievement, have been so intense that we have more and more substituted for the ideal of inner dignity and self-respect which lies at the heart of our institutions, the pseudo-ideal of competitive efficiencies, of victory over others. Our prevailing maxim for young people, as well as old, is not now "Be good" or "Do good," but rather "Make good." Under the guidance of that maxim we have become eager and aggressive in defense of our individual competitive rights. But our only effective common purpose is that of forever raising higher and higher what we call the standard of living. And the illusions, the meaninglessness inherent in that purpose have penetrated into every corner of our common life. That is the basic reason why the schools and colleges which are, presumably, commissioned to study and teach the ways of freedom are so weak, so confused, so ineffectual. My first remark is, then, that insofar as a society is dominated by the attitudes of competitive business enterprise, freedom, in its proper American meaning, cannot be known and, hence, cannot be taught.

And, second, this substitution of a false ideal for a true one has built up among us a national defect of disposition or of character which hinders all our attempts to educate ourselves. That defect is a strong defensive antipathy against self-criticism, an insistence upon intellectual conformity, an irrational fear lest by the use of our minds, we might discover that we are not, in fact, what we intend or profess to be. I am not here suggesting that we fear intellectual activity as such. We have, of course, no terror of the brilliant investigations which make possible the curing of our diseases, no dread of the scientific research or the technological inventing which enables us to create external wealth and power with enormous efficiency. But the men whom we fear because of their thinking are the critics, men who would question the value or wisdom of these intellectual achievements, who would block progress by standing, like Socrates, in the middle of the busy thoroughfare, asking themselves and others whose ears they can catch, where the road leads. Such men are, as of old, corrupters of our youth and deniers of our gods. They do not follow loyally and contentedly what we call the American way of life. They are dreamers, do-gooders, eggheads, to be ignored or laughed at; or, if that does not suffice, punished and suppressed. And this craving for intellectual conformity, this timidity of mind, more than any other single factor, has brought it about that our teachers labor in vain as they seek to educate the people of a Nation which fears and despises the very essence of what education is.

What, then, is American freedom? May I say to you, my fellow ex-collegers, that ever since you and I parted company twenty-five years ago, the major part of my time and energy has been given to the attempt to answer that question. In reporting to you now "How I fitted in," I shall not give you an organized lecture on my findings. I shall follow the usual procedure of the college by telling you of a series of questions and assertions which still puzzle me. I do so in the hope that we may discuss them together.

First, I mention a point on which there is, I think, some progress to report to you. Following a suggestion given to me forty years ago by Walton Hamilton, and worked out with my colleagues in the San Francisco School of Social Studies, I seem to have discovered that, as we study American freedom, the best reading material available for the purpose is found in the Federal Constitution and in the judicial opinions by which it has been interpreted. That material is filled with controversy and with significance for the understanding of our national life. I deeply regret that when we puzzled out a sophomore course of study in the Experimental College we had not realized how it might be used. If any one of you or any number of you should someday share in starting another experimental college, or in making more experimental one which is now conventionalized, I hope you will consider the suggestion I am now making.

My second topic is, in form, semantic. It has to do with the defining of the difference between the two terms "freedom" and "liberty," as they are used in the Bill of Rights. These two terms serve as instruments for defining the relations between individual Americans and the governing agencies which they have collectively established. And the Constitution has great value for our discussion

Alexander and Helen Meiklejohn at the reunion of the Experimental College held in Annapolis, Maryland, May 10-12, 1957. Standing with them are some of the men who served as faculty of the college: Delos S. Otis in the first row; Paul M. Herzog, John W. Powell, and Malcolm Sharp in the second row; H. H. Giles, Paul Raushenbush, and Ralph Crowley in the third row.

because, in its own reference, it sharply separates these two words which are commonly regarded as interchangeable. The first amendment speaks of freedom—freedom of religion, speech, press, assembly, and petition. And its tremendous assertion is that Congress and, by implication, all other governing agencies, are denied any authority whatever to abridge those freedoms. The fifth amendment, on the other hand, speaks of liberty. And liberty, it appears, is within the scope of governmental restraint. The Declaration of Independence, it is true, had made the flaming pronouncement that all men are "endowed by their creator with unalienable rights" and that "among these are life, liberty, and the pursuit of happiness." But the Constitution, in flat contradiction of the earlier document, soberly provides that, by action of the Government, all three of these rights, as we call them, may be taken from us, may be alienated. That may not be done "except by due process of law." And yet the fact remains that, when public needs seem to justify such action, and when it is done fairly and with proper procedure, men may be ordered to go into battle to destroy other men's lives, to lose their own; their business activities may be confined within this or that set of limits; they may be required to pay into the public treasury such unequal shares of their yearly income as the Government decides that it needs to take. But those men are still, in the meaning of the Bill of Rights, free men, whose liberties are properly abridged.

The third intellectual venture in which I invite you to join is that of defining the revolutionary conception of freedom which dominates the Constitution and which finds its most explicit indication, if not expression, in the first amendment. Why did our forefathers adopt the dictum, "Congress shall make no law respecting an establishment of religion, or prohibiting the free exercise thereof; or abridging the freedom of speech, or of the press; or the right of the people peaceably to assemble, and to petition the Government for a redress of grievances"? And why do we, when our minds are clear, hold fast to the same intention?

At this point in the argument, I am sorely tempted to draw you into discussion of the paradoxes and controversies into which, during the last fifteen or twenty years, I have been plunged by proposing an answer to that question. I would much like to have your help in holding my ground or your consolation if I am forced to give it up. But the lack of time forbids me to yield to that temptation. I can only try very briefly to tell you what, as I see it, is the idea for which the American Revolution was and is being fought and won.

The constitutional principle which, for purposes of warfare and rebellion had been effectively, though inaccurately, proclaimed by the Declaration of Independence was that of political self-government. For centuries our forefathers had suffered, and had seen other common men suffer, from the tyranny of being governed by others. Priests, kings, barons, nonrepresentative parliaments had, by superior force, imposed an arbitrary control upon them. But now the time and the opportunity had come to establish a political order in which the people governed would also be the governors. The rulers and the ruled would be the same persons. No man would be required to obey a law in the making of which he had not had an equal share with his fellow citizens.

Against this background, the first amendment finds its significance in the fact that the terms "religion," "speech," "press," "assembly," and "petition" refer to those activities of judgment-making in which the process of governing consists. And it is obvious that unless the judgment-making of the people is, individual by individual, completely independent, unless it can be kept safe from any external interference, the program of popular self-government becomes futile and a sham. Now it was at this point that the makers of the Constitution envisaged the danger that representative officials and agencies chosen by the people might, under the new regime, attempt, as tyrants had done before, to govern the sovereign people without their consent by exercising powers which had not been delegated to them. And it is to prevent that catastrophe that the first amendment makes its ringing declaration, setting an absolute limit to the power of the legislative body and, by implication, to the powers of all other representative agencies. The need for that provision and for its unqualified enforcement, was never more clearly revealed than during the war-tormented years through which we have passed since 1919. Just as the tyrants of old had always justified their acts of suppression by the plea that religion, speech, press, assembly, or petition, in this case or that, threatened danger to the general welfare or to the national security, so our officials and our courts of these current days have invaded our freedom, appealing to the same justification. But the first amendment will have none of it. Speaking for a society whose members have decided to be free, it denies and outlaws that plea of danger. If the amendment does not mean that, it does not mean anything. Whatever political freedom turns out to be, we Americans have decided to have it and to take it straight.

Fourth, I have just spoken with much enthusiasm concerning the first amendment. And yet, for the purposes of the teacher, for dealing with the questions with which we are here concerned, it is a strangely unsatisfying statement. It takes under its protection five different human activities, but gives no unifying principle which could bind them together into a common significance. But, even worse than that, its provisions are merely negative. It seeks to prevent something from being done rather than to get something done. It protects our freedoms, but gives no assurance that, in actual practice, we Americans have and use any freedoms which are worth protecting. The difficulty just suggested does not, I presume, trouble those who, under the spell of the Declaration of Independence, think of freedom as a gift with which all men are endowed from birth. But to those of us who have spent our lives, as teachers, in the desperate attempt to find some way by which Americans, including ourselves, can become free, that belief seems meaningless and negligible. Freedom is not a gift. It is an achievement. It can be won only by hard work and good fortune—the good fortune including normally much help from others.

Now, if these things are true it follows that our attempt to understand the Constitution must go beyond politics, must attempt to find elsewhere the goal toward which the education of our self-governing people is, or should be, directed. And here, the teacher, more directly than any other member of our community, must be able to serve as our guide, the interpreter of ourselves. The persons who are commissioned to lead our people, young and old, into the ways of freedom, must understand what freedom is. What, then, have they to tell us about it?

The College and Society

Before trying to answer that question, we must carefully note the fact that education, good or bad, is won from the personal and social influences of a surrounding community, as well as from the teaching given in schools and colleges. Which of these is more important, it would be hard to tell. But, in any case, they must be considered separately.

As a starting point for some brief remarks about schooling, I offer you a provocative statement concerning British teaching which I picked up when in Oxford three years ago. It was written by a master of Eton College in the days, three-quarters of a century ago, when Britannia still ruled the waves, and the upper class boys and young men who went to Eton and like public schools were being educated to rule Britannia. As a teacher in the service of that aristocratic governing group, William Johnson Cory wrote as follows:

"At school you are not engaged so much in acquiring knowledge as in making mental efforts under criticism. A certain amount of knowledge you can indeed with average faculties acquire so as to retain, nor need you regret the hours you spent on much that is forgotten, for the shadow of lost knowlege at least protects you from many illusions. But you go to a great school not so much for knowledge as for arts and habits; for the habit of attention, for the art of expression, for the art of assuming at a moment's notice a new intellectual position, for the art of entering quickly into another person's thoughts, for the habit of submitting to censure and refutation, for the art of indicating assent or dissent in graduated terms, for the habit of regarding minute points of accuracy, for the art of working out what is possible in a given time, for taste, for discrimination, for mental courage and mental soberness.''

That description of what should go on in the minds of persons who are being prepared to govern a community seems to me unusually significant and suggestive. What I have to say here about the teaching of freedom in our American schools and colleges may be said in a few brief comments on Mr. Cory's words.

Since we are, as a nation, committed to self-government rather than to an aristocratic tyranny, it is evident that, as contrasted with the special privileges of Mr. Cory's upper class group, all our citizens must, so far as possible, be equally educated. And that being true, it follows that our task of educating our rulers is immeasurably more difficult than that which confronted the public schools of England, seventy-five years ago. It implies, for example, that, for a long time, we as well as the Britain of today must accept a lowering of the standards of teaching achievement set by an aristocracy.

Further, in spite of the quantitative difference just suggested, Mr. Cory's words go straight and piercingly to the heart of our American teaching enterprise. Every phrase which he utters about the "arts and habits" of "making mental efforts under criticism" should startle us into awareness of the failure of our schools and colleges to provide the preparation needed for the "judgment-making" which free men must be able to do.

But a strange and striking feature of Mr. Cory's account of the purpose of teaching is that he does not mention the curriculum, the content of study, with which a school or college should deal. And the explanation of that fact is, I think, that, in the Eton which he knew, the choice of subject matter on which pupils should practice their arts and habits was made, not by the school, but by the compact social group to which, both by external and inner commitment, teachers, pupils, and school, all alike, belonged. In fairness, I must add that, in the life and manners of that group, as in its schools, there were great possibilities of smugness, of cruelty, of stupid and insensitive conformity. And yet it had a purpose and could teach it. I doubt that, in the making of the modern world, the public schools of Britain have been surpassed with respect to their success in teaching the arts and habits needed by those who govern.

It should also be said again that in sharp contrast with Mr. Cory's Eton, our American schools and colleges do not find in our society any such intellectual and cultural purposiveness as that which he could count on to give content and direction to his work. As a new and highly conglomerate people, still in the early stages of its making into a Nation, we have, it is true, a code of behavior which we call a way of life. But . . . that way of life is sadly unaware and afraid of its own meaning and intention. There is throughout our society, I am sure, a generous passion for freedom. But that passion, marching blindly on under the banner of liberty, drives us toward enslavement of our fellows and of ourselves, toward tyranny and, hence, away from freedom. Our national education is, as yet, in its crude and unformed beginnings. We fail to educate our children chiefly because we have not had time or integrity or courage to educate ourselves.

The fifth step in our argument should by logical sequence deal with the influence upon education exerted by nongovernmental attitudes and agencies. I can, however, take time merely to mention two or three of these. Supporting our teaching is the intense but often misguided American belief in the usefulness of scholastic learning. But on the other side, our attempt at understanding is blocked and misdirected by a wide array of privately managed activities which are clearly hostile to education in self-government. One of these forces against which the colleges especially need to be protected at the present moment is the insatiable greed of the corporations and other business agencies for an output of technologically trained scientists as well as of potential business executives. At a time when our private colleges are suffering from financial stringency, that greed threatens their teaching with a fundamental distortion. And, further, correlative with this threat to the colleges is the dreadful effect upon public attitude and opinion which comes from the mass-communication industries, as they are conducted by business enterprise. In my opinion, those agencies, and especially radio and television, are, day by day, year by year, doing more damage to the minds of our people than the schools and colleges are doing good. They have made dominant again in our society the mental trickiness, which, long ago, Plato saw corrupting the mind and spirit of Athens—the trickeries which can prove (that is, make plausible) any belief, whether true or false, can, at a price, make the worse appear the better cause. Because of them, our national intelligence is, I believe, steadily losing ground. Madison Avenue is more powerful and more dangerous than the hydrogen bomb. What shall we do about it in defense of our freedom?

And now, in conclusion, I must summarize my argument by telling of the mortal combat which, during the sixty years of my teaching, has been waged in the American college. If I had the art for doing it, the story might be told in the form of a medieval mystery in which God and the devil contend for possession of the souls of men. The devil, one of whose favorite devices is that of raising for men the standard of living, thereby succeeds in lowering the standard of human intelligence. Since the battle, as we see it, takes place within colleges, it is fought in the field of the mind. Two sets, two kinds of intellectual activities are at war with one another. In spite of their hostility they are strangely akin in origin and in character. After all, the devil is, as you know, an angel. But he is a fallen angel, a rebel. He must, therefore, be subdued, brought back to fellowship and sanity. Can it be done? How can it be done?

The two contestants, as seen within the college, are the passion for knowledge and the passion for understanding. In one camp are the intellectual strivings by which men seek to add new knowledge to the vast stock of it which, in various departments, we already possess. In the other camp are the intellectual strivings to so interpret and reinterpret what we now know that it will play its proper part as the servant of an understanding which plans for human welfare. The question at issue is not "Shall knowledge be destroyed?" It is, rather, "For what ends shall knowledge be used, and by what kind of thinking shall the using be done?"

As I phrase that question my mind goes back to the days when, in 1897, my teaching began. Through the strange, mechanical, and, shall I say, devilish, device of an elective system, the old classical curriculum had been giving way before the inroads of a new scholarship. And I can still feel the thrill of excitement and hope, mitigated by a confused anxiety, with which we younger teachers welcomed the broadening and deepening, which the new forms of investigation promised to bring to our learning and teaching. We began to speak proudly and confidently of our newly devised university college which, through the addition of specialized graduate teaching, would fuse together the pursuit of knowledge and the pursuit of understanding on a higher level of intellectual enterprise. But today, so far as I can see, that hope is dead. The two elements did not fuse. Scholarship has not informed and inspired the search for understanding. On the contrary, stimulated and made powerful by its strong appeal to the externalized and competitive impulses of American life, it has specialized in disconnectedness, in lack of meaning. It has thus obscured the older purposes of the college and driven them from the field. The curriculum has now become merely a vast collection of mutually unintelligible subjects. The members of the faculty have, professionally, little if any intellectual acquaintance with one another. And pupils are encouraged to pursue each his own separate studies, without regard for or interest in what, in other classrooms, his friends may be doing. The combining of the university and the college into a university college has torn into fragments the community of learning which the older college intended to be.

How shall the damage be repaired? How shall the college become again a place of understanding? First of all, it must be separated from the university, must become a distinct and independent institution, aware of its own purpose, which is radically different from that of the university, and resolute in the pursuit of that purpose. And, further, the college must be small enough and coherent enough to be in a vital and dominating sense, a community which will bind together all its teachers and all its pupils in the carrying on of their common enterprise.

I have said that the pursuit of knowledge has heretofore invited disaster by tearing apart what we know about men and their world into relatively meaningless fragments. As against that procedure what we now need is that in pursuit of understanding there be cultivated and practiced an equally severe and rigorous intellectual discipline which will endeavor to put the minds of men together again into a pattern as meaningful as the facts allow. That pattern will not be created by mere good will. The needed unity can be won, only as the total body of human knowledge and purpose is brought within the scope of an organizing group intelligence. The brilliant achievements of scholarly investigation must be matched, they must be surpassed, by the concerted efforts of intellectual interpreters. The college must think its way through knowledge toward wisdom.

I need hardly add that if this transformation of the college is to be attempted, the demands made upon the teacher whether he works in Ghana or Russia or England or Israel and so on, will be radically changed and magnified. His work will be both more important and more difficult than that of the investigator. He will no longer be merely an instructor in English composition or banking or chemical engineering or foreign language. He will be, in the measure of his ability, one of the world's thinkers, just as all free citizens should be, grappling with the world's problems, carrying assurance to his pupils and to the surrounding community that it is a free man's business to do what he can with his mind in relation to these problems. He must think and teach in the interest of freedom for all men.

The situation which now faces the teacher and all of us is one of tragic severity.

It is possible, as we all know, that this blundering untutored race of men, through the sudden access of brutalizing power which knowledge brings, will soon destroy itself. But there is also hope that for the first time since man began his education among the carnivores, we may by patience and intelligent use of knowledge construct a world that sensitive and timid natures could regard without a shudder. . . .

Critique of Protestant-Capitalist Society

Alexander Meiklejohn challenged the basic aspects of U.S. society—its materialism, individualism, and pragmatism. In *Education Between Two Worlds,* published in 1942 when he was seventy years old, Meiklejohn used the phrase "Protestant-capitalist" society to indicate the individualism that he saw underlying both the Protestant and the capitalist traditions. Protestants believed that individuals could work out their salvation alone. Capitalists believed that the common interest could best be served by individuals pursuing their own interests. But Meiklejohn did not believe this. The common problem of creating a self-governing society that worked for everyone could not be solved by individuals pursuing their separate ends.

For him, capitalism was too competitive. It accepted as necessary that each person should be at every other person's throat. That belief had no appeal to a man whose serene parents had managed to weld eight sons into a harmonious, cooperative group. Meiklejohn had spent the first eight years of his life in Rochdale, England, where textile workers were creating a cooperative economic scheme that would eliminate the horrors of working class life under a capitalist arrangement. Though Meiklejohn seldom spoke in public about this experience, when he did he stressed its importance in shaping his adult outlook (selection 6).

When Meiklejohn began to teach at Brown, alternatives to capitalism were being widely discussed in the United States. Immigrants from Europe, fleeing wretched conditions there, were bringing ideas for other ways to organize society and economic life—socialism, anarchism, syndicalism. In the 1890s the Socialist Labor Party blossomed in New York. In 1901 the Socialist Party organized in Indianapolis. The Industrial Workers of the World organized in 1905 and held their dramatic strikes of western miners, loggers, and textile workers.

117

In the years just prior to World War I socialism was a growing movement capable of winning elections. The socialist Victor Berger was elected to Congress by Milwaukee in 1910. In the elections of 1911 socialist mayors were elected in thirty-three cities, including Milwaukee. In 1912 Eugene Debs ran for president on the Socialist Party ticket; he received 900,000 votes, six percent of the total vote, the largest percentage ever received by the Socialist Party in a national election. Socialists promoted their ideas on college campuses through the Intercollegiate Socialist Society, a group formed in 1905 by Upton Sinclair, Jack London, and others. From 1913 to 1919 it published *The Intercollegiate Socialist.* During World War I it was practically snuffed out; it re-organized in 1921 as the League for Industrial Democracy in order to expand its influence beyond college men and women.

At Brown Meiklejohn did not take a public stand on social and economic issues. But at Amherst he took his stand, publicly stating his belief that social and economic arrangements in the United States were not what they ought to be and that liberally educated people should be considering alternative ones. In 1918 Meiklejohn raised questions about the economic order in his speech commemorating the 250th anniversary of Pawtucket, Rhode Island (selection 4). He encouraged students to consider these questions by instituting a freshman course in "Social and Economic Institutions," by organizing students to give classes to workers, and by inviting speakers who challenged the prevailing order, notably the great English socialist R. H. Tawney.

Not being an economist, Meiklejohn did not try to specify how business should be owned and operated, but as a teacher he asked the questions and presented the alternatives. As an administrator, he made activities more cooperative and decision-making more inclusive. Especially he wanted students to run their extracurricular lives. Even his struggle for a common curriculum may be seen as implementing his belief that studies should be cooperative rather than wholly individualistic.

World War I set back all attempts to think about economic alternatives. Most anticapitalist groups, believing that wars are created by capitalists to increase their profits and keep workers subjugated, opposed the war, at least initially. The Bolshevik Revolution in 1917 and strikes involving more than four million workers in the United

States at the end of the war alarmed capitalists into taking the offensive. Laws were passed enabling the jailing and deportation of people who opposed capitalism. Meiklejohn himself was probably a victim of this reaction. His insistence that college students consider socialism as one possible alternative to capitalism proved too much for Amherst's trustees.

It was several years after his dismissal from Amherst before Meiklejohn relocated at the University of Wisconsin, where his Experimental College got underway just two years before the Great Depression of 1929. Many of the faculty he assembled there had some kind of socialist orientation. They asked students to read the English socialists, Russell and Tawney, and the U.S. social critics, Louis Brandeis, Henry Adams, and Helen and Robert Lynd. When Meiklejohn addressed Chicago businessmen in 1930 he called his speech "What Ought We to Think About?" He told them in no uncertain terms that they had better think about redistributing wealth, about putting more people in charge of their destiny, about reducing the ugliness resulting from the industrial scheme, and about avoiding war. In the San Francisco School for Social Studies, Meiklejohn set up discussions around Marx, Veblen, and John Strachey's *Coming Struggle for Power*. Always in his role as teacher, Meiklejohn raised the economic questions and organized discussions to insure the expression of different opinions.

Being at the University of Wisconsin in the late 1920s and early 1930s meant being at the source of some significant developments. Wisconsin's economists played a strategic role in the economic thinking of this period. Perhaps the most influential of them, John R. Commons (1862-1945), had come to Wisconsin in 1904. When socialists won the election of 1911 in Milwaukee, they asked Commons to examine their city's government, and they accepted practically all his recommendations. Commons created U.S. labor history with his eleven-volume publication from 1909 to 1911 of *Documentary History of American Industrial Society*. Commons' views gradually changed from espousal of socialism to believing that capitalism could be made satisfactory if ameliorated by reforms. Many of his students wrote and shaped the legislation of Roosevelt's New Deal. Edwin E. Witte and his graduate student Wilbur Cohen (a member of the fourth class of the Experimental College), went to Washington to write the Social Security Act of 1935. Another of Commons' students, Arthur J. Altmeyer, directed the program set up under the Social Security Act. Paul

Raushenbush, who had studied with Commons and taught in the Experimental College, stayed on in Madison to write and administer the first state unemployment insurance legislation that later became the model for national unemployment legislation.

Although some of Wisconsin's socialists became reform capitalists, Meiklejohn did not. He voted regularly for Norman Thomas except in 1936, when he felt that Thomas was softening his platform too much in his attempt to attract more Roosevelt Democrats. The New Deal did not go far enough for Meiklejohn toward curbing the competitiveness of capitalism.

When the Experimental College came to an end in 1932, Meiklejohn wrote down in *What Does America Mean?* what he really believed about the U.S. experiment in democratic government (selection 5). He thought it possible to change the economic system without resorting to violence. He did not see the proletariat as the primary vehicle for bringing socialism, for he felt certain that as people of all classes studied their social problems they would come to view some form of voluntary cooperative commonwealth as in their common interest.

Six years after *What Does America Mean?* was published, World War II restored prosperity to the United States, stilling most criticism of the American way of life. Prosperity did not reassure Meiklejohn, who continued to warn against the inherent defects of capitalism. Men were dying for freedom, but if by that they meant the free enterprise system, then Meiklejohn was certain they were dying for something that would not make them free.

Meiklejohn was never active in a political party. Rather than join the Socialist Party, he joined the socialist-oriented League for Industrial Democracy, in which he served as vice-president from 1928 until his death in 1964. He did not write pamphlets or make speeches for the League for Industrial Democracy, but its leaders were his friends, and he was pleased to be named an officer.

The League for Industrial Democracy never took hold on the West Coast. In order to have a strong liberal organization in California, Meiklejohn helped found the Northern California chapter of the American Civil Liberties Union. Some of the leaders of the new chapter were concerned when members of the Communist and Trotskyite parties joined. The leadership did not attempt a so-called united front. They feared that including Communists would drive away some people who believed in civil liberties and felt that Communists did not. Nevertheless, Meiklejohn persistently defended the right of members of the Communist Party to sit on the national board of the ACLU, to teach in high schools and universities, and to serve as union leaders. (See the fifth section, "Liberty and Freedom," for further elaboration.)

In 1943, in an article in the Communist magazine, *The New Masses,* Meiklejohn discussed the question of why liberal progressives and Communists in the United States had seldom been able to cooperate effectively with each other. He analyzed several possible explanations, rejected all of them, and concluded:

> What, then, is the source of the difficulty? It is, I am sure, one of tactics rather than one of goal. There is no basic incongruity between the ultimate aims of the Communist Party and the fundamental principles of the Constitution of the United States. But there is a basic incongruity between the tactics of the "class-struggle" theory, as now interpreted by the American Communist Party, and the American program of democratic political action. The difference is one between the tactics of war and the tactics of peace. I am well aware how much bitter and unscrupulous warfare underlies the processes of American political and economic life. I am not denying the existence here of the class struggle. And yet the fact remains that, as a people, we Americans are committed to the belief that even the fiercest and most fundamental conflicts among us can be settled by peaceful political action. Our majorities and minorities, our parties in power and parties out of power, are working together as well as working in opposition to one another. But the Communist Party seems, at present, unable or unwilling to accept that political faith. It believes that our American society is at war within itself and that, therefore, tactics of warfare are necessary in dealing with its problems. For that reason, the Party adopts the procedures of the military mind, both in its own internal discipline and in its relations with other groups. The bourgeois liberal, whom it invites to join in cooperation, is potentially or actually an enemy rather than a friend. That is why he can be used and then dropped. And this means that when the Communist asks for cooperation he is asking for something which he cannot give in return. And, further, it must be remembered that

men who are at war, no matter what their personal integrity, cannot be trusted to mean what they say. War is deceit. That is why the Communist asks for himself in America civil liberties which, when occasion arises, he refuses to others. He would like the liberals to be at peace with him while he is at war with them.

Meiklejohn concluded with the hope that "the day will soon come when, free from suspicions and hatreds, the Party will take its place as an active and recognized sharer in the democratic procedures of American political life." (*The New Masses* [October 19, 1943]: 16-18.)

4

The Machine City

In 1918, while he was president of Amherst, Meiklejohn spoke at the celebration of the 250th anniversary of the founding of Pawtucket, Rhode Island. A city of almost 64,000 in 1918, Pawtucket was located on the coast four miles from Providence, a city of 235,000. Pawtucket was the site at which the first spinning machinery operated in the United States. England tried to prevent the export of its textile know-how, but an English mechanic came to Rhode Island, drew the plans of the Arkwright spinning machine from memory, and from them a Pawtucket blacksmith built a successful machine in 1790. Meiklejohn's father came to Pawtucket in 1880 as an expert in the technology of color design for textiles. During the last decades of the 19th century a continual stream of workers from the English textile industry arrived in Pawtucket.

From 1898 to 1901 Meiklejohn served on the Pawtucket Board of Education, as his father had before him. What Meiklejohn had to say on the occasion of the 250th

anniversary follows. Meiklejohn had it published in his col-
lection of speeches and essays, Freedom and the College
(New York: Century Company, 1923, reprinted by Books
for Libraries Press, Freeport, New York, 1970).

I am asked to speak to you tonight on the future of this city. I know
only one thing certain about its future, namely, that no one can tell
what it will be.

This is, in an extreme degree, a machine city. I do not refer, Mr.
Mayor, to the nature of its politics, but to the source of its power, the
nature of its social forces. This city has been made by machines. Here
Jencks set up his forge, here Slater began the manufacture of cotton.
And since their day this group of people has led the way in the build-
ing and using of machines for the making of goods which men desire.
We are a machine city. It is our strength, our glory— and our prob-
lem.

If one could tell the future of such a city as this, one could answer
many urgent questions concerning the modern world at large. Modern
civilization, especially in our Anglo-Saxon section of it, has likewise
been made by machines. We have become an industrial people. What
is to be the future of an industrial civilization is a problem which
vexes and tortures the spirit of any man who honestly and intelligently
studies it. I should like tonight, on this occasion of our celebration of
two hundred and fifty years of great achievement, to ask you to look
with me at some of the implications which this achievement carries
with it.

Machines have brought to men results, some of them aimed at,
some of them quite unintended and unnoticed. May I give a very partial and hurried list of them?

First, machines have increased the numbers of our population and,
at the same time, the supply of material wealth for the use of the
population. The machine magnifies human work, makes it more
efficient, multiplies it, in its effect, by ten, by a hundred, by a
thousand it may be. It needs more people for its work; it can support
more people by its products. As a result of the machine mode of life,
we have more people in our communities, more wealth at their service.

But again, the machines have claimed the people themselves as
parts of the machinery. They have made human life more mechanical.

The machine which extends the power of the human body at the same time makes that body a part of itself. Men and women are taken into mills and shops and offices to be used, more than they were before, as tools, as instruments, as parts of a machine technique. The human life which uses machines is, in turn, used by them.

Again, machines have broken down the continuity and stability of towns and cities. They have changed the town from a settled group of individuals and families into a place through which people flow in constantly changing streams. The machines of transportation carry people off to other places in search of wealth and opportunity, while, on the other hand, the machines in the mills are ceaselessly dragging other peoples in from the ends of the earth to take their places in the mills. Our communities are no longer places of settled abode. They are changing, flowing streams made up of elements novel and strange and foreign each to the other, and ever replaced by others strange to them.

And still again, the machine has cut the family into parts, has broken down its continuity. Parents and children separate and go their different ways, different work, think different thoughts, choose different friends; they scatter and separate, live unrelated lives far more than families have before.

And through all this one other change has run in varying forms. While individual men have wandered and scattered, the net which holds them all has drawn more tightly in. The world is bound together in certain external, mechanical ways. We saw this in the recent war. That was no war of groups or tribes or even nations. It was the world at war, two huge, enormous forces fighting for mastery of our industrial power with every ounce of strength the world and its machines could give, being used to turn the scale. It was a war so great that all men had and all they were seemed to depend upon the issue, so great that many of us lived in ghastly fear that human life as we now have it would smash and go to pieces. Machines brought on the struggle, and when it came they made it monstrous in its power.

In these and other ways machines have changed our life under our very hands. But, now, what of the future? What will they make of us in days to come?

No man can tell what they will do to us. But we can tell what we will do to them. We will not let them use us as their tools. We will use them as tools of ours.

Mr. Mayor, I have a suggestion to make to you. It is that this city which has taken the lead in the development of the machine industry of this country shall now take the lead in making sure that that industry contributes properly to the life of the people whom it pretends to serve. We must understand our machines if we are to use them, must find out what they are for, whether or not they serve the purposes for which we made them, whether they are bringing about evil results which we had not intended. We must understand these machines and their consequences if we would use them properly.

I would ask, Mr. Mayor, that you select a commission of twenty-five or thirty of your best men to study human living in an industrial town. There are three essential questions about human life: (1) what ought it to be, what is its proper form: (2) what things further, what things prevent its being as it ought to be: (3) what measures can we take to make it right, to smash aside the things that make it wrong? Those questions this city should study. What of the people in the mills, the shops, the offices, the banks, the homes, the schools? What of men and women and children? Are they as fine and right and happy as human beings ought to be? If not, why not? And what can be done to make them better?

Mr. Mayor, if our industrial civilization does not begin to understand itself and its machines, it must of course go down in ruins. The forces which it makes and finds are far too great to be let loose to run amuck without our human guidance. We must take them in hand by understanding them, by knowing ourselves and them, by making them our servants. If you, my friends, in this strong city will seek for wisdom to match your strength, you will be taking the lead in what the modern world must do if it would keep itself a proper abode for men, for women, for children. I ask you, Mr. Mayor, to take the lead in seeing that studying such as this is done.

There are one or two explanations which I should like to add to this proposal.

I am not advocating any theory as to men and their machines. I am not pleading for Socialism or Radicalism, for Conservatism or Americanism. I am pleading for honest study by honest men, of human living. Study is not for scholars only, not for colleges and universities alone. Study is an attempt at intelligence in dealing with human life. Study is the activity of a man who has something to do and who wishes to do it well. When studying is needed, they who neglect it are not simply failing to be scholars; they are failing to be men; they fail where a man should be ashamed to fail without a desperate struggle.

And again, though it be somewhat ungracious, may I remind you that Rhode Island, industrial Rhode Island, seems to have special reason for self-examination. If one may take as they appear statistics from the surgeon-general in Washington, Rhode Island more than any other State failed in supply of proper men when men were needed for the army. For each one thousand men, the army found among you here a greater number of "defects," a greater number of men unfitted for its service than any other State supplied. The facts suggest at least occasion for our study.

But finally, a word that bears more closely on my theme. You ask me of Pawtucket's future. What of its children then? They are its future. What do you make of them? I said just now I had no program of reform. But at this point I have a program. We are not taking proper care of our children in this industrial life of ours. Wealth pours itself into our hands, and we are spending it in every way except in that which really counts — the making of children's lives as strong and fine and right as they might be. What we may do for them determines what our future is to be. If I were here among you as of old and serving again upon the School Board, I would ask the people of the city to multiply the school appropriation by ten; and then if that were not enough, to multiply again for taking proper care of children.

But, Mr. Mayor, I do not wish to interfere or dogmatize. I am not here to blame or criticize. Rather I glory in the strength and cleverness that have built up this place of industry. But now I ask for wisdom, too. I beg of you that here as elsewhere men make sure they have their living under control. I ask that you, the men who make machines and make them run, shall try to know what they are running for, shall make them serve their proper ends, shall make them serve the children, the women, the men, whose instruments they are. Make human living right in this old town. To make it right you must attempt to understand it. Pawtucket's future would be a glorious one if it could lead the way in such an enterprise as that.

5

What Does America Mean?

In this book, his first that was not simply a collection of essays, Meiklejohn had a chance to present his case fully. His students and colleagues in the Experimental College had pushed him to the wall about what he believed to be the meaning of U.S. civilization. He had found many who denied meaning to the term "Spirit," and in this book he wants to restore that meaning. He distinguishes between the outer and the inner life and defends the existence and power of inner realities such as spirit, ideals, excellence, and liberty.

In his first section Meiklejohn discusses what an ideal and a spirit are, and what the U.S. ideal is, namely, liberty. Then he analyzes the meaning of liberty, arguing that liberty is for people, not for property. He made this distinction between external and internal liberty in order to argue that the external liberty to make money and be comfortable is not the real ideal of the United States. Later in his thinking, but not yet in this book, he uses "freedom" for internal liberty and "liberty" for external liberty.

I have chosen from the beginning of the fourth section, called "The Illusion of Independence," in which Meiklejohn continues his analysis of confusions about liberty. The final excerpt comes from his concluding section, "What Shall We Do?" W.W. Norton & Company published What Does America Mean? *in 1935 and republished it in paperback in 1972.*

The more obvious of our two confusions about liberty is that which makes it an object of desire rather than an object of admiration or of obligation. It confuses a craving with a commitment. It is a form of mistake which we Americans very easily make.

In external ways we are an active and vigorous people. We are therefore impatient of restraint. We want to be free to do as we ourselves may choose. We resent interference with our actions. In this our attitude toward life is very much that of boys at play. One of our keenest delights is that of managing our own affairs. Life loses its zest for us if we must do as we are told. We have a passionate craving for independence. Is this desire, this impatience, a love of liberty? Clearly it is not. And yet habitually we identify the two. Men whose one dominating impulse is that of escaping control, whether that control be wise or foolish, necessary or important, think of that impulse as if it were a spiritual commitment to the cause of freedom. May I try to point out how inaccurate that self-interpretation is?

Let us suppose that a hundred men form a community by common agreement. And if we ask what that agreement is, let us suppose that some one answers, "I join this group because I want to be free to do as I may choose. I am here because I am assured that no one will interfere with what I do." Shall we then say that such a community, based upon such an agreement, expresses the passion for human freedom? Each man, it is clear, desires his own liberty of action. They are all alike in that. But what does each desire for his ninety-nine companions? Are they also to be free from interference? On that point, so far as desires are concerned, nothing has been said. Each man, so far as we are told, desires only his own freedom. Each has, it would appear, one one-hundredth part of a devotion to the liberty of the group. These men have no common love of liberty to bind them together. On the contrary there are among them one hundred sets of separate, conflicting desires, ready, on occasion, to tear them apart, to plunge them into warfare, to break into pieces the community as a whole.

Nor is the situation much improved if some one says, speaking for all, "Of course I am willing that every other man shall have his freedom too, if he can get it." Such "willingness" as this is neither desire nor devotion. The interest which it expresses toward the freedom of other men has none of the passion, the ardor which runs through one's own individual demand. Each man's desire is still only for himself. It is still merely a self-centered desire. There is in it no commitment, no sense of obligation, no eagerness to sacrifice oneself for a cause which is dearer than one's own being.

But the desire argument is commonly given a form which is, at least, more plausible than this. Any one can see, we are told, that the policy of "Every man for himself" will not work. We dare not, for the sake of our own interests, act with indifference to the liberties of other men. I must then help my fellows. Unless I join with them in securing their freedom they will not join with me in securing mine. And in that case we shall all be slaves together.—If a man, or a society, uses that argument of "enlightened" self-interest, shall we take it as revealing a genuine love of liberty? How can we do so? As the argument stands, the only freedom in which any member of the group expresses interest is his own. Each man prizes the liberties of other men so far, and only so far, as they serve his own purposes. They and their freedom are, for him, nothing for which he cares as he cares for himself. His fellows are for him instruments, social contrivances, which he may use. Freedom, as something for them as well as for him, a quality of behavior, to which he and they alike owe allegiance, a human value by which all human institutions must be justified or condemned—such freedom, in such a community, does not exist. The miracle simply cannot be performed. We cannot make, out of the desires of a man or of a hundred and twenty-five millions of men, who care only for themselves, that spiritual passion, that love of liberty, which make both men and their societies worthy of admiration. Selfishness is not generosity. Indifference is not friendship. Desires are not ideals. Individual independence is not liberty. External cravings, even though kept in order by external agreements, differ utterly in meaning from the spiritual commitments of men. And the thinking which confuses these two has eaten the clarity out of our American devotion to liberty. When we think in these confusions, the words are on our lips, the impulse in our veins, but our minds, our guides of action, have lost direction. We have made of self-seeking independence a gospel for the strong against the weak. It has come to mean that shrewd and powerful and unscrupulous men, who are able and eager to interfere with other men, shall be free from interference in their doing so. Freedom to destroy freedom is what it means in practice. This is the kind of social doctrine which men make when they confuse desires and admirations, cravings and obligations, the outer with the inner, matter with spirit.

I need hardly add that I am not here attacking as unworthy the individual desire for freedom. I am condemning, not the desire, but the mental confusion which identifies it with something wholly different from itself. When freedom is at stake, it is one thing to say, "It is mine; I want it; no one shall take it from me; I will fight to the death to keep it." But it is quite another thing to say in the same situation, "Freedom is right for men; I acknowledge its claim upon me; wherever that right is threatened I will defend it, whatever may be the cost to myself; I want liberty for all men." Out of the first of these two attitudes, a free society cannot be made. Wherever it prevails, every social group is, at bottom, an attempt by its members to enslave each other. Self-interest, no matter how enlightened, is and must be the source of strife. Out of the second of these attitudes, on the other hand, has come whatever of peace and order and justice and freedom our human societies have achieved. Nothing could be more disastrous, then, than to class together as alike "Wants," as alike "Responses to the Situation," this desire and this obligation toward freedom. One might as well say that since Heaven and Hell are alike defined as places of human habitation, the differences between them is, for human purposes, of no importance. The desire for independence is allowable but is not admirable. Let no man think, then, that because he is impatient of restraint he is, therefore, a devotee of liberty. Freedom is not something which each man wants for himself. It is something to which any man, worthy of the name, will gladly offer up his fortune and his life. . . .

My third suggestion has to do with economic policy. In that field we are facing a crucial national decision. Has capitalism broken down? Must we try to put in its place some form of social management of business? Shall we attempt to patch up the old economic order of free competition or shall we experiment with one of the new forms of socialization, of cooperation, which are being suggested to us? It is not my purpose to discuss this issue in economic terms. I do not know whether or not capitalism can be made to work. I doubt it very seriously. But my doubt comes chiefly from moral rather than from economic grounds. The essential defeat of the capitalist order is, in my opinion, that it is revolting as a form of human behavior. It makes the men who engage in it ashamed of themselves. It is hostile to liberty. It does not make men free. It makes them slaves.

The primary question, then, about capitalism is not, "Can we maintain it?" but "Do we want to maintain it?" The question is not, "What is going to happen?" but "What do we decide shall happen?" And when the question is put in that form I find two exceedingly powerful reasons which seem to me to make imperative a decision on the side of the social directing of industry.

First, the scheme of free competition is too insistent in its appeal to human selfishness. It is twisting our human nature out of its proper shape. In the last resort, the economic struggle rests upon human fear, human suffering, human cupidity, human ambition, human ruthlessness. It requires of each of us that, to the limit of his ability and his endurance, he take care of his own interests. I know that there is, at the bottom of the scheme, the suppressed major premise of "the general welfare." I know that men justify it ultimately in terms of human generosity. But I am equally sure that the "suppression" is too costly in terms of our own human quality. It is not safe that men should, to this extent, be used by "an invisible hand." They must themselves express, in their own planning and action, the generosity of their dispositions. Constant preoccupation with strife against their fellows cuts them off from experiences of inner peace and of genuine fellowship. Inevitably we become what we chiefly do. The spirits of American men and women, as I know them, are starving to death for lack of expression along the lines of their deepest convictions, their strongest commitments. Our economic scheme is not suited to our spiritual nature. I am sure that we must radically transform or wholly abandon it. We must adopt forms of business practice which will not destroy our own personal quality.

My second reason will, I fear, sound absurd. And yet it is to me overwhelmingly convincing. I am certain that, on intellectual grounds, the competitive order is wholly unsuited to the purposes of a democracy. Free competition and democratic living have, I think, been found to be quite incompatible. We must choose between them. And I, for one, unhesitatingly choose democracy.

It is fundamental to free institutions that all men and women shall have an active and responsible share in the making of the common decisions. Governments must be "by the people." But, for this purpose, the essential defect of a competitive society is that common people cannot make the decisions which are needed. They cannot understand what is going on. The system is too complicated for them. Most of us when confronted with the bewildering complexities of prices, wages, profits, rent, interest, capital, credits, currencies, inflations, cannot tell what is being talked about. And this means, of course, that we cannot play our proper part in the life of a democracy. We cannot make the decisions which the citizen of a free society must make. Democracy, therefore, breaks down.

Now it is one of the curious anomalies of the capitalist order that, at this point, it has failed to keep its promises. Its theory was that, in the field of industry, no fundamental popular decisions would be needed. The economic machine would run itself. It was to be automatic. All that was required of each of us was that he accept his place as a cog in the machine, let it grind out the plenty which it was so well fitted to provide, and meanwhile seize of that plenty as large a share as he could get. But, in that extreme form at least, free competition has failed us. In the ordinary running of the machine, millions of people are crushed down to penury and despair. And even with that sacrifice paid, the monster cannot properly care for his devotees. He sweeps forward in huge rushes of success and then, apparently defeated by his own achievements, he staggers and sinks down into overwhelming catastrophes. And when this happens, when the idol fails us, we men and women cannot escape the making of decisions. We must patch him up. We must set him going again. Who knows how that shall be done? Who knows what the trouble is and how it may be remedied? I have said that "common people" cannot answer these questions. But our aristocracy of brains seems to be equally bewildered by them. Our economists, our experts in government, men of high ability and high character, are in the same way, if not to the same degree, baffled and beaten. And the result is that, with no common ideas available, no common plan of action agreed upon, we are thrown back into the chaos of a welter of conflicting and selfish interests, in which action is determined, not by reasoned and generous planning, but by the sheer, brutal mastery of the strong as against the weak, the cunning against the unsophisticated. The purpose of a democracy is lost. Men do not share in the making of common decisions for the very obvious reason that no such decisions are really made. We cannot decide because, practically speaking, we cannot understand.

I am not here suggesting that a democracy should have no experts, that free people must live without leaders. That is very far from my thought. But I am saying that unless the general scheme of action within a nation is intelligible to the people as a whole, unless they can choose their leaders, can intelligently approve and disapprove their administration, it is plain nonsense to speak of that nation as democratic. And it is to that pass that the intricacies of our competitive order have now brought us. Our national mind is stultified and beaten by its own scheme of economic arrangements.

What, then, is the alternative? It is the establishment of an economic order whose underlying motives and principles of action are intelligible to the common mind. And it is the meeting of that demand which seems to me one of the two crowning virtues of a socialistic program. When people join together in the production of goods, not for a competitive market, but for the use of the community as a whole, when the scheme of distribution is not that of the blind play of conflicting desires and capacities, but that of reasoned planning for the human needs of all the members of the community, decisions must, in both fields, take on a directness, a simplicity which brings them within the general understanding of all of us. Such a society is intelligible as well as generous. In such a society it would be possible to be a business man without belying the greater part of one's own nature. In such a society men and women could be bound together by the sharing of common purposes, common ideas, which would make them, in some real sense, members of a community. I am not saying that technical questions would be answered by non-technicians. I am saying only that fundamentally we would understand ouselves and each other. We would have an intelligible society. Life, under those conditions, would be worth living, as it is not worth living now. We might begin to make a democracy. And in that case we might understand what it is that we are trying to do. To accomplish that would be to transform the quality of American living. The confusions and frustrations by which we are now beset would largely remain, but we would be working at them together. In my opinion, the spirit of America will not find itself so long as our present competitive economic order prevails.

My last suggestion has to do with class warfare. Can we, by use of that method, bring about the social changes which are needed? There are, I am sure, situations in which men and women are driven to warfare, situations in which they are so cornered and abused and misunderstood that no other form of action is, for them, available. And yet, fundamentally, the method is a bad one. On the whole, it loses more than it gains. We cannot count upon it, as a general method, to make America right.

The first requirement of any method is that it shall agree, in motive and idea, with the end which it serves. And the program of class struggle fails exactly at this crucial point. It takes over the principles which it is trying to destroy. It fights the Devil with his own weapons. And the terrible disappointment involved in that procedure is that when one wins he has lost. The Devil asks for nothing better than that his foes should adopt his way of fighting. He is, in essence, nothing but that way of fighting. If he can get men to hate each other, to misunderstand and misrepresent each other, to regard hate and struggle as the essential principles of human nature, his victory is won. It is that, and only that, which he wants. We will not get a classless society in America by urging that the deepest law of human society is the conflict of classes one against another.

I am not here saying that there are not economic classes in America. Our competitive scheme does create class warfare. It does divide men into two groups, the exploiters and the exploited. So far as that scheme has any intentions, it intends that these two groups shall struggle one against the other. Its principle is that of the balance of contending forces. Just as the rich are inevitably driven, and are expected, to band themselves together to make good their gains, so are the poor and the oppressed compelled, in sheer desperation, to organize and fight for self-protection against their economic masters. And, further, it is idle to ignore the fact that, as the struggle has been carried on in America, the conflict has not been an equal one. The odds have been very heavily on the side of the exploiters. If, as men say, justice is to be achieved by the equal balance of conflicting interests, then justice has not been done. Men as workers and consumers have not had a fair chance against men as owners and profit-makers. In the face of that situation, the under-dogs have no choice except to fight. And as they do so, no humane person can fail to take sides in sympathy and in action with the weaker group. One welcomes, eagerly and heartily, any successful attempt that group may make to build up economic and political power, to meets its foe on equal terms, to get for itself some semblance of a "square deal."

And yet this is not the heart of the matter. We will not destroy the competitive system by accepting its conflict-principle as valid. The only real victory over it is to show, both in theory and in practice, that the scheme of competitive struggle is futile as well as false. If that is not true, then all our efforts toward liberty and justice are foredoomed to failure. If we say that human nature is such that no economic class ever voluntarily gives up its power, then nothing will be gained by putting another class in control of our social order. That class, too, will take for itself the spoils of victory, will cut down its enemies, will suppress them by brutal and violent action. And, further, when its enemies are liquidated, the controlling group will itself break up into hostile factions, each fighting for the mastery, each seeking to drive the others down into servitude and exploitation. If the law of a social order is that of war it is idle to ask, "How shall we establish the rule of peace?"

But the "war" theory of human nature will not ultimately work because it is not ultimately valid. It does not explain the essential facts in the life of America. When a nation pledges itself, as we have done, to keep the activities of wealth-seeking within the bounds of liberty and justice, it denies that theory. When a people takes as its program a scheme of life in which men are to be equals and brothers, it has rejected the law of the jungle. And, however blind and confused has been and still is our action, those are our intentions. It is only the heedless unreflectiveness of a frontier life which has brought us into conflict with our own convictions. It is only the superficial thinking of an over-busy, externalized mind which has persuaded us that liberty is economic and that justice is that division of possessions which ensues when men have fought each other to the finish. To believe these things is to deny all the human significance which the life of America contains. It is in line with much of our action. It is not in line with our traditional, our deliberate present intention.

I should not like to be misunderstood in what I am here saying. The method of class warfare seems to me bad because it is terribly ineffectual and self-defeating. If, as a temporary measure, it would give results, if, as a form of surgery, it would remove evils which defy our ordinary ways of caring for the social order, I would, whatever the immediate cost, accept it. But, even as surgery, it is a dangerous expedient. It cuts at the very heart of our social process. It destroys what it seeks to cure. And, on the other hand, I am sure that our ordinary processes can be made far more effective than is violence. A democracy can take care of itself, when it is aroused to action. The human spirit, when it is stirred to life, is not a weak and pitiful and helpless thing. It is efficient as well as magnificent. Or rather, it is magnificent in its efficiency. The method of freedom and justice is not a sentimental dream. It is the hard and tough and shrewd common sense of a race which, through the ages, has seen the futilities of beastliness; which has, in some measure, come to awareness of its own situation and its own purposes. It is the way which, on the whole, America has chosen and must follow.

And so, at the end of the argument, as at the beginning, I answer back to the students who challenge me. In America, as in all human living, there are standards of behavior. We Americans have ideals to which we owe allegiance. And high among these is the passion, the reasonable passion, for liberty. Because of that passion America has been, and will continue to be, a great venture of the human spirit. Never, in the history of the world, had a nation so favorable an external situation as is ours. But it is correspondingly true that never, in the history of the world, were temptations so alluring, confusions so bewildering as are ours. Our greatest danger is, I think, that of over-hasty, superficial solutions. The human being who, ages ago, differentiated himself from himself, set for his successors a vastly complicated human problem. To divide the world of one's activities into the realms of spirit and body is to involve all one's activities in a doubleness of meaning which fills our living with strain and conflict and dilemma. And yet it is just the creating of those difficulties which has made men human. We are compounded of obligations as well as of delights. Our cravings for pleasantness are finely balanced by our commitments to excellence. No single human life is understood except as both these elements are found within it. Nor is the life of any nation. If we would know what America means we must see her both as body and as spirit. We must see these two in right relations to one another.

And, finally, we Americans must face the fact that our task is an immensely difficult one. As a nation, we come to our strength, to our opportunity, at a time when the body of mankind has been built up to gigantic proportions. Upon us is laid the necessity of creating a spirit to master that body. It cannot be done if we plunge still more madly into external activities, trusting to Fate to care for our spiritual interests. Those interests must be our constant, our major preoccupation. America cannot be herself unless she thinks as well as acts, unless she meditates as well as plans. America is a spirit in bodily form. It is important that we be happy, that we have power and wealth, comfort and convenience. But it is more than important— it is imperative—that we be admirable, that we act in ways of which we need not be ashamed. Can we make of America a thing "beautiful in itself'' and, it may be, ''an example of beauty to others''? To try to do that is to know what America means.

6

I'm an American

The following interview is the only record Meiklejohn left in which he spoke of his childhood. It reveals much about the roots from which his criticism of Protestant-capitalist society grew. NBC broadcast the interview on Station WBZ from Boston, Massachusetts, on Sunday, August 10, 1941. At the time Meiklejohn and his wife were in the east spending the summer with Evelyn and Roger Baldwin at their home on Martha's Vineyard. Europe was fighting World War II, and four months later Japan would bomb Pearl Harbor. This excerpt constitutes about one-quarter of the interview; the remainder was devoted to discussions of the role of the United States in the international struggle.

NBC: Mr. Meiklejohn, Americans have known you for many years as the former president of Amherst and through your writings as one intensely concerned with preserving the democratic way of life. But they don't know much of your life story. Won't you tell us where you were born and when you came to the United States?

Meiklejohn: I was born in England, Mr. Dimock. I was the youngest of eight sons in a Scottish, Presbyterian, working-class family. My mother and father emigrated twice. Three years before I was born, they went from Scotland to England. When I was eight years old, they came from England to America.

NBC: Apparently you have had three countries, Mr. Meiklejohn! How have they affected your ability to say: ''I'm an American''?

Meiklejohn: I am glad you spoke of that, Mr. Dimock. Loyalties belong, I think, not so much to countries as to the principles and causes to which the countries are dedicated. Out of my boyhood experiences there came to me two loyalties I have never lost. They are woven deeply into the texture of my devotion to America.

NBC: Won't you tell us about them, Mr. Meiklejohn?

Meiklejohn: My earliest allegiance was to the Scottish culture which centered about the Bible and the poetry of Robert Burns. You see, the first family migration had made me the only English-born member of a Scottish family. I could, therefore, be called by teasing brothers an outsider, an alien, a Johnny Bull. Out of the distress of that situation my first argument, so far as I can remember, was constructed. It ran as follows—"You could be born in a stable, but that wouldn't make you a horse." You can see how passionately I wanted to be a Scotsman! My second loyalty came from my father's occupation. From boyhood to old age my father worked, as a color-designer, in the textile industry. My mother and father were early members of the Rochdale Cooperative. I played cricket and soccer with the boys and men from the mills. The textile-workers were my people. I was proud of their achievements. I rebelled against their wrongs. The sense of the injustice done them has never left me. One of my most passionate desires is to do what I can to help transform, in legal ways, the competitive system of free enterprise which has dealt so cruelly, so ungenerously, with the working people of England and America and Scotland.

NBC: I wish you would tell us, Mr. Meiklejohn, from your experience in three great democracies, some of the changes which must be made.

Meiklejohn: May I say first that when I criticize my three countries, I am not disloyal to them, nor am I afraid that they will accuse me of disloyalty. Whatever their failures Britain and America have succeeded at one essential point. They have developed the high political art of self-criticism. They do not demand of their citizens blind approval of what they do. They believe in freedom of speech. They welcome difference of opinion. As democracies, they expect that every man will think as straight as he can and will speak fearlessly and honestly, what he thinks. No people is free unless it thus provides for the criticism of its own actions.

NBC: Tell us, then, Mr. Meiklejohn, what you have in mind when you ask for democracy in the lives of the working population of England and America.

Meiklejohn: Well, Mr. Dimock, I can give you a few suggestions of what I mean. A recent book by Francis Williams tells us that at least a half of Britain's people regularly lack proper food. Six percent of the population owns eighty percent of the capital wealth. For every baby that dies from pneumonia or bronchitis in a middle-class home, five hundred and seventy-two die from the same causes in poor homes. And my own field, that of education, repeats the same story. England has always had two sets of schools, one for the upper classes and one for the lower classes. The minds and spirits of young people are starved and stunted even more than their bodies. That is not justice as a democracy interprets justice.

The Reality of Values

From 1897 until 1911 Alexander Meiklejohn taught philosophy at Brown University and learned to think as a philosopher. During those fourteen years he rose steadily to full professor of logic and metaphysics.

College philosophy in the United States reached its nadir about 1870. Its teachers distrusted their own subject. Most of them were Christian ministers who considered philosophy the handmaid of theology. They sensed that free inquiry about basic philosophical problems would produce questions threatening accredited religious beliefs. In consequence, in the usual philosophical course teachers stuck close to safe textbooks and protected their students, and themselves, from doubts.

This pattern of college philosophy could not long endure under the challenges of Darwin's theory of evolution, the scientific outlook, and the secularism of German universities. The department of philosophy at Harvard, under the leadership of George Herbert Palmer (1842-1933), took the lead in departing from tradition. Palmer had trained as a minister, and his own philosophy was a kind of moderate idealism. But he understood the task of philosophy to be untrammeled inquiry, and when he began teaching philosophy in 1872, he introduced two striking innovations: instead of using textbooks he took students to the original sources, and he offered an independent course in which he invited students to construct their own philosophies. During the 1890s his department contained the most brilliant of philosophic antagonists: William James, an empiricist and pragmatist; Josiah Royce, a rationalist and absolute idealist; Hugo Munsterberg, an ardent Fichtean; George Santayana, a skeptic and instinctive materialist; and others.

The philosophy department at Brown could not boast the showy brilliance of Harvard, but in the debate between God and science Brown did not cling to orthodoxy. Although it was a Baptist institution, Brown took pride in its open-mindedness about religious affairs. Indeed, by 1899 its leading professor of philosophy was an urbane agnostic—Walter Goodnow Everett, who considered himself a naturalist. He accepted the findings of science about the natural world, interpreted specific beliefs of traditional theology as expressions of the poetic imagination, and found justification for ethical behavior in the human and natural world.

Meiklejohn's Scotch Presbyterian family had carefully reared him in its religious faith. Though his parents had pointed out to the examining minister that Meiklejohn did not know his catechism as well as if the family had remained in Scotland, he had been confirmed into the Presbyterian church. As his intellectual powers became evident, his parents expected him to become a minister. He went off to college hoping to major in French but, at the urging of his teachers, switched to philosophy.

In philosophy Meiklejohn studied, both as an undergraduate and as a graduate, with James Seth, a Scot who taught moral philosophy at Brown from 1892 to 1896 and at Cornell from 1896 to 1898. For his dissertation Meiklejohn wrote on Kant's theory of substance, and Kant's metaphysical position became the basis of his own. Meiklejohn agreed with Kant that there are two worlds—an outer one of phenomena and an inner one of noumena. Meiklejohn acknowledged the existence of the outer world, yet for him the inner world was equally real and of greater importance. He accepted the scientific method as the best instrument for gaining knowledge about the external world, and in the conflict between science and orthodox Christianity he relinquished orthodoxy. In *Education Between Two Worlds* (1942) he expressed his resolution of the conflict as follows:

Theological ideas had made intelligence cosmic in origin and importance. For men who believed in God, the universe was an expression of thoughts and purposes of which the world had been made, for the sake of which it was carried on. But the Darwinian nontheological theory gives to intelligence no such cosmic status. Thinking is, so far as we know, man-made. No other thing, living or nonliving, shares in the conscious attempt to know, to appreciate, to control. The cosmos as a whole, out of which human life emerges, gives no evidence of being, or wishing to be, intelligent. The human spirit is alone in an otherwise nonhuman, nonspiritual universe. Whatever it has, or may ever have, of sensitiveness, of wisdom, of generosity, of freedom, of justice, it has made, it will make, for itself [pp. 199-200].

Many U.S. philosophers who at this time abandoned orthodox interpretations of Christianity thought of science and religion as adversaries. They were naturalists (not supernaturalists) and empiricists (not rationalists). They believed that truths are established by a combination of reason and experience (the scientific method), not by reason alone, nor by authority, God, or the church. Their philosophical positions ranged from reductive materialism (J. B. Watson and the behaviorists), to pragmatism (William James), to instrumentalism (John Dewey).

Some materialists held that only knowledge gained through the bodily senses such as sight, sound, and touch is scientifically verifiable. They believed that knowledge of good or evil— of values—cannot be verified, since it rests on emotion or the teachings of one's culture. Some of their followers tended to glorify technology and to identify progress with the achievement of a higher standard of living.

For Meiklejohn, the problems of philosophy could be formulated in terms of the principle that there are two ways of knowing the world, each of which yields a form of knowledge, both of which are valid. His own conviction was that knowledge of the world as known in terms of meaning, purpose, and value is "far deeper and truer" than other forms of knowledge (selections 7 and 8). Because he accepted the methods of science for dealing with the external world, he called himself a "naturalistic Idealist."

Meiklejohn met stiff opposition to his Idealist position from other philosophers. At the University of Wisconsin he enjoyed the spur of argument with cogent pragmatists—Max Otto in the regular department of philosophy and Carl Boegholt, jointly in the regular department and the Experimental College. But it was John Dewey whom Meiklejohn finally challenged. Meiklejohn eventually came to believe that Dewey was causing so much intellectual mischief with the ambiguity of his ideas that Meiklejohn devoted a section of *Education Between Two Worlds* to arguing with him. In this section, Meiklejohn made these assertions about Dewey's position:

1) Dewey gives two contradictory statements about the relation of knowledge to intelligence and allows both to stand, creating a fundamental ambiguity. He says both that intelligence is a procedure for rationalizing our passions, and he says that it is a procedure for testing our beliefs by objective intellectual criticism. The question not

answered is, "By what process of thinking is knowledge transformed into wisdom?"

2) Dewey entrusts education to the state, but he views the state as a policeman needed to settle arguments among competing pressure groups devoted to their self-interest. Such a state has no common purpose to teach, says Meiklejohn.

3) Dewey prefers democracy to dictatorship or aristocracy, but the reasons he gives do not stand up to examination. He said in 1927 that technological advances made democracy inevitable, but since then democracy has not been inevitable in Germany, Italy or Russia. He says that democracy must be judged by its consequences, but he gives no way to measure the value of its consequences. Does the "experimental method" mean that we should try both democracy and dictatorship tentatively and let them fight their way through to some victory? asks Meiklejohn.

After concluding that Dewey had a passion for democracy but no coherent theory of it, Meiklejohn constructed and defended his own general theory of democracy and education, basing it on two assertions—that all men are brothers, and that all activities summed up under the term "intelligence" are expressions of that kinship (selection 9).

Meiklejohn looked for generalizing ideas in the realm of values as a physicist looks for them among particles. For him the presence and operation of values in the everyday world was a fact as obvious as the presence of the sun. For pleasure he read the German and Scotch idealists—Kant, Spinoza, Francis Herbert Bradley— but his idealism differed from theirs. He made no theological assumptions; he overcame any hunger for cosmic support; he accepted the uncertainty and relativity of the contemporary human condition; and he was aware of the tragic dimensions and probabilities. He took ethical questions to be of supreme importance to philosophy, at a time when most leading U.S. philosophers had given up trying to think about purpose and value. Meiklejohn saw the achievements of science summoning people to their next great task—the creation of intellectual, moral and esthetic foundations sufficient to support the vast weight of scientific knowledge (selection 10).

Putting Meiklejohn into a category has proved difficult for reviewers and summarizers. He does not fit into the usual niches, because underlying most summarizing schemes is the assumption that

some necessary connection exists between empiricism and liberal, progressive beliefs, on the one hand, and idealism and conservative, traditional beliefs, on the other. Meiklejohn cannot be placed in a scheme based on this assumption. As Theodore Brameld put it:
". . .more than any other idealist educator he [Meiklejohn] projects his thinking in a radical direction." (*Philosophies of Education in Cultural Perspective* [New York: Dryden Press, 1955], p.253.)

7
_____

Philosophy

> *Meiklejohn served as president of the Eastern Division of the American Philosophical Association in 1925-26. What philosophy meant for Meiklejohn, how he approached it, and where in its permanent battles he took his stand, he laid out simply in a pamphlet he wrote that year for the American Library Association. It was published as* Philosophy *(Chicago, Illinois: American Library Association, 1926) and was part of a series, "Reading with a Purpose," designed to introduce the general public to academic disciplines and to help them get started reading independently in these various fields. By 1934 the American Library Association had published sixty-seven titles and had sold 800,000 copies. Meiklejohn's pamphlet totaled a succinct fifty-one pages, of which this selection constitutes the last twenty.*

. . . .It is not the purpose of this paper to give a complete or orderly account of all that philosophy does. We are trying rather to show the position and the attitude of the study in order to see what it might say to evolution and to religion as it finds them in controversy. It will perhaps serve this purpose if we state as briefly and clearly as we can two or three of the specific problems upon which philosophical thinking has been focussed.

One of the most important problems has been already suggested. It is that of the logical unity of the mind. If we say that the mind has different methods of thinking and that each of these gives a different account of the world then we are driven to ask whether the mind of a man is logically one mind or many minds. How can one mind know in different ways? How are our different ways of thinking related to one another? Are they in conflict; or are they indifferent and irrelevant to each other; or have they such meaning for each other that their results can all be united into a single set of ideas for the mind which includes them all? It is evident, I think, that we are here asking about the unity of the mind itself. And the question is whether the human mind is an intellectual rag-bag or a single unifying activity with a single meaning running through all its activities. In another form, the question is whether there is one truth or many truths, whether truth is absolute or is made up of many relative truths which are unrelated and disconnected with each other. This question is, in all its forms, a difficult one, and I must not attempt to deal with it here. There are however two remarks which may be made in passing.

First, whatever its multiplicity and variety there can be no doubt that human thinking is dominated by its own demand for unity. If it is a rag-bag it is an uneasy one. If there are in the mind ideas or sets of ideas which have no meaning for each other, which cannot therefore be brought into the orderly comprehensions of a single set of ideas which includes them all, the mind which thus has the ideas without understanding them must, and does, regard itself as failing in its work. To think is to unify. And in so far as difference defies unification, the mind is balked and beaten by its own content.

And second, it is evident that two different kinds of thinking in the same mind and about the same objects cannot be wholly indifferent to each other. If, for example, I am perceiving a series of qualities as reds, blues, greens, yellows, etc. and the physicist is at the same time describing those same qualities in time-space terms, the two descriptions must at least vary together. When I see red, he will find one time-space set of relations. And as his qualities change into other speeds and lengths, so does my red give way to blue or yellow or green. From this it follows that we can always infer from the one series to the other. And in fact that is just what our "explanation" seems to be in such cases. A fact described in one set of qualities is said to be explained when it is translated into the terms of the other set of qualities which another description gives. In very large measure our explanations of the world are just such "translations" into another language.

A second problem is one which has puzzled men ever since they discovered themselves. It is that of their relations to the other objects in the world. Perhaps the most baffling and the most desperate riddle of all human thinking is that of the place of Man in Nature. Am I a part of the physical world? Or am I something quite different from it and alien to it? Is a man a soul, a self, a mind, or is he a collection of atoms or cells or tissues and organs? On this issue two views meet in open conflict. On the one side, it has always seemed clear that a man is a part of the material world, made of the same stuff, created by the same processes, erased by the same forces. But it has seemed equally clear, perhaps more clear, that a man is something wholly different from "nature" as we commonly know it—a thing of quite different character and quality. If the reader would meet this question in its simplest form let him ask himself what is the relation of his mind to his body. His body is a part of the material world. But what is his mind? Is it a part of the body? If so, how big a part is it and where is it located? Does it act upon the body and is it acted upon in return? Common experience seems to make quite certain the fact that a blow on the head does something to one's mind and also that a decision of the mind can set the body in motion and guide its action. But, as against this, our sciences seem equally sure that nothing except a body can affect a body or be affected by it, nothing except a bodily thing can occupy a bodily frame. The two conflicting statements, I say, seem equally clear and certain. First, I am a mind, in some relation to my body. But, second, my body is so completely accounted for in terms of its relations to other bodies that the supposed relation to a mind is quite superfluous and unintelligible. This latter view is at present stated by the Behaviorist psychologist who condemns and abjures all reference to a "mind" in the explanation of the nature of a man. When the natural sciences explain what a man is they can, without a "mind," account for all the facts and make all the parts of their explanation intelligible for one another. But, on the other hand, it is equally certain that men know themselves in terms of mind. We are selves, persons; we do live lives of conscious purpose and self-direction. And, further, it is in these terms that the essential relations of life are lived and must be lived. It is in these terms, even that one decides to be a Behaviorist. How shall this riddle be solved? Again, I cannot, in these pages, attempt to offer a solution but can only make one or two remarks on the situation as we pass it by.

First, it seems fairly clear that in the description of body and mind we have a typical instance of the meeting of two different methods of thinking. And the problem must be solved, if solved at all, by discovering those kinds of thinking, defining their presuppositions and their procedures, and so determining the meaning of each, for the other and for the mind as a whole.

And, second, I would suggest an analogy between the problem of the self and that of the meaning of a poem. If as one sees a poem on a page, one should ask how big the meaning of it is and where it is, one would have in another situation the problem of mind and body. If one could tell in what letters or letter the meaning is contained; if one could discover that certain parts of the letters are the meanings, then one might tell what part of the body the soul is. But if the meaning is not a part of the letters then the self is not a part of the body. If the mere listing and counting of letters will not reveal the meaning, neither will the discovering of bodily machinery reveal the self. In both cases there are two different modes of thinking which clash and separate without understanding of each other. But in both cases that understanding must be achieved. To do that is a characteristic task of philosophy. To attempt that task, whether one succeeds or fails, is to engage in philosophy.

The third problem which I have in mind is that of the acceptance or rejection of the theory of Idealism. We have just seen that when the world is described in the terms of the natural sciences the self, the conscious person, is left as it were flapping in the wind. Those sciences seek for a set of terms in which the whole world can be described and in which, at the same time, all the descriptions can be brought together into the order and coherence of explanation by law. And their achievement is the building up of that orderly thing which we call the world of nature—the world of which the body of man is an integral part. But, as I have said, from that world the self, the conscious person, is excluded; he is thrust out from nature just as color and sound and odor are expelled or reduced to illusion by the time-space explanations of the physical sciences. Now Idealism is simply the retort direct to this Materialism. It suggests a world of reality from which all material things are as such expelled or reduced to the status of appearances. It proposes that the whole world should be interpreted in terms continuous with those in which we know our own minds. It suggests that the world which the sciences know as a great mechanism of material forces shall be construed as the play of meanings and values. If this could be done then the conscious self, the person, would no longer be left an isolated and disconnected fragment. He would be at home in a world essentially akin to himself. The world of matter would become a world of appearance. The world of mind would be the reality to which that appearance belongs. I have said, "If this could be done," and our argument may well leave the suggestion there. Whether or not it can be done, to what degree of plausibility Idealism can attain,—that has been a permanent problem of the philosophic mind. To some of the greatest thinkers the theory has seemed to be the necessary and the solid basis for all other thinking. They have seen it explaining all the facts of human experience and making them all genuinely intelligible. The most familiar statement of the position for an English-speaking world is that of Bishop Berkeley. He interpreted the world as a set of relationships between a Divine Mind and the minds of men. For him God was speaking to men and they with their peculiar ways of thinking were reading his messages in terms of matter and color and sound. But all such qualities were simply the appearances to men of a world of mind in which they themselves and a Divine Mind were the real beings. I am not disposed at present to argue the validity of this position. My point is simply that throughout the history of philosophy the suggestion of Idealism has been a dominant one and men have ranged themselves in opposing schools as they have supported or attacked it. And today it is still before us, still open to support and to attack. It is the most exciting and the most significant of the suggestions arising from the query as to which of our different kinds of thinking reveals to us the real nature of that world which appears to us in such different forms.

As I now try to bring this discussion to its close may I remind the reader that the three problems just stated are simply three illustrations of a principle in terms of which all the problems of philosophy are formulated. In its simplest form that principle is this—we have different ways of knowing the world and each of these ways gives a description quite different from those which the others give. The one world which

we are trying to know becomes many worlds as our thinking deals
with it.

Now there is in this situation very great danger of the dogmatism
of the partial view. When a mind has described the world in one way
as having a given set of qualities, it is tempted to say, "This is what
the world is." Such dogmatism is, of course, a too hasty and uncritical
settling of the question of Reality and Appearance. And we, with our
variegated minds, are in constant danger of it. It is chiefly with this
danger in mind that I turn to ask what philosophy shall say when two
conflicting sets of ideas are advocating the claims of evolution and
religion. There are, I think, three or four things which may be said.

First, we must repeat that such conflicts cannot be settled by warfare or voting or compromise. Whoever attempts to discover the truth
in the midst of such a controversy must do so by intellectual means.
If one would pass judgment upon the issues here involved he must
know the kinds of thinking by which the conflicting ideas are
achieved. He must do his work by genuine reflection.

Second, the philosophic mind will deal with the opposing ideas not
as enemies but as friends. At least it will insist that they are both
friendly to itself. These sets of ideas are both within the same mind
which is trying to understand them, they are its own; each is its own
creation. And for any mind it is an essential demand that each of its
ideas shall be acknowledged to have such validity as it can rightly
claim. The mind, when philosophic, will not arbitrarily adopt one of its
own points of view as the truth, condemning the others to outer darkness. But it will assign to each such kind and such measure of truth
as its way of thinking is qualified to achieve. Philosophy is, in this
sense, an attempt at justice in the realm of ideas.

Third, the mind when philosophic will sharply rebuke its own dogmatism on either side of the issue. On the scientific side it often finds
a dogmatism which is destructive of genuine study of the problem.
Men say, "The world can be described in scientific terms: it is therefore what those terms describe it as being." And then they proceed to
ask, "Where in such a world can you find minds or values or colors or
meanings?" In our day, uncritical as it is, men simply take it for
granted that the sciences reveal what the world really is. And in the
face of this dogmatism all other descriptions are reduced to appearance and illusion. The argument is—matter has no meanings; hence
there are no meanings. But to this dogmatism philosophy gives sharp

rebuke. To say that in time-space terms the world can be described with greater accuracy and completeness than in any other terms does not mean that the world really has a time-space character. It may be that we are most accurate about the least important matters. It may be that our deepest and most significant modes of knowledge are also the least successful. But in any case, no method of knowing can find within itself evidence that it is better than its fellows. The question, which way of knowing is the best, must be answered by a study of all ways of knowing, by an objective judgment which all alike must respect.

And in like manner, the philosophic mind mourns over the dogmatism of religious thinking. Men say "The *Bible* is true; the world is a place of meaning and values, of selves and destinies." And if you ask "How do you know that?" they answer "By Faith." But if you question further "What is the method of Faith, how does it decide between the true and the false?" you find men simply accepting from some traditional source a set of opinions which they have never questioned by any active method whatever. They know without inquiry that certain opinions are true. And different sects, in exactly the same way, know that different opinions are true. So far are they removed from the spirit of questioning that they make the asking of questions a sinful and wicked thing. Now here again, philosophy must try to put an end to dogmatism. If one knows the history of human thinking one knows that religious opinion is, like scientific opinion, the result of honest and persistent thinking by human minds. In general our religious creeds are the summing up in popular forms of the results achieved by the philosophic schools of Idealists. But the trouble is that the creed-makers and those who wish to build their lives upon the creeds are driven by sheer practical necessity to give to the creeds a finality which thinkers cannot justify. And so they confront the living, striving, advancing thinking of the sciences with a mode of believing which is by choice atrophied and inert. To such dogmatism, as practiced in the name of Faith, the philosophic mind refuses to entrust the cause of religious belief.

To sum up in a word the issue of dogmatism, a philosophy must give to the two partial thinkings each its proper rebuke. To a religion which says "The human problem was solved for all time two thousand, or ten thousand years ago," philosophy says "To take that position is intellectually to desert the cause of religion; it is to stop thinking." And to a science which says, "We moderns have achieved a form of understanding compared with which all earlier forms are superficial and imaginative," philosophy says, "That achievement has been made too many times before to be taken very seriously this time."

But finally, what has philosophy to say in positive contribution to the settlement of the controversy between evolution and religion? It will not accept the uncritical dogmatism of either party. But what has it to put in the place of those dogmatisms? At this point I cannot pretend to speak on behalf of the many-minded guild of philosophers. I can only give my own results so far as I have any. And these can be summed up under three statements.

First, there is no reason to believe that the physical or natural sciences do get at the real nature of the world. It seems to me practically certain that the world is not a time-space world. Nor do I think that the Behavioristic account of a man tells what he really is. Those accounts of nature and of man have value but it is not the value of Reality as against Appearance.

Second, it is idle for those who think in non-scientific terms to quarrel with the sciences in their own fields. The sciences are simply our best ways of dealing with certain questions of fact. And a religion or a philosophy or an art which disputes the facts of science is simply inviting disaster. It is merely fighting good science with bad science and the outcome is never in doubt. Did the world of matter come into being? If so, when and how? Did the human organism develop from other forms? If so, when and how? These and countless like questions deal with matters of fact which are discoverable, if at all, by the technique which the sciences are devising. We who are outside the fields of the sciences must simply accept their results as the best which honest and able thinking can at present achieve. To fight living science with dead science; to oppose to honest and eager investigation mere uninformed and idle assertion is not only futile; it is disastrous in its effect upon the credibility of the cause which one is attempting to serve.

And third, the method of thinking from which Idealism springs, on which therefore religion rests, seems to me far deeper and truer in kind than those of the sciences. Wherever we do know the world in terms of meaning and purpose and value I am sure that we get at Reality far more closely, than we do in the more external descriptions of it; when we know men in those terms we know them as they are rather than as they appear. But on the other hand it must be said that, as compared with the vast achievement of the sciences, the results of Idealistic interpretation are tentative and fragmentary. They are genuine so far as they go; but how far do they go? It is here, I think, that one finds the proper meaning of the word "Faith." In every age the human mind reflects upon its knowledge. Always the practical issues of life center about the question, "Can this knowledge which we have made in various ways be so translated that the whole world shall have meaning of the kind which, in fragmentary ways, men find within themselves?"

And age by age the problem changes as knowledge advances. During the last century or two our scientific techniques have gained an accuracy of observation and a breadth of inference which have swept from the field the older scientific views with which an earlier philosophy had to deal. For philosophy and so for religion, our present question is, "Can we make a new metaphysics for the new science?" That is what in every age philosophy has had to do. It is what we must forever do as the mind finds and applies new techniques for the creating of scientific knowledge. As new accounts of the external world come into being, the mind must ask again, "What does this world mean, what is it worth for us?" It is not enough to say that science does not give the final truth; we must be forever seeking that truth beneath and through the knowledge which the sciences make. Only thus are we loyal to a past which has done the same.

And so may I say in conclusion that in my opinion metaphysics is not a weakness of the ancients. It is the next great struggle to which the human mind is summoned by its own achievements—that of finding intellectual and moral and esthetic foundations sufficient to support the vast new weight of science and craft and institution in which the human spirit has found its outer expression. If one would be a good American today—if one would be a good man—then let him study philosophy.

8

Postscript to
What Does America Mean?

Meiklejohn's reference to the realm of ideas, values, and spirit created difficulties for educated Americans, who by the 1930s tended to dismiss this realm as suspect—one where the methods of science could not apply. Meiklejohn struggled again and again to make his meaning clear. His most extended attempt at clarification occurs in the following chapter, a postscript to his book What Does America Mean? *(New York: W.W. Norton & Company, 1935, reprinted by Norton in paperback in 1972). In it he combats materialism, cultural relativism, and hedonism.*

Throughout the course of this argument I have used the term Spirit in relation to men and to nations. And on every occasion on which the word has appeared I have been shuddering with terror because of the misunderstandings which it has, in actual use, gathered about itself. In the history of that word there is written, I am sure, the truest record of our human blunders. When it is not used, the lives of men have no meaning. As it is used, one sees the meaning of life confused, distorted, contradicting itself, denying its own purposes, as well as coming to awareness of them. It is the glory of the human race that it has insisted on interpreting itself in terms of spiritual significance. It is the pity of our living that we have had as yet so little success in our most magnificent undertaking.

It is not my purpose in this postscript to add to the argument of the book. I should like merely to disclaim the holding of some opinions which are commonly attributed to those who try to deal with life in spiritual terms.

First, when one says that a man is both a body and a spirit, one is not saying that he is two bodies, a big one and a little, with the latter somewhere inside the former, like a beetle in a bottle. To say that is, of course, to make the notion of a spirit quite ridiculous. And the men who specialize in "external" explanations are today very skillful

153

in the use of such ridicule. The trick is very simple. One demands that everything be stated in bodily terms. When that is done, it appears that there is no "spirit" to talk about. One then asks, "What is the external relation between spirit and body?" And the laugh which ensues is the solution of the problem. But as against this easy victory, may I insist that to say that a man is both a spirit and a body is not to say that he is two different men, two separate bodies? On the contrary, it is the very fact that one man, the same man, is both spirit and body which creates the problem. One gains some amusement but very little wisdom from such attempts of the human spirit to ridicule itself out of existence.

There is, however, a valid sense in which we do separate outer and inner activities. We do this on the basis of the intention by which any given act is dominated. If, for example, we are educating a person, are trying to develop his courage or intelligence or fairness, our work, however external its methods, is inner in purpose. But if, on the other hand, we are trying to change an external situation, to deal with things and possessions, our action is, in the corresponding way, outer in character. In this sense, education is always a spiritual venture, and industry always a material occupation. Whenever we are concerned directly with the quality of a person himself, our interest is inner. Whenever our attention is directed to the external forces which play upon life, our interest is outer. It is in this sense that we try to make the outer the servant of the inner.

Second, to say that a man is a spirit does not mean that he is static and unchanging. The body of a man, as seen by the physiologist, is in process of constant change. But it does not follow from this that the inner life is changeless. If anything follows, it is quite the contrary, since the two are the same man. So far as one can see, the spirit of a man changes as does his body. It is born and lives and dies. It waxes and wanes. Now it is cold and sluggish. Later it is hot and passionate. To deny that it changes would be to deny that it is active. And to say that of a spirit would be to say that it does not exist.

And, third, to say that men are alike spirits is not to say that there is present in all men, in all groups of men, some common mysterious "entity" which is throughout the race completely identical with itself. Just as bodies differ, so do spirits. Just as, within a general background of similarity, our physiological processes assume the infinitely varied forms of life, so do our spiritual activities. The child is not a senator. Nor is the savage a reader of Amiel's *Journal*. Nor is the coward, in the same respect, a hero. Men, as such, resemble other men but, in addition to this, each is his own peculiar, changing, individual self. They are alike, but also, in multifarious ways, they differ.

Still another group of false interpretations has gathered about the use of the term "Obligation." I have been saying that men are committed to enterprises, that these have valid claims upon them. I have even ventured to suggest that America, a vast nation of many people, has something to do, something which she is in honor bound to be accomplishing. . . .

Now the misinterpretations of which I am speaking have all one feature in common. They give to obligation an external meaning. In their view, a spiritual commitment becomes a requirement, enforced by authority and by penalty from without. If I say, "You must: you are obliged," they answer, "Who says I must: what external body has the right or the power to tell me what I ought to do?" And since very clearly the inner demands have no such external authority, they are taken to be meaningless, to have no authority whatever. Could any conclusion be more tragically false than this? The claim of duty is not an external compulsion. It is not enforced by penalties. The citizen who obeys the law in order to keep himself out of jail does not thereby express his respect, his regard for the law: he is merely revealing his preference for the out-of-doors. The man who is kept by fear of Hell from robbing the widow and orphan does not show himself to be bound by obligations of justice and mercy. We discover in his conduct only his sensitiveness and timidity in matters of temperature. If only the American mind of our day could see that external compulsions of any kind are forever irrelevant to the activities of the inner life, it would realize how little of our current thinking is done in spiritual terms. To act from pain, from fear, from desire of pleasure, from hope of reward—these are all ways of being driven by external forces. They are as little spiritual as is the experience of drowning when one's head is thrust and kept beneath the water. To think of an obligation as being a requirement is to miss its meaning altogether.

Again, to say that we human beings are "committed" to an obligation does not mean that we are bound by "the Past," by our ancestors. There is a sense in which we owe loyalty to the men who prepared the way for us, whose enterprises we, in our turn, are carrying on. But that does not mean that we, contrary to our own judgment, are required to think their thoughts, to accept their decisions. The sense of obligation of which I am speaking is and must be our own. In this realm, nothing has authority over us except as it is the expression of our own judgment, except as it stirs us in our own natures to admiration and emulation, except as, in our own experience, its opposite arouses us to disapproval and contempt. No statement is valid for us because it was uttered by Moses or Confucius, or Jefferson or Marshall. If we accept it, as they did, it is because we judge these men to have been right. But it is we who today are judging—not they.

But, at this point, we shall be sharply challenged. "If your obligation has no authority from the Past," men say, "if it has no power or force outside your present self, has it then any validity other than that of the passing mood of the passing moment?" And from this it seems to follow that our commitments are arbitrary and capricious, that they are worth nothing more than the whims, the moods which come upon us as the varying influences of human experience bring us under their varying controls. Does this conclusion follow? I do not think so. It does not follow unless we assume that all the present experiences of men are and must be dominated by whim and passion. But why should we assume what is clearly false? Men, as we know them, sometimes try to think: many of them seek to be dispassionate, accurate, objective, reasonable. They are not always willing to be dominated by whim and caprice. Rather, the men whom we admire study their commitments, reflect upon their duties, consult together about their obligations, search diligently in the records of the past for wisdom as to their undertakings. Surely there is something wrong with the argument which says of such critical, patient, objective studies as these that, because they are present and personal, they are therefore capricious and willful! One can justify that conclusion only by a denial of all tests of validity, by so destroying all arguments that one's own argument goes down in the common ruin. It is one of the most common, as well as one of the worst forms of the "external" fallacy. . . .

And, finally, may I insist that to prefer excellence to happiness is not to condemn happiness as undesirable. It is not even to disparage it as unworthy of our seeking. On the contrary, both these sets of "goods" are valuable to us. Neither can be given up as worthless. It is essential only that we do not confuse them, that we do not allow either to get out of its proper relation to its fellow value. That relation is, as I have said, difficult and paradoxical. May I then, in conclusion, state as clearly as I can the elements of that paradox?

With respect to the relation of excellence and happiness, four apparently contradictory statements seem to me to be true. They run as follows:

First, the satisfying of desire is desirable.

Second, excellence of behavior is more than desirable; it is imperative.

Third, as human living becomes excellent, it thereby becomes, other things being equal, more happy.

Fourth, even when excellence does not create happiness, we still choose it, still acknowledge its prior claim upon our action.

It is, I think, only as one faces the conflicts which these statements involve that one tastes the full flavor of what it is to be a man. To solve these difficulties by quick and arbitrary reduction of one set of goods to terms of the other is far too simple-minded to be a valid account of what men have to do in order to be true to themselves. Happiness is not reducible to excellence. Nor is excellence reducible to happiness. Human nature, in spite of all its eager and persistent striving for unity, is still essentially dual in its dealing with its world. May I, as the "closing word" of our argument, reemphasize this point as it arises out of the four observations which I have made?

First, it is of course quite impossible to deny that, for human beings who have desires, the satisfying of those desires is desirable. The man who shivers in the cold does regard the coming of warmth as good. The man who cowers under the condemnation of his fellows does yearn for the happy day when men will smile instead of scowling when he and they meet. And, further, it must be recognized that the excellence of behavior of which we are speaking consists, on one of its sides, in the skill, the persistence, the devotion, with which a person tries to get for men the things which they want. If a father provides shrewdly for the care of his family—for food and shelter and health and education—we admire his prudence and affection in so doing. So, too, the passion for justice, which today we exalt as perhaps the most timely of our virtues, is concerned very largely with land and power and rents and prices and wages and living conditions of every sort. Our admiration goes out to any one who, in regard to those "goods," works efficiently for himself and for his fellows. In a word, the achieving of excellence is not, in intention, hostile to the satisfying of desires.

But, second, to interpret a human being simply in terms of satisfactions is nothing else than to take Hamlet out of the human drama. And to think of a nation in the same terms is equally false and disastrous. When that is done all spiritual value is lost. And, in the last resort, it is the spiritual values for which we most deeply care. If any one of us says that what he wishes for America is that all its people should, in the external sense, be satisfied, he seems to me to take out of the lives of other men all their artistry, all their creative quality. This is, as I have said, the vicious aristocracy of the "We—They" fallacy. The man who thus plans for his country is generous and high-minded. He would be ashamed of himself if he were not. But he is lacking in imagination. He thinks of other Americans, not in the terms of admiration and contempt which he applies to himself, but in terms of a craving for satisfactions and enjoyments which he himself gladly puts aside, denies, destroys, whenever the situation makes such action imperative. It is true that we must plan and work for our fellows. To do other than that is unworthy of any one of us. But to ignore in our planning their likeness to ourselves, to plan for them as if they were not likewise trying to be generous and high-minded, to plan for their happiness without regard for their excellence, is an insult to them which is wholly unforgivable. It is not enough to try to make people happy. It is imperative that we give each other respect. When that is done we are all joined together, on equal footing, in the attempt to make, whatever the cost, a national life worthy of men's admiration.

But, third, it is also true that such willingness of an individual or a nation to lose its own happiness is a very efficient way of finding it. No human effort can, of course, be wholly successful in keeping men safe from disaster. Death, disease, calamity, frustration, wait upon all of us. And that being true, the experiences of suffering, of anguish, of fear, of disappointment, cannot be altogether avoided. But however bad the situation may be, it is made better when men work together in the attempt to improve it. And this happens in two ways. First, since human thinking, human action is not wholly ineffectual, we do succeed in removing causes of anguish, in creating sources of pleasure. And second, far more important, as we strive to make others contented, the fellowship of common striving brings with it the joy, the delight of human comradeship. I suppose that among all our joys, none ranks higher on our scale of preference than those which we experience when congenial people are fused together in friendly endeavor. There inner and outer values are magnificently blended. It is toward the realizing of that experience for the one hundred and twenty-five millions of our population that our planning for America should be chiefly directed.

But, fourth, even when the way of excellence is not that of happiness, either for the individual or for the group, we are, none the less, bound and willing to choose it. It is not imperative that any individual, or any nation, or even the race itself, should continue to be happy, should even continue to exist. It is imperative that so long as we live, we do so with taste and intelligence, with fineness and generosity. Many things are worse than unhappiness. But nothing is worse than being contemptible. We must save America from that fate. We have no right to hope that she will escape external misfortunes or that she will exist forever. Presumably she, too, like other nations of the past, will have her day and cease to be. It would be madness for us to set our hearts on the expectation that our country will be, in the external, temporal sense, the "Eternal City" of human aspiration. But we may, and must, plan that here and now America's part in the world drama shall be well played. If men ask, now or later, "What does America mean?" the answer must be found, not in the outer, given facts of our career, but in our own inner creative activity. America means whatever meaning our spirit brings into being. Our country is not a possession which we may take and keep. It is an opportunity, an obligation, a commitment. Its chief enterprise is the making of men and women free.

9

Education Between Two Worlds

> *Meiklejohn's major theoretical work, in which he attempted to construct a theory of democracy sufficient to carry a general theory of education, was his book* Education Between Two Worlds *(New York: Harper and Brothers, 1942, reprinted by Books for Libraries Press, 1972). The following selection is the final of twenty-one chapters, called "The General Theory of Education."*

The human road, we have said, leads from barbarism to civilization. So far as they are intelligent, men seek to establish reasonable relations with their fellows. Such relations are not possible with mosquitoes or tornadoes or trees. But they are possible with normal human beings. And the human task, so far as men are moral and intellectual, is that of extending the scope of reasonable co-operation to its widest and deepest limits. The final goal of that attempt would be the creation of a world-state, in which the appeal to reason would have replaced the resort to violence in the relations of all men to one another.

1

If we accept for humanity the goal which our argument has suggested, the ruling motive of education becomes clear. Learning is not merely the acquiring of mastery over intellectual subject matter. It is, first of all, initiation into many social groups and, ultimately, into one social group. The teacher leads his pupil into active membership in a fraternity to which he himself belongs. The motive force of that fraternity is found in a common devotion to a common, co-operative enterprise. Just as, in the home, each child learns, or should learn, to play his part in the family circle, so, in our schools and colleges, every citizen of the world should become "at home" in the human "state." He should acquire a sense of what humanity is trying to do, and a will to join in doing it.

The calling of the teacher, as so defined, is one of infinite difficulty. But it's also infinitely significant. He is commissioned to form and fashion both human society as a whole and the individuals of whom that society consists. He acts for the state with a completeness of responsibility which is equaled by no other official.

As he engages in his task, the teacher needs two kinds of equipment. He must acquire command, both of method and of content. On the one hand, he must be expert in the technique of his art. To this end he must know human nature just as any artist knows his materials. He must have considered the principles and practices which are propounded in Rousseau's *Emile*. He must understand how intelligence grows and is kept from growing. In each specific case he must assess capacities and incapacities, powers and impediments. He must discover how to cultivate powers and to remove impediments. Like Comenius he must seek to provide for the plants which he is cultivating good soil in which to grow, a sunny place whose warmth will stimulate their powers to action. Unlike Comenius, the modern teacher will find his sun, not in the mind and will of God, but in the human fellowship which, against frightful odds, mankind is trying to establish.

2

We have said that a teacher should read Rousseau's *Emile*. But it is far more important that he read, and study, and read again, the *Social Contract*. One of the greatest failures of our contemporary training of teachers is that they become mere technicians. They learn the tricks and devices of the classroom. But they do not learn the beliefs and motives and values of the human fellowship for the sake of which the classroom exists. The primary question of teaching theory and practice is one of purpose. Why do we teach? What should we teach? For whom do we teach? What is our goal, and what is the source of its authority over us? Those are the questions which must be answered if our teachers are to be themselves members of the fraternity into which they seek to initiate their pupils. Only as those questions find solution do our schools and colleges understand what they are doing.

3

The argument of this book has centered around the contention suggested by Rousseau that education is, and must be, carried on under the authority of some social group. It is an expression of the will of some social "organism, instinct with one life, moved by one mind." Teacher and pupil are not isolated individuals. They are both agents of the state. They are called upon to go about the business of learning. And, as they do so, the truth, beauty, and goodness with which they deal, come to them, not from some foreign source, not from their own separate experiences, but from the "state" of which they are members. The content of teaching is found in the modes of behavior, the "patterns of culture," which are approved, and criticized, by the fellowship for which the teaching is done. And, that being true, it is clear that the fundamental question with regard to any system of education is, "By what social group is it given; what are the purposes of that group; why does it will that its members be educated?"

4

In the course of our argument we have touched upon four different answers to this basic question. And these four answers give as many "general theories of education."

First, the answer which Comenius gave to the question of authority and purpose was direct and unequivocal. His pupils were the children of God. His teachers were servants of God. Schools and colleges were, therefore, commissioned to follow after the mind and will of God. The Divine purpose was directed toward the making of a human community. It required peace rather than violence, reasonableness rather than selfishness, intelligence rather than stupidity. The "world-state" was established by the Divine will. And a common citizenship in that state prescribed a common curriculum of wisdom and piety for all mankind.

But, with the weakening of theological beliefs and sanctions, our culture has faced the task of providing a "secular" authorization for the purposes of teaching. We moderns have, therefore, tried to describe, in "scientific" terms, the relation between an individual, whether pupil or teacher, and a social consciousness which is wider and deeper than his own. These scientific accounts of human behavior have followed three lines. They suggest, therefore, three different types of educational theory which are now competing for our acceptance.

5

The disorganic theory, in its most extreme form, finds an individual life to be related to the conscious life around it as a drop of water in a stream is related to the current which carries it along. In this figurative description, the total stream of consciousness, as it flows, has no intention of doing so. It does not choose its course. It may, at points, become aware of its own process. But that awareness is merely cognitive. It is a recognition of conditions and their consequences as mere facts. Each individual drop of consciousness, therefore, as it is swept along, may feel what is happening to itself and to others. It may even recognize the influence of this set of conditions or that as determining the course of events. But it cannot participate in the purpose of controlling that course, for the simple reason that there is no such purpose in which to participate.

When we say that this "scientific" account of human relations can never provide a basis for a theory of education, we are not denying its validity as "science." We are saying that knowledge, as such, does not express purpose. It describes happenings. Knowledge of conditions and consequence is necessary for the directing of education. But it is not sufficient. It is only as knowledge, being used for the purposes of human brotherhood, becomes intelligence, that it serves the purposes of the teacher. Pupils must learn, not only what they are and how they act, but also what they have to do and be. They must see themselves as participating in enterprises which have a right to their allegiance.

6

A second, less extreme form of disorganic theory, does not exclude purposes from the stream of events. But it finds them to be scattered, multifarious, episodic. They occur on specific occasions. They appear and disappear as individuals and groups are stirred to "adjust" themselves to their situation, to adjust their situation to themselves. This is the point of view which Dewey expresses when he describes the "conscious" activities of men as dealing with a "plurality of problematic situations." Each of these situations requires purposive action. But each is dealt with separately as the specific conditions may require. They do not fuse into a single situation. It is true that a number of individuals may become a social group, that their many enterprises may become one enterprise. But these groupings also, are separate and episodic. At the best, they give us only a multiplicity of conflicting pressure groups, each going its own way. The stream of events is marked here and there by eddies or currents of conscious purpose. But, in its general flow, it remains merely a stream which rushes along with no conscious control of what it is doing.

This view of human behavior is, likewise, inadequate as a basis for a theory of education. As already noted, it gives us, not one human education, but a vast multiplicity of separate and unrelated educations. It finds in the circumstances and interests of each individual life the materials and the needs which prescribe a peculiar and distinctive plan of teaching. But it does not express that general will of the state, that devotion to the common good, which is required if the members of a social group are to be properly prepared for reasonable co-operation in the life of the community.

7

As against extreme naturalism or partial pluralism, this book has insisted upon a continuous purpose which runs through the course of human experience. We have not said that that purpose dominates the total course of events. But we have said that it seeks such domination, so far as it is humanly possible. The race of man has before it the possibility of being civilized. And it is that possibility which defines the course of education. All women and children and men may become intelligent, loyal members of a single social group. And it is for that group that teaching should be done. Teaching itself should be intelligent and loyal. It should recognize that the will to reasonableness has critical authority over all individuals and all groups which are found in the ranks of humanity.

It follows from what has been said that all human beings should have the same essential education. This assertion does not deny that they should have different educations as well. The drummer and the violinist have different techniques to acquire. But they must also learn to play together. It would be disastrous if, in the midst of a symphony, either drummer or violinist were found unable to make his instrument play. But it would be at least equally disastrous if either of them should play with vigor and efficiency but with no regard for the score which had been placed before his eyes.

Humanity has, I insist, one intelligence. That intelligence, it is true, is only "in the making." Its making is a difficult and precarious venture. It may at any time collapse. And yet, the statement that all men may share in a common enterprise is both true and significant. It tells us, in part, what the world is. It tells us, in part, what men are. And it is upon that basis of fact that any proper plan of human education must be based. It is the lack of that basis of fact which has made our current theories of teaching so negative, so lacking in positive direction. There is a fellowship of civilizing intelligence into which every human being, so far as he is capable of it, must be initiated. Each of us must have loyalty to that company. As pupils, we must turn aside from the resort to violence. We must acquire skill in the appeal to reason. We must become citizens of the world. Education is the fitting of people, young and old, for the responsibilities and opportunities of that citizenship.

8

If we accept the belief that the whole world of human behavior can be dealt with as a single enterprise which a single cooperative human intelligence is trying to direct, and if we regard all lesser enterprises as finding their basic justification and criticism as participants in this all-inclusive attempt, some general conclusions concerning education seem to follow.

First, governments, local, provincial, national, and supernational, are equipped to teach. The handing over of the control of education from the church to the state has not been a fatal blunder. The state is not Moloch. It is not "nothing but your worst, nothing but the worst of us, lifted up." On the contrary, the state is the best of us, trying to control and to elevate the worst of us. It is ourselves seeking to be reasonable, to live in justice and freedom with one another. Man, at his best, is a political animal. His wisdom creates manners and morals. The same wisdom, when institutionalized, creates laws, roads, hospitals, parks, pensions, peace, schools. But these two expressions of wisdom are not hostile to one another. They are one in purpose, one in idea and value. And since that is true, education by the government is radically sound in principle. As our culture now stands, no other institution can equal the state as the representative of those purposes and beliefs which are the fruits of human reasonableness. We do not understand what a state is unless we see that it is both a student and a teacher. We belie its essential nature when we regard it as a policeman.

The statement just made does not mean that "private schools" may not do good teaching. After all, the thinking of the race is done by individuals. And groups of individuals who are disinterested, who are moved to teach, not by private interest or party bias, but by zeal for public intelligence—such groups may teach successfully. On the whole, however, the drift of circumstance is against them. Under current economic conditions private schools and colleges are, almost inevitably, agencies of special privilege. They give to a few advantages which are denied to the many. And that very inequality is destructive of education in reasonableness. It is hard to teach justice when the selection of the students must be recognized as unjust. Inequality of educational opportunity does not conduce to the inculcation of a zest for equality. Actions teach more effectively than words. And for this reason the role of private education seems sure to be a dwindling one.

At this point it may be objected that schools, when conducted by a government, are, of necessity, "plunged into politics," that they are used by "the party in power" for the furthering of its own selfish purposes. And that objection will hold good so long, and so far, as we Americans can see in political life, only the strife of contending pressure groups. That prevailing social philosophy has done enormous damage to our schools. But, on the other hand, that philosophy is false. And our actual social practice rises, at some points, far above it. In the organization of the state university, for example, our governments have devised a system of administration which combines, with amazing success, the independence of the teacher, and the responsibility of the institution to the public as a whole. The essence of that system of administration is found in the belief that men who are qualified to study and teach can be trusted to do so in the public interest. As against this, in other fields of political action, we Americans have dealt with our public servants on the theory that they cannot be trusted. We have assumed that they need to be watched, to be kept under constant pressure by us. And the inevitable result is that we have had as public officials the kind of person who needs to be watched, who responds to pressure. Every teacher knows that suspicion breeds trickiness and guile. Persons who are not trusted become unworthy of being trusted. That "pressure" philosophy will never give us a democracy. It must be abandoned. Mutual confidence is the prerequisite of freedom. Unless men can trust each other, there is no hope of reasonableness between them. I do not mean that a democracy should give up control over its representatives. But I do mean that such control should not be degrading and hence self-defeating. Our national and state legislatures give constant illustration of that degradation and self-defeat. They represent, not democracy, but a crude and stupid individualistic falsification of it which, while keeping the forms of freedom, has made men themselves unfit to be free.

As we attempt the sadly needed revision of our processes of government, we may find valuable suggestions in the structure and procedure of our state univerisities. We have, in those institutions, men who, in the public interest, are seeking for the truth. They are, in the best sense of the term, "responsible public servants." And yet, it would, on the whole, be meaningless to "subject them to pressure," to send telegrams telling them what truth to find, as we do with the members of our legislatures. The public servant of a free society must himself be free. That fact our pressure-group philosophy has disastrously obscured.

9

Our first conclusion has been that teaching should be a government activity. But, second, which of our governments shall take charge of it? Shall it be the village or the town or the county or the state or the nation or the world-nation? Each of these "states" represents a level of reasonableness. Each of them has its own "pattern of culture." And the choice among them is, in effect, the choice of the subject matter of our teaching. Shall we teach young people to live in a village or in a nation or in the world? The answer to that question must not be oversimplified. Every human being needs to learn how to live in all the social groupings to which he "belongs." And yet, if our argument is valid, one principle emerges from it which is of primary importance. Fundamentally education belongs to the world-state. The reasonableness of that institution includes and criticizes all the lesser reasonablenesses of our experience. Every human being, young or old, should be taught, first of all, to be a citizen of the world, a member of the human fellowship. All other lessons are derivatives of that primary lesson.

The statement just made branches out in two different directions. It tells us, first, that all education should be given "for" the world-state. It tells us, second, that all education should be given "by" the world-state. If we can explain those two assertions, our attempt at a theory of teaching will have reached its goal.

10

The need of so transforming our plans of education that our pupils will learn to participate in the total human enterprise is thrust upon us as we see the dictatorships of Germany, Italy, and Japan at work in the field of teaching. They have built and are running educational machines which torture and twist the minds of their people out of all resemblance to the forms of human reasonableness. Those nations are guilty of many crimes. But the deepest and blackest of all their offenses are committed against their schools. It is not true, however, that they are the only sinners. The democracies, too, in more subtle ways are like-wise guilty. Our localisms and provincialisms do not so obviously and brutally undertake to root out of our minds the appeal to reason. But they are, nevertheless, effective in doing so. It is not enough today to teach a young person to play his part in the life of Indiana or Boston or the South. It is not enough to make him a loyal Pole or Japanese or Canadian or Brazilian. The world is in crisis. There has come upon us all the necessity, as well as the opportunity, of creating a world-state, of making reasonableness prevail for all humanity. And we must have schools which will serve that purpose.

As I write these words my mind goes back to Comenius and to the Christian faith which was for him the basis of education. He saw *all* young people as the children of God. He saw them all, therefore, as having the same life to live. He, therefore, wished to provide for all alike, rich and poor, girls and boys, noble and ignoble, the same lessons in the same scheme of instruction. And that insight, in the new setting which the advance of secularism has brought upon us, still holds good. If we are to have an effective human fellowship, the pupils in every corner of the earth will have the same basic lessons to learn. They need to know each other. They must become aware of the humanity of which they are members. They must become acquainted with that whole human undertaking which we sum up under the phrase, "the attempt at civilization." Only by having that common knowledge, can they become reasonable in their relations to one another. "The proper study of mankind is Man."

11

The second implication of our principle is that the control of education, its planning and basic administration should be in the hands of the world-state. It is, I think, obvious as we plan for the future, that the nation which is to include all the nations and rule over them must have military force sufficient to give it mastery over its members. It must have a legislature and an executive. It must have courts of justice. It must have an equitable and stable system of finance and trade. But more pressing than any of these is the need for a universal scheme of instruction, whose driving force shall be the purpose that all men shall live together in peace and freedom, with reasonable regard for one another. First of all, the world-state like any other state must be a teacher. If it cannot teach, it will do nothing else successfully.

I have spoken of the desperate urgency of the need that people be educated as citizens of the world. But not even that urgency must be allowed to lead us into the illusion that changes have been made when they have been written on paper or even when they have been voted by legislatures. No teaching can go far beyond the actual living, the prevailing pattern of culture of the group by which it is given. Schools, like churches, are too often used as mechanisms of compensation. We live by one code which, in our hearts, we condemn. And we try to restore the balance by having another code taught to our children. But that procedure in education is just as futile and disastrous as was, in an earlier day, Sunday preaching which was balanced by Monday practice. We cannot teach world fellowship unless we believe in it, unless we put it into action by the creation of a political organization which shall take charge of the fortunes and the virtues of humanity. To attempt it would be like trying to teach Shakespeare to young people in whose homes the only reading is found in the pulp magazines. It is not easy to teach children to despise their parents. Nor is it, perhaps, desirable.

12

At this point, our argument returns to the principle from which, at the suggestion of Rousseau, it took its start. Education is, and must be, an activity carried on by a social group. It is initiation into an existing "pattern of culture." And, as such, it depends upon the support and the authority of the group to which both the pattern and the pupil belong. But that means that we cannot teach world reasonableness unless there is a reasonable world. We cannot teach citizenship in a world-state unless a world-state exists. Are we Anglo-Saxons willing to recognize that implication and to act accordingly? Are we willing to put aside the hypocritical superiorities of the "White Man's Burden"? Are we able to stop the brutal pretense of giving "justice" to the "lesser breeds without the law," and to join with them as fellows in creating a law which shall be equal for all mankind? There is a curiously vital connection between teaching and the truth. If we practice justice and freedom we can teach them. If we do not practice them our words are like "the crackling of thorns under a pot."

13

If we are to have a world-state and to teach its lessons it is clear that the most difficult, as well as the most essential, education must be given, not to children but to men and women. As the new world takes form, the minds of children of every race and country will accept it as easily, more easily, than the chaotic, confusing, self-contradictory scheme of behavior which we now present to them. But that is not true of the grownups. We elders are caught in fear, in habit, in custom, in prejudice, in prudence, in common sense. It is we, therefore, who resist the education or re-education which we need. If we are to have the moral and intellectual reconstruction which are implied in the making of a world-state, the prime essential is an adequate process of adult education. Our minds will have to be refashioned. And we ourselves must do it. There is no one else to teach us. We, members of a common humanity, acting together as one sovereign people, must teach ourselves to do and to be what our common citizenship offers us to do and be. We must learn to so know and care for all our fellow men that we can participate with them in the one common cause. That task of human self-education our generation is called upon to begin. But it will be only a beginning. The road to reasonableness goes on and on.

14

From church to state! From myth to fact! —Can our culture make that transition? There can be little doubt, as Matthew Arnold has told us, that an old world is "dead." And for a long time now the new world has seemed "powerless to be born." And the essential guilt of "the three great democracies," Britain, France, and the United States, as well as of lesser democracies, has been their holding back in the face of the vast and terrifying possibility of a new birth. All over the world the new expression of the human spirit has been striving to break loose, to enter upon its career.

In China, so long abused and mistreated and contemned, there is new hope, new resolution, new achievement. The ancient wisdom is making contact with the modern world. In Russia, a new and relatively untried wisdom has come into action. And the magnificent loyalty and endurance and efficiency of the Russian people, in the face of overwhelming odds, give some suggestion of the power and majesty which a creative program might bring to us. India, too, is stirring. Her demand for justice and freedom will not be denied. She will not remain a subject people. Even the hysterical madness of the Germans and Italians and Japanese springs from the conviction that, the present chaos being intolerable, something better can be devised to take its place. The words of Adolf Hitler are madness. And yet that madness, as a power which threatens the peace and freedom of the modern world, does not spring primarily from the mind of Hitler. It is the madness of a civilization which has denied its own faith, which has been untrue to its own principles. If we believe in democracy we must practice it between nations as well as within our own nation. If we believe in freedom we cannot be content that other peoples shall be enslaved. If we believe in law and order we must join in establishing them for all mankind. If we believe in equality we cannot defend so desperately our own "higher standard of living." If we believe in reasonableness we must follow wherever reason may lead.

In the midst of all our agonies and uncertainties the new world is being born. It is that new world which gives meaning to education. Every pupil must be learning for it. Every teacher must be teaching for it. Every scholar must be thinking for it. Humanity is reasonable as well as unreasonable. It is the struggle between these two which defines the course of education. We know what teaching is only as we see and feel what the free spirit of man is trying to do and to be.

10

Under the Elms

*Meiklejohn gave this talk to the class of 1953 at Brown
University on a Friday afternoon, May 29, 1953, as part of
the traditional Class Day exercises which preceded commencement the following Monday—a ceremony that had
come to be known as "Under the Elms," since the exercises were held on the park-like campus, studded with elms.
Meiklejohn spoke representing his class of 1893, bringing
greetings and advice across the sixty intervening years.
Characteristically he looked, not back, but ahead sixty
years.*

*This talk is the only example included in this collection
revealing Meiklejohn's style in talking with students—an
imbalance, since much of his life's talking had been with
students. It was published in the* Brown Alumni Monthly
53 (July 1953): 15-16.

Brown Men of 1953: You are very kind to summon an old grad, out
of the distant past, to talk with you, Under the Elms. Speaking for
myself and for my classmates of 1893, I thank you for that courtesy
of young men to old.

What shall we talk about, you and I? Sixty years of living separate
your youth and mine. Have we, then, anything in common to talk
about? I am strongly tempted to evade that issue, to tell you stories of
the glories of the past, to boast of Bennie Andrews and our other
heroes. But that temptation I resist. I shall be speaking, not of our
sixty years, which are gone, but of your sixty years, which are yet to
come. I invite you to think, not about us, but about you. What are
you going to do and see and be in the sixty years which stretch
between now and 2013?

The Envy of an Octogenarian

Of one thing I am certain, men of '53. I envy you. I wish that I were twenty-one instead of eighty-one. I wish that I could be a member of your class and live the life that you will live. I hate to miss the game that you will play. There is a chance, which we have never had, a fighting chance, that, at the hands of you and your contemporaries, mankind may turn a corner, may clear away the rubble of a social order which has fallen to pieces, may start to build another to take its place. And you, winning or losing, will play that game. I do not promise you a quick or easy victory. Who wants to play a game that he is sure to win? But I do envy you your chance.

Why must men turn a corner? What is the rubble which you must clear away? What must you build to take its place? You will not expect me to answer those questions in these few moments of a summer afternoon. I only offer, for your criticism as college men, a loose and sweeping generalization about the present desperate crisis in human thinking.

Our colleges, it seems to me, are cultivating two very different kinds of thinking. They teach their pupils skills in doing things. They also try to teach them wisdom in choosing what things to do. The search for skill has, as its intended products, inventions, devices, tools, and gadgets, by which, whether in thought or action, men get things done. The search for wisdom has a different aim. Its hoped-for products are judgments of value, decisions about what should be done, and why; about what should not be done, and why.

And these two kinds of thinking have different intellectual sources. The inventions of skill grow out of the sciences. The search for valuation is guided by philosophical or humanistic studies. These two, as so defined, cover the total range of human thinking. Science discovers and invents. Philosophy interprets, for human welfare, the meaning of those discoveries and inventions. If we could see those two in right relations, we would know, not only what colleges are doing, but thereby, what human living is and ought to be.

What Do Inventions Mean?

To you who now are facing the planning and making of a coming world, I offer three observations about inventions and about their meaning.

First, inventions destroy a social order as well as share in its creation. The inquiring, discovering mind has given to men the use of earth and water, fire and air. It has fashioned the plow, the wheel, the road, the boat, the clock, money, the bank and credit, the multifarious uses of power, and, most powerful of all, new methods of mind by which still other inventions may be made. But each of these devices, in turn, displaces older devices, and thus shatters and renders obsolete some earlier mode of life, the customs and beliefs, the habits and values, which the earlier devices had kept alive.

Second, as inventions thus lead the way, the forces of wisdom tag along behind. Theirs is the task of reconstruction. They must, by reasoned, creative, imaginative thinking, bring into being new beliefs and plans, make out of chaos a new order of individual and social action. The inventions have widened out the range of human choice. And now, a new philosophy, informed by knowledge, but not directed by it, must make a plan of life to fit the novel situation.

But, third, in this our present "time of troubles," disaster has come upon our planning because inventions are being devised so fast that wisdom cannot keep the pace. Philosophy, the tortoise, is far out-distanced by Science, the hare. And for that reason, our civilization is now becoming more externalized, more mechanized in mind, more fascinated by gadgets and techniques, more avid for power, more barren of clearness of purpose, than any other which the world has seen. The madness of that external preoccupation invades even our colleges. In them the acquiring of skills now claims an equal status with the search for wisdom and may be substituted for it. The passion for knowledge dulls the zest for insight. Techniques of scholarship are cutting away the roots of liberal learning. And, to cap the climax, philosophy itself seems eager to be a science, to follow the current fashion of the mind.

Bet on the Tortoise

Men of '53, have you any philosophy in you? I have suggested, in these hurried words, that discoveries and inventions do not, as such, accomplish human welfare. But they do bring it more fully within our reach. During your sixty years, if you and your friends can, by rigorous thinking, understand and master the process of invention, there can be established a human community in which no woman or man or child will lack for proper food, or proper housing, or proper care of health, or proper education to fit him for friendship and mutual understanding with his fellow-men. That can be done, as basis for further advance, only if you will bet your lives and minds, not on the hare, but on the tortoise. It takes an act of reckless faith to lay that bet just now. But, sooner or later—so the fable goes—the tortoise wins.

As these words come to their end, I am thinking of that member of 1953—not yet selected, I assume—who, if this custom is continued, will, sixty years from now, stand here, "Under the Elms," and talk to 2013. I'd like to shake his hand and smile with him in friendly greeting. Meanwhile, the Class of '93 salutes the Class of '53; salutes, with high respect and admiration, our president and faculty; salutes the grand old college to whose "altar" we Brown men, whether of '93 or '53 or 2013, bring once again our "offering of praise."

Education for a
Free World

Even before the Experimental College had come to its end, Meiklejohn had begun to think about teaching adults. If teaching freedom requires developing self-governing adults who can think for
themselves, then a teacher must reach beyond the immature and
select group he finds in colleges to the governors themselves. Meiklejohn had long wanted to teach the basic skills of citizenship to
adults—both to those who had gone to college and to those who had
never had a chance at liberal education.

Earlier, at Amherst, Meiklejohn had shown interest in adult education when he organized students and teachers to conduct classes for
workers in nearby industrial towns. This seems to have been the first
instance of a regular college or university taking some responsibility
for workers' education. Later, in 1921, Meiklejohn spent a year in
Europe, where he learned more about workers' education, and in
1923 Alvin Johnson, director of the New School for Social Research,
asked him to help that school focus on adult education. Although
Meiklejohn was tempted by this offer, he did not feel ready to take up
adult education before trying out his educational ideas with undergraduates, and he turned instead to setting up the Experimental College
at Wisconsin.

The decade of the 1920s, however, was one of increasing national
interest in adult education. A burst of activity and a struggle for control of workers' education began in 1921. The basic question was:
Should workers support and control their own education or should
they attempt it through established universities, supported by big business? If workers supported their own education, should it be done
through their unions or through their independent political organizations? In the 1920s all three of these possibilities were tested. First, a
few universities tried to provide workers' education. The University of
California in 1921 created a program jointly with the California
Federation of Labor, directed by a Committee of Control on which
labor had five representatives and the university had four. This

176

program ran for eighteen years, complete with eight summer sessions and thirty labor institutes, but the unions never gave it whole-hearted support. In 1921 another influential university program began, the Summer School for Women Workers in Industry at Bryn Mawr. In 1924 the University of Wisconsin set up the Wisconsin School for Workers as part of its summer program. Despite its popularity, it never paid for itself, and the legislature cut its funding in 1939.

For decades workers had set up their own educational programs, through their unions and through their political organizations. One of the most sucessful union programs was that of the International Ladies' Garment Workers' Union in New York City, which began in 1916 after disaffiliating from the Rand School for Social Studies founded in 1906 by the Socialist Party. In 1921 an agency was created to coordinate workers' education sponsored by unions—the Workers Education Bureau. It became the educational arm of the American Federation of Labor and tended to be a conservative force, uncritical of existing social-economic institutions and hostile to proposals for serious change. It refused to cooperate with communist groups and eventually broke with all the independent efforts at workers' education. Many of these flourished in the 1920s; two of the best-known were Brookwood Labor School, Katonah, New York, founded in 1921 and Commonwealth College, Mena, Arkansas, founded in 1923.

In 1926 the Carnegie Corporation entered this struggle for control of adult education. It gave a five-and-a-half year grant of $137,500 to establish the American Association for Adult Education as a coordinating agency for all education past the collegiate level. Morse Adams Cartwright was elected president; ten years later he reported on the problems and progress of adult education in his book *Ten Years of Adult Education* (New York: Macmillan Company, 1935). Until the 1920s, and even through that decade, he found, most middle-class people thought of adult education as being classes in reading and writing for illiterate immigrants. He held two books most responsible for changing that notion —the popular *Why Stop Learning?* by Dorothy Canfield Fisher in 1927 and the scholarly *Adult Learning* by Edward Lee Thorndike in 1928. In 1929 the American Association for Adult Education began publishing its *Journal of Adult Education,* and in 1934 it put out *The Handbook of Adult Education in the United States.* Cartwright reported in 1935 that the Carnegie Corporation had made grants for adult education amounting to almost three million dollars over ten years.

When the Experimental College ended in 1932, Meiklejohn asked the Carnegie Corporation to fund an outside evaluation of the experiment. They refused, saying they did not want to risk repudiation by the University of Wisconsin. (The trustees of the University of Wisconsin had decided in 1927 to refuse gifts from private corporations, and although they reversed this decision in 1930, the foundations were still wary.) In 1937-38 the Carnegie Corporation gave Meiklejohn a grant to expand the work of the San Francisco School of Social Studies.

When Meiklejohn's School of Social Studies was well established (selection 11), he threw himself into national and international promotion of adult education. From 1936 to 1943 he gave speeches around the country as they were arranged for him by the Adult Education Council of Chicago. From 1937 to 1939 he served as a director of the California Association for Adult Education. From 1938 to 1941 he was a vice-president of the American Association for Adult Education, and in May 1942, he was elected president to serve until October 1943. From 1944 through 1950 he served on the Executive Council of the American Association for Adult Education.

As president of this association, Meiklejohn wrote two articles for the *Adult Education Journal:* "Teacher, Teach Thyself" (July 1943) and "For International Citizenship" (January 1943). He developed his ideas about education for world citizenship in several other journals (selection 12) and in 1946 served as a delegate to the founding of the United Nations Educational, Scientific, and Cultural Organization (UNESCO). Meiklejohn realized that if people around the world were to become self-governing groups who appealed to reason rather than resorting to violence, then the magnitude of education that would be necessary was eluding the imagination of almost everyone. He pushed the idea of worldwide adult education as far as he could, but returned from London discouraged that even the delegates to the founding of UNESCO did not understand the quantity and quality of education such a project would require.

After 1950 Meiklejohn no longer served adult education in any direct ways. But one project in adult education that he and Helen always supported was the Highlander Research and Education Center in the Cumberland Mountains of Tennessee. Myles Horton started

Highlander in 1932 "to assist in the defense and expansion of political and economic democracy." Highlander was deeply involved during the 1930s in labor organizing drives and during the 1940s and 1950s in the civil rights movement. Its farm and facilities provided a residential setting where adults from different social, racial, and economic backgrounds could live together and discuss how to act together on the major problems facing them. The Meiklejohns never visited Highlander, but many of their good friends did, and Myles Horton always visited them when he was in Berkeley. In the 1950s the Meiklejohns became sponsors of the Berkeley Friends of Highlander, a committee to publicize Highlander's work and to raise money for its support.

11

Adult Education: A Fresh Start

Progress Report on the
San Francisco School of Social Studies

> *Meiklejohn wrote the following report after the San Francisco School of Social Studies had been operating about six months. More a plan of intentions than a report of results, it was published in* The New Republic *80 (August 15, 1934): 14-17. In 1936 Meiklejohn turned over the direction of the school to John Powell, who wrote up the whole story in* Education for Maturity *(New York: Hermitage House, 1949).*

The time has come for the establishing of a new branch of public education in America. It is no longer enough that we teach children. It is not enough that we lead many of our young people through high school and a few of them through college. Every day makes it clearer that the amount of learning, and the kind of learning, that an American needs for proper living cannot be won in the years before twenty-one. Our scheme of government and of life can succeed only if, in their more mature years, men and women will engage in careful, enthusiastic and guided study of common values, common dangers, common opportunities. In a word, we must have a comprehensive scheme of adult education.

The end to be served by this new teaching will not be vocational. We Americans are already well able to train ourselves for jobs. There is no need for a fresh start along that line. On the other hand, the purpose is very badly described as that of "fitting people for the new leisure." That notion has in it too much of individual irresponsibility, too much of mere escape from obligations—from significant loyalties and endeavors—to serve as a basis for a national movement in popular teaching. The primary aim of adult education goes far deeper than either of these relatively superficial glimpses of meaning. That aim is the creation of an active and enlightened public mind. The deepest question in American life today is not economic or political; it is educational. It is the question of the thinking power of a democracy. Can our people understand and direct their own living or must someone else do their thinking, make their decisions, for them? As a democracy we are pledged to try the first of these two programs. And to make that attempt successful is the aim of adult education. At this point we do need a fresh start.

It should be noted in passing that the program here suggested is not that of the indoctrination of Americanism. We need the practice of democracy rather than the preaching of it. And the practice of democracy in teaching is one of "free inquiry." It seeks to create and develop the will and the capacity for independent judgment. It regards its own beliefs as open to study, to criticism, to revision. To fall short of such self-criticism is to betray the deepest principles of our American life. There is among us no treason so black as that which would, by methods of insinuation or of violence, "impose" democratic principles, keep them safe from hostile opinions. We cannot teach democracy unless we trust it in action, practice it in our teaching.

It need hardly be said that the task of creating a national system of adult education is a very difficult one. In terms of quantity, the difficulties are obvious enough. Into the field in which newspapers, churches, libraries, theatres, lecture platforms, books and magazines, art museums, radio centers, concert halls, are already at work, teachers must go. And they must go in sufficient numbers and with sufficient clarity of purpose to criticize and modify these other agencies as well as to cooperate with them. Theirs will be the primary responsibility for making vivid and attractive the studying activity in which every good American should be engaged. To do that will be, in sheer quantity, an enormous undertaking.

But the qualitative difficulties are even greater. How shall a people that has not built up the habits of study be led into the forming of those habits? Who shall be the teachers? What "materials" shall be used? What "methods" shall be followed? Here is a teaching problem as difficult as it is important. A democracy must arouse and sustain the creative intelligence upon the postulating of which its whole scheme of government and of living rests, with whose success or failure its own existence stands or falls. How shall it be done?

As we face so overwhelming a task we may find some encouragement in the success of like ventures in at least two other countries. In Denmark, we are told, the Folk Schools have had a powerful influence in making for that country a mind of its own. They have brought many people together into the sense of common interests, common conditions, a common destiny to be studied and so mastered. And, in a more limited range, democratic living has, in like manner, been created by the tutorial classes of England. In those classes "intellectuals" and "workers" have helped each other. Their teaching influence has gone through and through the working class of an industrial society and has, perhaps more than any other single factor, raised it up into self-conscious, intelligent participation in English life and English administration. At both these points in the struggle for democracy, adult education has won outstanding victories. They tell us that our own task, difficult though it is, is not an impossible one.

In America, many adult teaching agencies have been, for longer or shorter times, at work. Lyceums, chautauquas, evening schools, extension classes, correspondence courses, public libraries, have established themselves among us. And recently, chiefly through private initiative, there has sprung up a great variety of teaching enterprises. But the most striking feature of these activities, when taken as a group, is their planlessness. In them, our teaching policy has risen very little above the level of giving to each student such subjects as will appeal to his own immediate personal interest.

It is true that such organizations as the American Association for Adult Education and the Workers' Education Bureau have given valuable assistance and suggestion. Powerful minds, such as those of [Joseph Kinmout] Hart and [Eduard Christian] Lindeman, have struggled for coherence. And yet the fact remains that our adult teaching is a vast conglomeration of classes in labor tactics, typewriting, history, dancing, economics, painting, etc., which are bound together by no dominating ideas or purposes. And the time has now come when such "elective" incoherence simply will not do. We Americans have a very definite piece of adult teaching to do. We have common problems which must be thought about. Unless we can be aroused out of our distractions, out of our ignorance, into the attempt at understanding, our venture in democracy must come to a speedy and disastrous end. Can we do what needs to be done? Can we train ourselves to think about our problems? Can we create and sustain a national system of adult education?

It is a commonplace of educational theory that teaching method must vary with the nature of the human purpose that is sought and with the conditions that, from within and from without, are playing upon the minds of the pupils. Just as Denmark found her way of teaching and England her own quite different procedure, so we must find ours, one to fit ourselves and our intentions. It is the purpose of this paper to suggest that we are now beginning to see what, in its essentials, the American method may be.

Ten years ago the American Library Association appointed a commission to investigate how our popular reading might, by proper guidance, be made more serious and valuable. The same motive found expression in the "Great Books" course at Columbia and again in the similar venture carried on at Chicago by President Hutchins and Professor Adler. It was the dominating idea in the course of study of the Experimental College at Wisconsin. Basic to all these enterprises was a principle which, though constantly ignored, is as old as teaching itself. It seems to me to be the soundest idea that we can find for use in the field of Adult Education in America, *viz.,* that the best external help in learning to think about human problems is to get into living contact with the ablest men who have thought about these problems. One learns to play well by playing with the best players. Americans would learn to study if they would read properly the great books.

During the past academic year, the San Francisco School of Social Studies has been trying to plan and conduct a scheme of teaching on the basis of this principle. A small faculty of college rank has been conducting twenty classes with about three hundred pupils. As the outcome of their experiences a fairly definite scheme begins to emerge.

The first task of the teachers has been that of selecting the books in which the best minds of our civilization have expressed themselves upon our common problems in ways suitable for popular reading. In the nature of the case, most of our technical, scholarly books will not serve the purpose. But the "Dialogues" of Plato, the Bible, the Constitution, the writings of Emerson, Whitman, Adam Smith, Karl Marx, Emily Dickinson, Dreiser, Jeffers, Dewey, Veblen, Tawney, Brandeis, Turner, Beard, Lenin, Bourne, Mumford, Dos Passos, these and a host of others in poetry and prose, tell us of the attempts of our intellectual leaders to solve the human problems that we in America now face. Out of these a course of study may be made.

The second task of the faculty has been to furnish guidance in the study of the books selected. To this end groups have been formed with six and fifteen as the lower and upper limits of membership. At weekly meetings the books have been discussed chapter by chapter, all the members being pledged to careful reading of the assignment in advance. The reading time of a single book has ranged from five or six to twelve weeks.

In the guiding of the discussion, the teachers have tried to avoid two opposing evils. On the one hand, they have not "lectured," have not undertaken to explain the books, to tell the pupils what they mean. Lecturing, here as elsewhere, would invite the student to passivity rather than to activity; it would inform or excite or stimulate or amuse rather than challenge to the enterprise of independent reading and judgment. The purpose is to develop in the student the power to do his own reading and to discuss it with his friends. On the other hand we have not been willing to devote the meetings to mere "discussion." To do that, to encourage people to strive for victory with respect to opinions they have not really tried to verify or understand, is to help in the fixing of prejudices rather than to train the capacity for thinking. It is true that the books are read for the sake of the ideas they advance and that the reading is justified only as it leads the reader to better thinking, to better ideas of his own. But the first step in that process is an honest, painstaking attempt to understand what an idea means when presented by another mind—in this case, by a mind far superior to one's own. In the field of study, independence is essential. But, in the proper uses of the terms, honesty, humility and accuracy are essential as well.

With respect to more external arrangements the attempt has been made to construct the simplest possible scheme, with a minimum of overhead both in expense and administration. No fees have been charged, the expenses being met by the subscriptions of a group of private citizens. No credits have been required for admission and no credits given at the end of the course. Student groups have been formed in two ways. First, existing organizations in the city, such as labor unions, churches, teachers' associations, women's clubs, political organizations, have been invited to form groups from their own membership. Second, individuals applying at the school office have been formed into groups by the teachers. The groups have varied much with respect to homogeneity and the effects of this difference are being carefully watched by the teachers. The student age has ranged from eighteen to sixty-five. Practically every type of occupation has been represented and every type of political and social attitude. Previous education has ranged from grammar school to professional and graduate university training. For the most part, meetings have been held in rooms furnished by the students or by their organizations. Attendance has been amazingly regular and the preparatory work seriously done. Twice as many students applied as could be taken by the present teaching force, and the number of applicants is constantly increasing. So far as can be judged by student activity and enthusiasm, the work of the school has fully justified itself.

One further feature of the plan remains to be mentioned. In the minds of the teachers the separate books are not regarded as separate and unrelated fields of reading. If they are to do their work they must be so related that, taken together, they give the elements of a coherent and unified study of community life as a whole. What we would like to develop in the city is the sense that there are certain central problems with which every mind should be dealing, certain leaders of intellectual activity with whom every intelligent American should have acquaintance. We need, in our American cities, what might be called a common culture of ideas, of interests, of problems, of values. We need to be brought together into unity of interest and understanding so that we may have the materials, the methods, the acquaintance with ideas that would make possible for us the experience of genuine thinking together. We are at the present time a curiously multifarious, unrelated collection of individuals who do not know each other. And we are rendered ineffectual in our common living by the lack of any common thinking. Such a school as I have been describing dreams of planting here and there throughout the city groups of persons who may begin to remedy that evil. In such a city as San Francisco there should be hundreds of such groups at work, and they should be linked together in active cooperation. In every other American city there should be like associations, reading the same books, thinking about the same problems, grappling with the same ideas. And to this there should be added some central organization in the different states and in the nation as a whole which would keep the separate activities in acquaintance with one another, would unite them in generous cooperation. If that could be brought about it would do for us what the folk schools have done for Denmark, what the tutorial classes have done for the workers of England. It would have in it the beginnings of the making of an American mind. To say these things is of course to speak of dreams rather than of present achievements. But such dreams define the direction in which our efforts may go. As such they may be of value in the planning and creating of a democratic America.

12

Education as a Factor in Post-War Reconstruction

Once Meiklejohn had stated his general theory of education in Education Between Two Worlds, *he wrote article after article expounding the consequences of his theory even amid the realities of a world at war. The following article appeared in* Free World, *a monthly magazine published in New York City from 1941 to 1946, which sprang to life as a forum for discussing the war, democracy, and what the world would be like after the war. Editions were published simultaneously in Havana, Mexico City, and Montevideo. Its international Honorary Board included: Max Ascoli, Madame Chiang Kai-shek, Albert Einstein, Harold Ickes, Max Lerner, Thomas Mann, Gunnar Myrdal, Reinhold Niebuhr, and Dorothy Thompson. From 1946 to 1949 the magazine continued as* United Nations World. *Meiklejohn's article appeared in* Free World *5 (January 1943): 27-31.*

In the making of plans for international peace and justice, three sets of factors must be dealt with. I list them in order of increasing importance, which is also the order of increasing difficulty. They are first, economic; second, political; and third, educational. As to the first of these, all men now know that the time has come when we must create and administer a unified economic world order. Economic chaos is no longer tolerable. It is no longer necessary. But second, this ordering and controlling of our business activities implies and requires that we create and administer a unified political world order which shall be equal in scope, but superior in power, to the forces of economic procedure. The production and distribution of wealth must be under public control. A world economy without a world government spells strife and disaster. But third, political institutions in turn must be sustained and controlled by adequate education. The nature and quality of a government depends upon the nature and quality of the intelligence of its citizens. The tragic experience of Adolf Hitler has shown us that no dictatorship can endure unless it can teach its people to be slaves. But, it is equally certain that no democracy can endure unless it can teach its citizens to be free. A unified world economy, authorized and controlled by a unified world government, implies, as a basic postulate, a united system of world education.

When I speak of world unity in economics and politics and education, I am not thinking of a unity which ignores or denies the facts of multiplicity. I am thinking, rather, of unity in multiplicity—a unifying activity which, as it faces the varieties and complexities of human experience, endeavors to save them from sinking down into chaos and meaninglessness and brutish strife. What we must have in economics, in politics, in education, is an ordered multiplicity— an economic order, a political order, an educational order. These are three inter-dependent phases of a single human enterprise. They are three sides of that endeavor by which—if I may borrow a phrase from Rousseau—the human being "ceases from being a stupid and unima-ginative animal and becomes an intelligent being, and a man."

Now, if what I have said is true, then two serious dangers beset the planning of the United Nations for post-war reconstruction. First, our economic experts working in isolation may be tempted by "the bias of happy exercise," to devise an economic world order without placing it under the control of an adequate political world order. Second, our political experts, influenced by the same bias, may attempt to create and maintain political institutions without giving them a solid founda-tion in an adequate system of popular education. If those dangers are not avoided, then the outcome of our struggle for the Four Freedoms will be the establishment of more than four slaveries. Our economic arrangements will fail because they are not supported and controlled by adequate political institutions. Our political institutions will fail, because they are not rooted in the understanding and good will of their citizens. If those evils are allowed to come upon us, catastrophe is inevitable. The greatness of our opportunity will be the measure of the greatness of our failure to meet it.

The economic danger of which I have spoken can be very simply though, on this occasion, very abstractly indicated. It has to do with the choice between public and private control of business. If we say that an economic world order is created, what we are really saying is that some human mind, or some group of human minds, has taken control of the economic forces of our civilization. Order, as here used, means control. To say that the play of economic forces has become orderly is to say that someone has taken charge of them. Someone has so studied them, so measured and charted them that they can be directed to work together for the realization of assigned ends. Forces in themselves have no order. Order is a human contrivance. It is a human achievement. If, then, the world of business becomes a world of order, the first question to ask is: "Whose order is it? By what methods and toward what ends is it directed?"

And to that question two sharply different answers are possible. The control of the world's business may be in public hands or in private hands. It may be exercised with common consent or without common consent. It may belong to the common people or to the masters of the common people. If the first of these alternatives is adopted, if the production and distribution of the world's wealth is made subject to the common judgment, the common will of the citizens of the world, then world government, in some form or other, is established. But the danger which now threatens us is that our economic experts will lead us in the other direction. Men who through special knowledge have the inside track, and especially the shrewd and aggressive minds of our Anglo-American business world, will be sorely tempted, without the consent of their fellows, to take into their own hands the domination of the economic process. Such men do not always realize what they are doing. They commonly regard themselves not as our masters, but as the servants of natural forces which work through them. It is not by accident that the men who dominate our Anglo-American economic life have so generally believed in Natural Laws as governing human society. But that belief is, more or less unconsciously, simply a cover for the brutal fact of their own domination over the lives and fortunes of their fellows. These men, if they are not subjected to the authority of political institutions, will lead us into disaster. I do not on the whole challenge their good intentions. But I do challenge their understanding of what they are doing. I do not deny the need of economic leadership. But I do protest the futility of self-appointed, dictatorial leadership. Government, whether economic or political, must be by consent of the governed. If control is not public, then it is private. And a world economy in private hands means war—and war again. Only under a free world government is a free world economy possible. There is only one device by which human beings can escape the evils of dictatorship. That is by governing themselves.

But secondly, the enterprise of government has its own perplexities and dangers. If it be decided that an international economy is to be politically controlled, if its problems are to be dealt with by common consent, then all the difficulties of human education come rushing upon us. How shall the citizens of the world give consent, or refuse to give consent, to measures which they do not understand? Two thousand years ago, Epictetus stated the principle underlying this dilemma when he said: "The rulers of the state have said that only free men shall be educated; but God has said that only educated men shall be free."

Here, then, is the second, the greater danger which threatens the plans which our experts are making for the organization of the world. To arrange that a world government shall be conducted by the consent of the governed implies and requires a system of world education. If we are to have a free world community, the citizens of the world must learn what free institutions are and how under actual conditions they can be achieved. To say this is not to deny that in the first instance the problems of an international society must be dealt with by "experts." These problems must be studied with all the finesse of scholarly investigation and with the wisdom which comes from wide political and economic experience. But for the purposes of free self government such study is not enough. The same problems must be studied on the popular level. "Experts" may recommend. But "citizens" must decide. And that means that the citizens of a world order have much learning to do. They must become able to comprehend and to pass judgment upon what their leaders say. Even more important than that, they must learn to know each other, to think together, to understand the common enterprise. In the last resort, political institutions can succeed only as they grow out of and give expression to fundamental agreements of idea and purpose. But that implies mutual acquaintance, mutual understanding—in short, a common education. A free world government is possible only if from one end of the world to the other, free men and women are engaged in widespread, well organized, and persistent study both of the *end* to be realized and of the *conditions* which are favorable and unfavorable to its realization. Just as a government must rule its business, so must a people rule its government. On any other basis than that we shall have dictatorship and with it the wars, the injustice, the slavery which dictatorship, whether open or concealed, inevitably brings.

II

If now we turn from the negative side of our problem to its positive side, from the dangers which threaten post-war reconstruction to ways of overcoming those dangers, I venture to suggest how a beginning might be made in the establishment of a system of world education adequate for our economic and political needs. I have in mind the creating of an International Institute of Education, somewhat analogous in kind, though differing in function, to the International Labor Office in the planning of the League of Nations. The positive considerations from which that suggestion springs are somewhat as follows:

1. It is I think essential that from the start international planning shall include as an organic element in its procedure provision for general popular education. And, especially, teaching must be devised for those mature persons who are to have the rights and responsibilities of world citizenship. As men plan for a world order, economic, political, and educational institutions must grow together. We cannot practice justice and freedom unless we can teach them. To impose economic and political arrangements upon citizens who do not understand them is to plan for the renewal of world conflict.

2. The international education which we need cannot be limited to provision for intellectual co-operation among scholars. Nor can the need be met by the establishment of one or more universities. Scholarship is essential. But it is not sufficient. The task which lies before us is that of cultivating among all the common people of the world such knowledge and good will as will weld them together into an international community.

3. It follows from what has just been said that, in its initial stages at least, international teaching must be done chiefly in the field of adult education. The citizens of the world must learn what it means to be a citizen of the world. They must learn to use their minds, to enjoy using their minds, for the making of a free human society.

4. The education of which we are speaking must be, in the democratic sense, free. It must present to its pupils not the solution of a problem but the problem itself with all its perplexities. Such teaching forbids the use of propaganda. The common people of all countries must be led into a common study of a common enterprise in which they are together engaged.

5. It is equally certain—though the statement of the fact seems paradoxical—that in all countries the same basic education must be given. Amid all the varieties of circumstance, the same lessons are to be learned. Chinamen, Englishmen, Indians, Russians, Peruvians, Javanese—for all these the same fundamental problems must be presented, the same teaching methods applied, the same intellectual materials used. The first essential is that learners shall recognize that from one end of the world to the other the same human struggle to

devise and maintain law and order is going on. To be educated is to be fitted to participate in that struggle.

On the basis of these considerations it is, I think, possible to draw in outline the form which an Institute of International Education might take. One can see also certain forms which it must not take.

1. The teaching we need cannot be given by the separate nations, acting separately. It must be given by the international organization itself as a fundamental part of its own procedure. All genuine education is initiation. It is the attempt of some social group to fit its members, old and young, for participation in the activities which the group is carrying on. The world government itself must study and teach what it is doing. No other group, no separate groups, can meet that responsibility.

2. It follows from what has just been said that the financial support of world teaching must come from the world government. That teaching must be free from all the restrictions and conditions which direct financial support from local or national sources might lay upon it. And in the same way the international organization must take direct and unqualified responsibility for the intellectual and administrative control of the teaching process. The world government must do its own studying, its own teaching.

3. The staff of an Institute of Education would be drawn in part from the administrative staff of the international organization. It would include also other scholars and teachers who are trained for the critical examination and interpretation of the principles of world order. If these two groups could be fused together into a unified faculty clearly aware of its responsibilities, we might achieve that integration of intellectual and practical activities which is so sadly lacking in much of the scholarly work, much of the teaching which is now going on.

4. The pupils of the Institute would be drawn from universities throughout the world. They would be young scholars who have completed in some special field of study the intellectual training ordinarily required for admission to teaching on the university level.

5. These young scholars would have at least a year of training at the Institute. They would study there the work of the international organization, its aims and methods, its general principles and its specific problems, its successes and its failures, its hopes and its fears. They would be fitted to become, in the forms of adult education, interpreters of what the international organization is trying to do.

6. On the completion of their training, the Institute would send these young scholars throughout the world as teachers of its citizens. Acting in collaboration with local authorities, they would go from community to community, staying two or three or even four months in each place. But the Institute would keep them in close touch with each other and with itself. It would endeavor to make of them a well-integrated teaching body, clearly aware of its own purposes, ready to promote the realization of those purposes in the midst of all the differences of circumstance into which they might come. These international interpreters would learn as well as teach. In them and in their work, the motives, the ideas of world peace and world justice would find an approach at least to adequate expression.

III

Anyone who has engaged in actual teaching knows how fragmentary are the suggestions which I have made. The path of education is not an easy one. The task of devising and administering a scheme of education for the citizens of the world will be a long and perplexing one. And yet, fifty years of the achievements of adult education in many countries indicate the lines which we may at the beginning fruitfully follow. I mention here three of these:

1. As our teachers enter local communities, public meetings would be held at which various phases of the international enterprise would be presented, together with the intellectual materials bearing upon them. Such presentations would be supplemented by discussion at the meeting and on other occasions.

2. More important, however, than listening and discussing are the activities of careful and sustained study. To this end, small study groups would be formed in which leaders and pupils together would read and reflect upon the great books and the decisive documents in which international issues find their most enlightening formulations. The far-off goal of this method would be that every adult citizen of an international society should be an active member of such a group. That goal will not soon be reached. But only as we approach it are we making headway toward an international society.

3. In the new forms of communication and travel, the radio, the film, et cetera, there are opening up vast new possibilities of teaching achievement. These must be tested and developed. They are for the first time in history making possible the creation in intellectual terms

of a single, unified human society. In fact, so great are their promises and so great their dangers that they must not be allowed to develop without public criticism and control. They can be made to serve as instruments either for the elevation or for the degradation of the intelligence and generosity upon which in the last resort all human attempts at cooperation must rest. It would be a primary task of the Institute to explore and to develop the teaching possibilities of these agencies.

IV

As I close this plea for an Institute of Education in the field of world government, two final words must be spoken. The need which I have presented is immediate and urgent. If adult education is to be ready to play its part in post-war reconstruction, decisive action must be taken at once. It will not do to wait until the experts in economics and politics have finished their work. The plans for teaching must modify and be modified by all other types of planning. The Institute of Education must take form and assume responsibilities step by step with all the other agencies which will appear as the general project moves forward. To that end, official and unofficial conferences should be now under way. Too much time has already been lost.

As we plan for the education or re-education of the nations of the earth, let us not think it is only our enemies who will have new lessons to learn. That theme has been much played in these days of bitter strife. But in sober fact it must be said that if, as we hope, we are to be the victors in the world conflict, it will be we, rather than our foes, who stand in greater need of teaching. Defeat brings its own lessons. But victory in battle has never been a good teacher. And we Anglo-Americans have been terrifyingly successful in the struggles of the modern world. Seventy-five years ago, Matthew Arnold told in bitter, hopeless words the impenetrability of the successful British mind to the forces of education. "One has often wondered," he says, "whether upon the whole earth there is anything so unintelligent, so unapt to perceive how the world is really going, as an ordinary young Englishman of our upper class."

I quote these words not because of their peculiar reference to the ruling class of England. They apply to all individuals and to all nations who have won predominance over their fellows. The greatest danger to the United States is that as its power and success grow greater, there will come upon it the same blindness to its own need of education. The lessons of freedom and equality are not easy for nations accustomed to superiority and domination. It is the victors who must be educated. It is upon them that an International Institute of Education must lavish its efforts. It is idle to plan for a free world and, at the same time, to plan that we shall be masters of it. A free world is a world of equals. All men, all nations must be educated.

Liberty and Freedom

Some of those who knew Meiklejohn as an educator found it perplexing that he concentrated his last twenty years on defending free speech, while those who knew him from 1946 to 1964 were often surprised to learn of his career as an educator. The connection between the two careers was clear to him:

> The basic problem, then, of a democratic scheme of teaching is, "What kinds of thinking, what subject matters of knowledge must a person study in order to become equipped for membership in a free society?" These common studies are the content of a liberal curriculum. In a self-governing society, the liberal arts are the required arts. What then are they?. . .We cannot know how to prepare our people, young and old, for participation in the common venture toward happiness and peace and justice and freedom unless the outlines of that venture are clearly and validly conceived. Our teachers must understand our national enterprise, must see how far it has succeeded, at what points it has gone astray, along what lines our common studies must proceed if we are to advance it toward its goal. Education is today, as it has always been, a branch of politics. It no longer expresses the politics of the universe, as it did in the days when schools and colleges were conducted by the church. But it does express the politics of human society, wherever men have grouped themselves together for the furthering of common plans and the realizing of common purposes. (Written by Meiklejohn in 1957 for *Education for a Free Society,* pp. 2, 11, 12 of the manuscript at the State Historical Society, Box 38, Folder 1.)

Meiklejohn's interest in defending freedom went back at least to the days before World War I. He had been on hand for the founding of the American Association of University Professors in 1915. That year, at the annual meeting of the American Philosophical Society, a caucus of its members (among them John Dewey, Arthur Lovejoy, Harry Overstreet, J. E. Creighton, Morris Cohen, and Ralph Perry) organized the AAUP. When these friends of Meiklejohn appeared on

195

the second day of the regular meeting, they told him that he was not eligible to join the new organization, since he was not a professor but a president. Meiklejohn did not submit tamely. He argued that they were planning to enter into a conflict with trustees in defense of freedom and that it would hurt their cause to eliminate presidents from their side. They did not relent, so Meiklejohn defended academic freedom from outside their organization.

U.S. universities developed a tradition of academic freedom different from that of their German models. In the German tradition teachers were expected to take sides and to try to persuade their students within their classrooms, but in the political life of their community they were expected to be neutral. In the United States, on the other hand, teachers were expected to remain neutral in the classroom and to take sides, if at all, outside in the political arena of their community. This reverse position reflected some U.S. realities—the preeminence in the universities of science and empiricism, which held that value judgments should not enter into competent thinking, and the greater political freedom outside the classroom than was available in German traditions.

Meiklejohn agreed with neither of these traditions. He argued that neutrality was not required of teachers in either realm, classroom or community. What is required of teachers, he believed, is that they avoid propaganda. A teacher is responsible for raising issues, for showing more than one way of approaching the question, for demonstrating how sound arguments are constructed, and for encouraging divergent points of view. But teachers can do this and still take their own stand. Indeed, teachers are irresponsible if they remain safely neutral. By refusing to take a position, they teach their students to remain neutral and thereby encourage them to avoid all the most important and difficult decisions inherent in human living. What position teachers take does not matter, in their role as teacher, as long as a school or college carefully insures that its staff includes forceful advocates for the full range of opinions on the basic issues (selection 13).

When the suppression of noncapitalist ideas began in earnest in the United States, Meiklejohn consistently defended the rights of members of the Communist Party to be heard both inside and outside the classroom. After World War II two positions emerged regarding Communist teachers. The first held that evidence of membership in the Communist Party was sufficient to prove unfitness for teaching. The second position held that Party membership alone was insufficient to justify dismissal, that unfitness had to be demonstrated by a careful examination of how individuals dealt with argumentation and whether they excluded other points of view from their classrooms.

These two positions received their classic statement in a debate in the *New York Times* between Sidney Hook and Alexander Meiklejohn following the dismissals of professors at the University of Washington in 1949. Hook held that membership in the Communist Party was *prima facie* evidence of academic incompetence. Since the Party directed its members to use their positions to promote the current Party line, he believed, members could not think for themselves. Hook concluded that a teacher whose thought was controlled could not be academically free, and therefore the dismissed professors were themselves "guilty of violating the principles of academic freedom." Meiklejohn, on the other hand, insisted that dismissals solely on the basis of Party membership were a gross violation of academic freedom. He denied Hook's assertion that the Party could control the thoughts of its members, and he pointed out that three of the six accused at Washington had already resigned from the Party. "How could they have done that," he asked, "if, as charged, they were incapable of free and independent thinking?" (selection 14).

The following year the Regents of the University of California tried to purge their faculties of any Communists by requiring a loyalty oath. In April 1950, the Regents changed the usual oath required of teachers at the University of California at the beginning of their service, attesting to their loyalty to the constitutions of the United States and of California. They added a contractual clause that had to be renewed every year and that covered not merely loyalty but also advocacy: "I do not believe in and am not a member of nor do I support any party or organization that believes in, advocates or teaches the overthrow of the U.S. government by force or violence." A group of professors refused to sign, were fired, and brought a case that resulted in the State Supreme Court ruling in their favor two years later. By then the Regents had rescinded their oath; the state legislature, however, had instituted one for all state employees.

Meiklejohn advised the professors who resisted the loyalty oath, and he wrote the statements of the Northern California branch of the ACLU opposing the loyalty oath. The issue of loyalty, Meiklejohn held, was being totally misunderstood by the Regents. Under the U.S. Constitution, loyalty requires all persons to obey the laws but not to believe in them or to say they believe in them. While obeying them, anyone may advocate their change, even by force. According to Meiklejohn, the Constitution recognizes only two forms of disloyalty: 1) the attempt to dictate what other people shall believe or say, and 2) submission to that dictation. This position Meiklejohn stated succinctly the following year in a letter to the chief of the San Francisco office of the Federal Bureau of Investigation (selection 15).

But it was Sidney Hook's position that found broad support during the Cold War. Both the National Education Association and the American Federation of Teachers barred Communists from membership and took stands against their teaching. In 1953 the Association of American Universities, consisting of the presidents of thirty-seven leading U.S. universities, agreed with Hook that membership in the Communist Party extinguishes the right to a university job. Meiklejohn's position was that of the Academic Freedom Committee of the American Civil Liberties Union and of the American Association of University Professors, which in 1952 asked Meiklejohn to address their annual meeting on the topic "The Teaching of Intellectual Freedom."

The major organization defending freedom of speech from World War I to World War II was the American Civil Liberties Union, founded in New York in 1920 by Roger Baldwin, Elizabeth Gurley Flynn, Albert de Silver, Walter Nelles, and others anxious to redress violations of the rights of pacifists, labor unionists, and aliens. Meiklejohn was elected a member of the sixty-five-person National Committee of the ACLU in 1927-28, a position to which he was re-elected through 1962-63.

Six years after becoming a member of the ACLU's National Committee, Meiklejohn helped to found a local chapter in San Francisco. He and Charles Hogan, a teacher in the San Francisco School for Social Studies, saw the vigilantism and other abuses of civil liberties used against the strikers in the San Francisco general strike of 1934. Meiklejohn and Helen Salz canvassed their wealthy, influential friends. The national office of the ACLU made a grant of $500 and sent Ernest Besig from their branch in Los Angeles. The San Francisco branch opened in the summer of 1935 with Charles Hogan as chairman, Meiklejohn as vice-chairman, and Ernest Besig as executive director. Meiklejohn remained vice-chairman of the Northern California chapter for thirty years, until his death in 1964. Between studying judicial opinions on the Constitution with citizens enrolled in the School for Social Studies and taking an active role in choosing which legal suits the local ACLU should bring to court, Meiklejohn tested his legal mettle and found it up to the task.

A major schism in ACLU leadership occurred in the early 1940s. The signing of the Hitler-Stalin Pact in 1939 engendered contention on the national board about whether members of the Communist Party should serve the ACLU. No open member of the Communist Party had ever been elected to national office in the ACLU, but one person, Elizabeth Gurley Flynn, had become a member of the CP fifteen years after she had helped found the ACLU in 1920, as a labor leader and former Wobbly (Industrial Workers of the World). She had been re-elected to the national Board of Directors after she had joined the CP. The chairman of the ACLU's board, Dr. Harry Ward, professor at Union Theological Seminary, was also chairman of the American League for Peace and Democracy, a united front group that included Communists. Many of the people on the board of the ACLU had been stirred by Marxist ideas and had believed or at least hoped that the Soviet Union would generate a more nearly just society.

Some of these people had been increasingly disillusioned by Stalin's policies in the 1930s, and the USSR's signing of the Hitler-Stalin Pact was the final blow to their hopes. They rejected the Communist position that the pact was a defensive measure by the Soviet Union, to which it turned to gain time after the defeat of its efforts for collective security with England, France, and the United States against Hitler. It seemed to them that no member of the CP could serve the ACLU in good faith, for supporting the denial of civil liberties in the USSR and now in Germany seemed too flat a contradiction to supporting their extension in the United States.

Meanwhile, in October 1939, the two general counsel of the ACLU made a verbal agreement with Rep. Martin Dies, chairman of the recently established House Committee on Un-American Activities, that he would stop claiming that the ACLU was a Communist organization in exchange for the ACLU's cleansing itself of its Communist members.

Roger Baldwin, executive director of the ACLU, composed what came to be known as the purge resolution. In part the resolution said: "The Board of Directors and the National Committee of the American Civil Liberties Union. . . hold it inappropriate for any person to serve on the governing committees of the Union or its staff, who is a member of any political organization which supports totalitarian dictatorship in any country, or who by his public declarations indicates his support of such a principle. . . ." On February 5, 1940, the National Committee passed it, though only eight of the forty-three members were present. A few days after the adoption of this resolution Dr. Ward resigned, and on May 7, 1940, the executive committee expelled Elizabeth Gurley Flynn because she belonged to the CP.

Meiklejohn vehemently opposed the purge resolution from the beginning. With two colleagues from San Francisco on the National Committee, Bishop Edward Parsons and George West, he tried to convince other members of the committee that it was totally inconsistent for a group defending civil liberties not to permit freedom of belief on its own board. Characteristically, Meiklejohn remained friends with Baldwin and others who succeeded in passing the purge resolution, but he did not waver in his opposition. In 1948-49 the national office requested that the Northern California branch adopt the same resolution, and it refused, saying that the best test for association with the Union is a person's willingness to defend the civil liberties of all persons without distinction. Much later, national boards viewed the purge of Elizabeth Gurley Flynn as a blot on the ACLU's history, and in 1976 the national board repealed her expulsion posthumously.

From 1940 on, the Northern California chapter of the ACLU continued to resist policies of the national ACLU in three major areas: the rights of people of Japanese descent in the United States, the relation of power between the national office and its affiliates, and the rights of Communist Party members.

In 1942 the Northern California chapter hired its own lawyer to challenge the detention of Japanese and Japanese-Americans because the national office refused to tackle this issue, and Meiklejohn went to Washington to try to move the government on their behalf. He was not successful, and the suits were lost.

The ACLU had begun as a tight, centralized organization. As the number of affiliates increased, the national corporation was forced to yield them some power. In 1948 the Northern California branch joined two other branches in calling for a national meeting of affiliates; they complained that the national board did not even consult branches before issuing policy. At the meeting the branches asked for equal voting power, which the national board rejected, instead giving each of the seventeen affiliates, regardless of size, two votes on the corporation of 110 members (the National Committee of seventy-five and the Board of Directors of thirty-five).

This struggle persisted. Meiklejohn represented the Northern California chapter at the second national conference of ACLU affiliates in New York in May 1951. The national office tried to integrate local membership and finances with their own, but they abandoned this attempt. The Northern California branch continued to turn down national policy having to do with Communists. It rejected three positions taken by the national ACLU, namely, that federal loyalty oaths could be accepted with procedural safeguards, that Communists could be barred from holding office in unions, and that aliens who are Communists could be denied citizenship.

Throughout these organizational issues Meiklejohn searched for the unifying principles that lay within all the specific legal questions about free speech. In 1947, in the Walgreen lectures at the University of Chicago, he delineated the basic principles underlying free speech. During the late 1940s and the 1950s he applied these principles to specific instances, writing legal briefs and articles. Among these were his assistance on an Amici Curiae brief against the contempt of Congress convictions of the Hollywood Ten in 1949; "The First Amendment and Evils that Congress has a Right to Prevent," *Indiana Law Journal* (1951); "What Does the First Amendment Mean?" *University of Chicago Law Review* (Spring 1953); and "The First Amendment Is An Absolute," *The Supreme Court Review 1961.* His ideas came to be known as the Meiklejohnian or "absolute" theory of the First Amendment. A quick survey of the history of interpreting the First Amendment will show the significance of Meiklejohn's position.

The First Amendment, along with the other nine amendments that constitute the Bill of Rights, was adopted in 1791. These simple words carry the principle of a self-governing society:

> Congress shall make no law respecting an establishment of religion, or prohibiting the free exercise thereof; or abridging

the freedom of speech, or of the press; or the right of the people peaceably to assemble, and to petition the Government for a redress of grievances.

These words were directed at the U.S. Congress. Its first action challenging them was the Sedition Act of 1798, which expired in 1801 before it was tested against the First Amendment in the Supreme Court, but which later commentators have regarded as definitely unconstitutional. During the nineteenth century state legislatures frequently curtailed the speech of abolitionists, but they could not appeal to the First Amendment since it applied only to the national legislature. Its meaning and scope was first raised effectively in court tests of sedition and draft legislation during and after World War I.

Justice Oliver Wendell Holmes set forth a judicial interpretation of the First Amendment in 1919 when the case of *Schenck v. United States* reached the Supreme Court. The case tested how closely words had to be related to illegal acts to be themselves illegal. Holmes spoke for a unanimous court in upholding the conviction of the defendants, who had mailed circulars to men eligible for the draft. The circulars had declared conscription to be unconstitutional and had urged men to assert their rights. Holmes declared: "The question in every case is whether the words used are used in such circumstances and are of such nature as to create a clear and present danger that they will bring about the substantive evils that Congress has a right to prevent." The Civil War veteran added, "When a nation is at war many things that might be said in time of peace are such a hindrance to its effort that their utterance will not be endured so long as men fight and that no Court could regard them as protected by any constitutional right." This interpretation became known as the "clear and present danger" theory.

The doctrine of clear and present danger is sufficiently vague that it could be invoked in opposing directions. On the one hand, it could be used, as it was by Holmes in 1919, to limit free speech by arguing that there are some ideas whose expression is too dangerous to the nation's security under some circumstances, especially during a war. On the other hand, it could be used, as it was in later cases, to defend free speech by insisting that anyone seeking abridgment must assume the burden of demonstrating an emergency grave enough to justify limiting speech. During the Vinson Court Era (Fred M. Vinson served as Chief Justice from 1946 until 1953), Justice Felix Frankfurter tended to use Holmes' doctrine to justify limits on free speech, while Justice Hugo L. Black led the defense of free speech. Justice Black's arguments came at times close to those of Meiklejohn.

At the University of Chicago in 1947 Meiklejohn told his audience that:

> The primary purpose of this lecture is to challenge the interpretation of the freedom-of-speech principle which, since 1919, has been adopted by the Supreme Court of the United States. In that year, and in the years which have ensued, the court, following the lead of Justice Oliver Wendell Holmes, has persistently ruled that the freedom of speech of the American community may constitutionally be abridged by legislative action. That ruling annuls the most significant purpose of the First Amendment. It destroys the intellectual basis of our plan of self-government. The court has interpreted the dictum that Congress shall not abridge the freedom of speech by defining the conditions under which such abridging is allowable. Congress, we are now told, is forbidden to destroy our freedom except when it finds it advisable to do so. (*Political Freedom: The Constitutional Powers of the People,* pp. 29-30.)

Meiklejohn broke through all the fine distinctions and challenged both wings of the "clear and present danger" doctrine. He argued that the First Amendment sets an absolute prohibition against the abridgments of freedom of speech, religion, press, assembly and petition. For the purpose of self-government all ideas bearing on an issue must be expressed, and the need for this expression is, if anything, greater in times of danger. The only debatable question is whether the time or place of expression is appropriate, not whether the idea itself is allowable. That, according to Meiklejohn, is the rock on which this government is founded (selection 16).

Part of the deep confusion in the United States about freedom of speech, Meiklejohn believed, was the tendency to give priority to individual, personal rights. In economic affairs many U.S. citizens assumed that the right to accumulate unlimited wealth was part of their basic freedom, somehow protected by the Constitution. Even in political affairs, many U.S. interpreters viewed the right to speak as an individual prerogative, deriving from the natural rights of man.

Meiklejohn disagreed. He was certain that the Constitution does not prescribe laissez-faire capitalism and that the right to own and operate property can be constitutionally limited by due process for the common good, as stated in the due process clause of the Fifth Amendment.

In the political realm Meiklejohn believed that "free speech" did not refer to the private right of individuals to talk. Free speech in a nation attempting self-government means that every possible idea bearing on a problem has a right to be heard, not that every individual has a right to say it. Meiklejohn had pointed out in 1947 the difference between freedoms that may constitutionally be limited (liberty) and those that may not (freedom). In 1957 he tried again to make this clear to a group who easily confused liberty and freedom— the American Civil Liberties Union. In 1960, when his lectures of 1947 were republished, he clarified his new emphasis by changing their title from *Free Speech and Its Relation to Self-Government* to *Political Freedom: The Constitutional Powers of the People.*

In the 1950s, people subpoenaed to testify before the House Committee on Un-American Activities often faced an agonizing decision. They could choose: 1) to discuss their own beliefs and those of others, or 2) to discuss their own beliefs and refuse to discuss those of others, or 3) to refuse to discuss their own and others' beliefs. They could base their position on one of two grounds: either on the Fifth Amendment, which states that no person has "to be a witness against himself in any criminal case," or on the First Amendment, which guarantees that "Congress shall make no law. . .abridging the freedom of speech." Or they could appeal, as many did, to both the First and the Fifth.

The courts usually acquitted people who exercised their constitutional rights under the Fifth Amendment, often on due process grounds, although they would be labeled "Fifth Amendment Communists" in an effort to ruin their reputations. The courts refused the claim of those who appealed to the First Amendment alone, saying that the ideas of the Communist Party threaten the preservation of the U.S. government and therefore the private interest of free speech must give way to the public interest of self-preservation.

Meiklejohn urged people in this dilemma to stand on the principle of the First Amendment, and several who might have gotten off if they had refused his advice and had relied on the Fifth instead of the

First, went to jail. The plight of these people weighed heavily on Meiklejohn's conscience, and in his article "The Barenblatt Opinion," *University of Chicago Law Review* (Winter 1960), he challenged the Supreme Court on their behalf. The following year he restated his arguments for an absolute interpretation of the First Amendment (selection 17).

13

Teachers and Controversial Questions

In the early 1930s Meiklejohn made speeches under the title "Should Teachers Discuss Controversial Issues?" His clearest statement of this question follows. It was published as "Teachers and Controversial Questions," Harper's Magazine *177 (June 1938): 15-22. The national head-quarters of the American Civil Liberties Union distributed free reprints of this article as a statement of their position on this issue.*

I had just been listening to the President [Franklin D. Roosevelt] of the United States. He was speaking at the celebration of the birthday of Virginia Dare, the first child of European stock born in this coun-try. He said to his far-flung audience of Americans that America has been, and still is, a place of controversy. Throughout the record of our three hundred and fifty years he found a conflict between the Many and the Few, between the mass of the common people, who wish to control and direct themselves, and the powerful group or groups who seek to take that control and direction from them. That conflict, the President seemed to say, that controversy, is the most striking feature in the political history of our people.

As I listened to the President's words they seemed to me especially important for the teachers of America. What have teachers to do with the controversy of which he spoke? Should they discuss it in their classrooms? Should they be partisans with repsect to it, line up before their pupils and the general public? Should they fight with their minds and wills on the side of the Many or of the Few, as may seem to them best? Or, on the other hand, should they keep clear of such controversies, as irrelevant to the business of teaching? If one is commissioned to prepare young Americans for living in America what has he to do with the crucial, the controversial isssues of his time and country?

I need hardly point out that this question about the teacher and his work is itself a controversial one. Around it passions gather and conflicts rage with a peculiar intensity. Just as we resent cruelty to a child more than cruelty to an older person, so do we resent the "misleading" of children more than the misleading of their elders. For a hundred different reasons, emotional and intellectual, we demand that our schools shall not malform our pliant youth, shall not destroy its capacities, or start them growing in wrong directions. And so it has come to pass that the American teacher is today a focus of controversial fury. The conflict which finds open expression in discussions about "loyalty" is raging in subtler form in every American community which is sufficiently aware of its schools to pass judgment upon what they are doing. Teachers and administrators are under constant pressure. As compared with the few striking, sensational "cases" which are noted by the press, the unnoted bulk of that pressure is enormous and overwhelming. It is that pressure which chiefly suggests our problem. I am not asking, however, whether or not a community should influence and determine the character of its schools. That it should do so seems to me both inevitable and desirable. But the real question is: "In what direction should the community influence its teachers? Should it expect them, encourage them, direct them to make their instruction relevant to the controversial questions of the time? Or should it forbid them to deal with those issues at all?" I am asking—let it be noted—not about the rights and privileges of the teacher, but about the welfare of the people.

When we say that an issue is controversial we commonly mean not only that people differ about it, but also that they "feel" about it. A genuine controversy splits a community into factions, into hostile groups which regard each other with such fruits of misunderstanding as hatred, distrust, and contempt. Such an issue cleaves like a sword through the life of a community and cuts it asunder. As an illustration of such a conflict, I should like to present an issue which arouses even more passion and misunderstanding than that formulated by Mr. Roosevelt. Perhaps I should rather say that it is the President's question stated in its most extreme, its most fury-raising form. I refer to the conflict between the Capitalists and the Communists. Should the American teacher, in the normal course of his teaching, discuss Communism as a possible alternative in America for our way of dealing with men and with their possessions?

I am assuming, as I state this question, that the conflict between Capitalism and Communism is now raging in America. It is not yet clearly stated as a question. No one can tell, I think, just what form it will take when it does come to focus. And yet, in the realm of feeling, if not in that of opinion, America is falling apart into two hostile groups. Two cultures, two plans of civilized living, are at war for the domination of our minds and actions. The issue concerns religion and art, poetry and morals, manners and philosophy, as well as economics and politics. On the one hand, there is the traditional tendency to trust our welfare to the play of private initiative. This is the way of the "individual," the way of competition, the way which demands freedom for private enterprise. No one supposes that we have had in America the unlimited acceptance of such individualism. But men have said, and do say, that the interference of the group with the individual should be kept as limited as possible. Competition, men say, is the "natural" form of human living: regulation of it is artificial, justified only by strong necessity; and, in the nature of the case, such regulation must be largely unsuccessful. And, over against this, the attitude which I am labeling "Communism" puts its faith in group action. It believes in the efficacy and necessity of the control of men by their government. It regards a polity which is based upon the private seeking of advantage as inherently selfish and immoral and as doomed to failure because of that immorality. These two tendencies are, I say, at war in America. In much more complicated form they are at war in Europe. In that place of bitter and desperate struggle there is not a single problem of international relations which does not take its form, its color, from that underlying controversy. To understand the Western world to which we belong is, in larger measure, to weigh the merits of these two proposed ways of dealing with human society. The still relatively unclear issue between Capitalism and Communism is the most far-reaching, the most deeply significant external factor in the interpretation of modern society.

May I explain, in passing, the use of the name "Communism"? There are many terms which might be used to indicate the second of these two conflicting programs. Social Planning, Collectivism, New Dealism, Socialism, Social Control—all these, as well as Communism, express opposition to the customs and presuppositions of private enterprise. Which of them then shall we select to indicate, not its own separate party meaning, but the field as a whole? I have chosen "Communism" because it is, for many Americans, the most hated, the most objectionable term on the list. For our purpose of finding out how we propose to deal with controversies it has a peculiar advantage. It sharpens the issue. Its ordinary associations are those of antagonism. It smacks, as now used, of the alien and the foreign. It suggests danger to religion and morals and good taste. In a word, it offends the popular mind of America. And it is this quality of mutual misunderstanding which is needed for the square and honest facing of our question. What do we, as Americans, propose to do about opinions which many of us deeply and passionately condemn? I know no better way of determining the essential meaning of our institutions than by inquiring how we intend to deal with "Communism" as I am using the term. What is the American plan for conducting controversies which bear upon our most cherished interests and beliefs?

II

If then we face the problem, "Should teachers be permitted, be encouraged, be directed to discuss the relative merits of Capitalism and Communism as plans for America?" my own response is quite unequivocal. It can be stated in three assertions. I should like, first, to express these as simply as possible and, then, to explain the views of teaching and of America by which they seem to me justified:

First, all our teaching, no matter what its field of interest, must be related to a controversy so fundamental as that of which we are speaking. Teaching which is irrelevant to such issues is irrelevant to the purposes of education. In America today teachers, in order to do their proper work, must bring before their pupils the conflict between Capitalism and Communism.

*Meiklejohn with Norman Thomas, whom he supported five of the
six times that Thomas ran for president on the Socialist ticket.*

Second, teachers must, so far as they honestly can, take sides on
the issue. The teacher must appear before his pupils as one who is
struggling with the essential problems of his time, and who is, in his
own way, forming conclusions about them. He must be going "left"
or "right." To be a teacher, a leader, he must be going somewhere.
He must be a believer in some plan of human living.

Third, school boards and trustees of colleges and universities have
a heavy responsibility. They must see to it that among our teachers
there is an adequate supply of "Communists," of able, fearless,
outspoken advocates of the unpopular view. It must be arranged by
the authorities that both sides of fundamental issues shall be
represented by teachers who believe in them. Under the actual conditions of democratic life the practical question facing a governing board
is not, "Shall we have any 'Communists' on our faculties?" but
rather, "How can we get enough 'Communists' to give proper expression of views which run counter to the general trend of habit, emotion, interest, of the community at large?" We must provide for the

criticism of our institutions as well as for their advocacy.

To get an understanding and, it may be, a justification of these three contentions, two matters must be considered—first, teaching, and, second, America. What is the task, the purpose, of the teacher? And, further, what are the peculiar conditions in American life which require that teaching here be different from that of many other countries? And, finally—putting these two together—what is it that we want done in our schools for the education of our children?

Among those who oppose the teaching of Communism in the schools one often finds a curious misunderstanding of what teaching is. We seem to regard it as a form of "salesmanship," in the popular sense of that term. The teacher is expected to "put something over" on the pupil, to get him to accept a definite set of opinions. Just as the church too often tries to "sell" religion, as an artist "sells" his painting, as all of us "sell" ourselves—that is, get people to accept from us something which it is to our advantage that they should take—so the teacher is expected to lure or cajole or force his pupil into the acceptance of habits and beliefs. By direction or indirection we equip the student with opinions which someone other than himself wishes him to have. From this standpoint, education is, to quote the words of Professor [Boyd Henry] Bode, "the art of taking advantage of defenseless childhood." And if this were sound doctrine, it would be easy to see why a predominantly Capitalistic community should object to the advocacy of Communism in its schools. Any good salesman wants an embargo on foreign goods.

But education is not salesmanship. No genuine teacher is trying to put something over. The human relationship between teacher and pupil differs, as does Heaven from Hell, from that in which one person is trying to use another for his own advantage or is hired by a third person to do it for him. Our teachers must be advocates, but they may never be salesmen or propagandists. The very existence of democratic schools depends upon that distinction.

What, then, is teaching? It is, I think, the initiation of pupils into a fellowship. Teachers are members of a guild. Their lives are devoted to the practice of an art. It is the art of creating and using intelligence for the improving of human living. And the first duty of a teacher, prior to whatever he does in the classroom, is to cultivate his own mind. No one can be a genuine teacher unless he is himself actively sharing in the human attempt to understand men and their world.

Teaching is not, primarily, a matter of tricks and devices and methods. It is the communication of intelligence. One cannot educate young people by bringing them into contact with uneducated teachers.

But, second, the teacher leads his pupil into the practice of this craft of his. How is that done? There is nothing mystical about the process and yet it is curiously compounded of interchanges which are emotional, active, personal, as well as intellectual. How, for example, does a man like Tilden teach tennis? The pupil must of course go out on the court and try to play. But he must also see and experience how his master plays. And as they play together there is built into the pupil the "feel" of the game. He becomes aware of his wrist as never before, and of the swinging leverage of his arm and the moving of his feet and the balance of his body. He sees the court as a field of infinitely varied action, senses the flight of the ball, the impact of the racquet, the strategy of the struggle. All these are revealed by the teacher who plays the game with him, who knows how to play it. It is never assumed that the pupil is to play just as the teacher does. That would be true only if their bodies were identical and their wits of the same brand. No one whose arms are short, whose legs are chunky, should copy Tilden's style. But it is assumed that both the teacher and pupil are intent on discovering what is the "right" style of play for that pupil, what he should do with arms and legs and wits and what he may never do with them. About this "rightness" and this "wrongness" the whole process of teaching centers. On the basis of them, habits are developed, faults are corrected, judgments are established. Under a good teacher one learns to play by a process of free, directed imitation.

What I have said of tennis is true of any art or craft. Only by such contacts with a "master" can one be helped in learning to wield a brush, or play a fiddle, or argue a case, or manage a kitchen. In all these one learns to play well by playing with a good player, just as one learns to play badly by playing with a bad one. And in like manner, in the classroom the craftsmanship of the mind is created by the joint activity of the teacher and pupil. In any good school or college a student learns to do what his master is doing. He becomes a member of his teacher's fraternity. What does that membership mean? It is a poor statement of it to say that the pupil learns how to think. Rather he learns to do thinking, to take an active share in the making and using of the world's intelligence. He undertakes a piece of work which will keep him busy as long as he lives. And, further, he recognizes and accepts the distinction of value upon which any art or craft must be established—the difference between lazy, careless, inaccurate, shoddy work and the kind of activity in which a man trains himself to do the best there is in him. The fellowship of understanding has standards. It makes demands. And the neophyte must acquire, by association with his leader, responsiveness to those demands. He enters a fellowship in which heart and will as well as mind, muscles and glands as well as spirit, are habituated and inspired into the using of a human mind for the doing of a man's work. It is that craftsmanship which he must learn from his teacher.

III

So much of education in the abstract. What now are the peculiar conditions, and hence the peculiar purposes, to which in America teaching must be adjusted?

There are in modern society two plans of life and of government, and the difference between them bears directly on the work of the teacher. The difference has to do chiefly with methods of settling controversies. One way is that of suppression and violence. The other is the method of free discussion. No country is of course completely committed to either of these policies, and yet, predominantly, societies are of one type or the other. And from this it follows that there are in the modern world two different kinds of education. It is one thing to learn to submit, to obey, to conform, to cringe. It is a very different thing to learn to join with one's peers in the discussion of common problems, the decision upon common issues. In both cases, as policy is determined, it is inevitable that one party shall prevail over another, that the weaker shall give way before the stronger. But the essential difference between the two programs is seen most clearly just at this point. In the regimes of violence the beaten party is expected to change its opinion when the decision has been made. It must come into line. If necessary, it is forced to do so. But in societies of free discussion, on the other hand, we expect that the minority will, in the main, hold to its view, that it will continue to criticize and to challenge the prevailing procedure. In such a society all men, whatever their party, are expected to obey the law, but it is not demanded that men shall think, or shall say, that the law which they obey is wise, that it should not be changed. Men's actions are controlled but their minds are free.

Now it is the crowning glory of America that we have, from the start, pledged ourselves to the creation of a program of government by free discussion. "Congress shall make no law," says the First Amendment, "respecting an establishment of religion, or prohibiting the free exercise thereof; or abridging the freedom of speech or of the press; or the right of the people peaceably to assemble and to petition the government for a redress of grievances." And that statement defines for the American teacher the nature of the society which he serves. It is for life in a community of free discussion that he must educate his pupils.

But the first principle of action in a society so defined is that all its mature members must understand the decisions which are made, must share in the making of them. Government is carried on by the active consent of the governed. And from this there follows the peculiar character of our education. Our pupils must learn how to make up their minds. They must acquire the art of making decisions. That art, as used by a democratic society, is a very difficult and paradoxical one. Young Americans must be taught to think independently, but they must also learn to think together. They must be partisans, but, in a deeper sense, they must also be impartial. They must come to conclusions, while at the same time recognizing that other men, for whom they have respect and affection, are coming to opposite conclusions. So far as minds are concerned, the art of democracy is the art of thinking independently together. Our teachers then must be adept in the practice and the teaching of that art. The purpose of the American school is not merely to teach arithmetic and literature and science as unrelated subjects. It is rather, through these and other means, to teach the art of living intelligently as one takes an active share in the experiences and decisions of a democratic society.

IV

The three contentions which were made at the beginning of this paper seem to me now to have been justified. They all follow from the principle that it is the purpose of school and college to train and equip minds to deal with living issues. If that be true, then education must relate itself to such a conflict as that between Capitalism and Communism. Again, teachers who are training their pupils to deal with that issue must themselves deal with it openly and frankly. And, finally, pupils must be exposed to the full force of both sides of a controversy with which they are getting ready to deal. A school or a college, to serve the interests of a democracy, must be a place of active, fearless, unhindered intelligence, at work upon the interpretation and direction of the society which it serves. Teachers and pupils must study actual human living.

These conclusions, as they apply to the teacher, can be seen from two different sides. For the sake of clarity I should like to speak of them separately.

First, it is obvious that the teacher must be free to do what he is trying to get his students to do. No one can teach an art which he is forbidden to practice. Slaves cannot teach freedom. If the members of our faculties are forbidden to make up their own minds and to express their own thoughts they cannot lead their pupils into the making up of their minds and the expressing of their thoughts. They can only teach what they do. To require our teachers to say to their pupils, "I want you to learn from me how to do what I am forbidden to do," is to make of education the most utter nonsense.

But far deeper in significance than the privilege of the teacher to use his mind independently is his duty to do so. There is a popular, sentimental view of the teacher which stresses his open-mindedness. He is represented as dealing fairly with all the conflicting answers to any question. When a problem has been formulated he can tell his pupils with cool, impartial, scholarly detachment just what opinions different men and groups have offered for its solution. He can give them all the materials which need to be considered in the making of a decision about it. Now I am not saying that this is not an essential part of teaching. Surely it is. The pupil must know, and know sympathetically, what has been thought and said on his problem. He must learn the ways of scholarly inquiry, must take advantage of the work which other minds have done and are doing. And yet such scholarly inquiry is only preparatory to his main task. He must, in a society of free discussion, make up his own mind, form his own judgment, take his own stand. And the primary task of the teacher is to help him in developing the power to do that. How shall the teacher give that help? By refusing to make up his own mind? By coming to no conclusions of his own? To say that is to say that the drama of teaching must be played without a Hamlet. Real teaching is guidance in the technic of judgment-making. And that guidance can be given only as a teacher and pupil play the game together, only by contagion, only by companionship in an activity which both are carrying on. In a classroom in which young people are being prepared to use their minds for the doing of the world's work, the open-mindedness which refuses to commit itself to plans of action is indistinguishable in its effect from feeble-mindedness. It prepares the pupil for deciding—nothing.

There are so many ways of misunderstanding the argument which I have offered that it seems hopeless to try to guard against them one by one. Freedom is not a simple matter—as is violence. And teaching is far more complicated than is propaganda. That is why what we call "common sense" is never adequate for the purposes of a democracy. That is why we must have in America an education, such as we have not now, which will train minds to deal with dilemmas and paradoxes and seeming contradictions. People cannot have a democracy unless they are willing and able to puzzle about it.

There is one charge, however, which I must try to meet. I have said that the teacher should be an advocate, that some teachers, at least, should be, in the schools, advocates of Communism. And sad experience tells me that I shall, therefore, be accused of saying that the teacher should be a salesman, a propagandist, of Communism. Since nothing in the world is to me more hateful than salesmanship or propaganda, nothing more alien and hostile to the spirit of teaching in America, I wish to try to answer that charge.

Should teachers in the American schools be allowed to "sell" Communism to their pupils, to propagandize on the "Left"? Certainly not! Any teacher who does that is unfit for his post. But the same statement holds true if a teacher is "selling" Capitalism, if he is "putting over" the doctrines of the "Right." Such a teacher should in either case be dismissed. And the reason for his dismissal is not that he is "left" or "right" but that he is not teaching. He is not doing the work for which our schools are maintained. The primary intention of the schools of a democracy is the development of the power, the capacity, of the student to judge upon such matters as Capitalism and Communism. And the fundamental sin of the propagandist is that he weakens the mind of his victim rather than strengthens it. He merely wants to use the pupil for the furthering of a cause. The teacher-advocate of whom I have been speaking is trying to get the student to use his own mind for the making of his own decisions. The propagandist is trying, by cajolery or trick or pressure, to get the student to accept opinions which the pupil has no adequate basis for believing. The teacher-advocate wants thinking done as the only proper way of arriving at conclusions. The propagandist wants believing done, no matter what the road by which the belief is reached. In the one case there is respect for human nature, regard for the integrity of the reasoning process. In the other case there is contempt for human nature, the subordination of intelligence to all the forces of passion and self-interest which can be used to confuse and becloud its vision.

The difference between these two methods can be seen in the practical work of any good classroom. When a teacher advocates a theory he does so because it is a good, an effective, teaching method. The teacher's primary reason for offering his own view is that it serves as an example to the student, stimulates him to the forming of his own view. And the characteristic quality of this method can be seen, in two ways, whenever it is put into action. In the first place, it is an unfailing mark of good teaching-advocacy that a very large part of the student response to it takes the form of opposition to the conclusions of the teacher. His advocacy in a field where opinions are known to differ is a challenge to his pupils to refute him, to establish other conclusions of their own. Teacher and pupils alike recognize that the generous clash of opinion is the normal state of mind of a democratic society. The teacher is saying to his students, "This is the way it looks to me; this is the platform on which at present I propose to live and act. How does it look to you? What do you propose to decide and do about it?" And so together they formulate problems, compile evidence, weigh opinions, reach, so far as they can, their own tentative and changing conclusions.

A second mark of good teacher-advocacy, as against propaganda, is that in any well-conducted classroom it quickly becomes apparent that the conclusions reached by the teacher are not of very great importance. We ordinary teachers are not the leaders of the world's thought. There are not many Platos or Kants or Newtons or Darwins among us. And, further, we differ among ourselves. It is largely a matter of accident that in this particular classroom the pupil has hit upon a Capitalist or a Communist. In some other classroom he will find the opposing view presented with equal advocacy. Why, then, should the words of the teacher be accepted as if they were words of authority?

That is not their function nor does it express the teacher's intention. Anyone who really teaches prizes disagreement from his pupils at least as highly as he prizes agreement. But deeper than either of them is the fact that the teacher is leading, inspiring his students to engage in the activity of judgment-making, to fit themselves for membership in a free society. To that end, the teacher must advocate. He must show what he wishes to be done by doing it.

V

I have argued in this paper that the health and effectiveness of our national education depend upon our keeping it in active touch with the fundamental controversies of our society. No one who studies our situation can fail to see that, in many different forms, the issue between Individualism and Social Control is now rushing toward its crisis in America. Within the lifetime of the young people now in our schools and colleges that issue must, in all probability, be decided. Very soon America will make a choice. She will turn "left" or "right." I do not mean that such a turning will be final or complete. But I do think it will be decisive as fixing the course of our national life. And the burden of making that decision will fall upon the pupils whom we are now teaching. In the face of that future and that responsibility, to forbid our teachers to lead their students into the consideration of controversial questions is madness.

But the question has still wider implications. It goes straight to the heart of our national institutions and our national integrity. Here, as always, the policies which we adopt for our children reveal the motives which we are following for ourselves. We, too, are facing our crucial issues. More urgent even than the question, "Shall we turn 'left' or 'right'?" is the question, "In what way shall it be decided whether we go 'left' or 'right'?" Will that choice be made by methods of violence or by those of free discussion—in our own way or in ways alien to us, subversive of our national spirit? And the danger which chiefly threatens both us and our successors in America is that, without realizing it, we shall desert our principles of freedom. Can our institutions stand the strain of the work we have to do? There is real ground for fear that, under the stress of conflicts now beginning to rage, we shall substitute methods of suppression and evasion and violence for those to which, in spite of many failures, we still give allegiance. If that happens it will not be because of our deliberate choice. On the contrary, the very denial and destruction of our freedom will invoke the spirit of freedom as its sanction. We shall not choose to abandon American institutions. Rather we shall drift into slavery. And the first, fatal, slip into such a drift is to be seen in the enslaving of our education. If at that point our nerve fails; if in our schools and colleges we do not demand of our teachers that they be free; then, whether we know it or not, we have chosen the way of violence. If we forbid our teachers to form their own ideas and to express them; if we try in this way to keep our young people innocently unaware of the problems which lie before them, then we have determined our own future. In the days to come, our crucial questions will be decided. But, if our teachers are shackled, they will be decided in blood and carnage rather than in the ways indicated by the Constitution of the United States. The questions will then be answered by persons who are intellectually unprepared for dealing with them. They will be answered, therefore, in terms of passion and prejudice and misunderstanding, rather than in terms of free, democratic discussion.

Our teachers must discuss controversial questions. There is no other program by which the education of a free people can be carried on.

11

Professors on Probation

Should Communists Be Allowed to Teach?

In the following essay, written eleven years after the previous one, Meiklejohn again interpreted academic freedom. By this time the witch hunt for "subversives" had begun in earnest. Governments, both state and federal, had begun to suppress "dangerous" speech. The FBI had built up a system of espionage by which hundreds of thousands of people had been listed as holding this or that opinion. Legislative committees had been set up to investigate "un-American activities." The Department of Justice had listed sixty or more organizations, association with which might be taken to raise the question of "disloyalty" to the United States. In 1947 President Truman had issued his Loyalty Order. The assumption underlying these actions was that Congress may rightly abridge the freedom to hold beliefs it judges to be dangerous. In his essay Meiklejohn takes an uncompromising stand against this interpretation of the First Amendment as it applies to college teachers.

This essay was written in response to that of Sidney Hook, "Should Communists Be Allowed to Teach?" in the New York Times Magazine, *February 27, 1949, in which Professor Hook argued that membership in the Communist Party alone disqualifies a teacher. Meiklejohn's essay appeared in the* New York Times Magazine, *March 27, 1949. It was reprinted in: Alexander Meiklejohn,* Political Freedom: The Constitutional Powers of the People *(New York: Oxford University Press, 1965), pp. 133-141.*

The President and Regents of the University of Washington have dismissed three professors and have placed three others on probation. That statement fails to mention the most significant feature of what has been done. The entire faculty is now on probation. Every scholar, every teacher, is officially notified that if, in his search for the truth, he finds the policies of the American Communist Party to be wise, and acts on that belief, he will be dismissed from the university.

In one of the dismissal cases, the evidence is not clear enough to enable an outsider to measure the validity of the decision. But the other five cases force an issue on which everyone who cares for the integrity and freedom of American scholarship and teaching must take his stand. Cool and careful consideration of that issue should be given by all of us, whether or not we agree with the teachers in question, but especially if we do not agree with them.

The general question in dispute is that of the meaning of academic freedom. But that question has three distinct phases. The first of these has to do with the organization of the university. It asks about the rights and duties of the faculty in relation to the rights and duties of the administration. And the principle at issue corresponds closely to that which, in the government of the United States, is laid down by the First Amendment to the Constitution. Just as that Amendment declares that "Congress shall make no law abridging the freedom of speech," so, generally, our universities and colleges have adopted a principle which forbids the administration to abridge the intellectual freedom of scholars and teachers. And, at this point, the question is whether or not the President and Regents at Washington have violated an agreement made in good faith and of vital importance to the work of the university.

The principle of academic freedom was clearly stated by Sidney Hook in the *New York Times Magazine* of February 27, 1949. After noting that "administration and trustees" are "harried by pressure-groups," Mr. Hook concluded his argument by saying, "In the last analysis, there is no safer repository of the integrity of teaching and scholarship than the dedicated men and women who constitute the faculties of our colleges and universities." On the basis of that conviction, the Association of University Professors has advocated, and most of our universities, including Washington, have adopted, a "tenure system." That system recognizes that legal authority to appoint, promote, and dismiss teachers belongs to the President and Regents. But so far as dismissals are concerned, the purpose of the tenure agreement is to set definite limits to the exercise of that authority.

This limitation of their power, governing boards throughout the nation have gladly recognized and accepted. To the Association of University Professors it has seemed so important that violations of it have been held to justify a "blacklisting" of a transgressor institution—a recommendation by the association that scholars and teachers refuse to serve in a university or college which has thus broken down the defenses of free inquiry and belief.

It is essential at this point to note the fact that the fear expressed by the tenure system is a fear of action by the President and Regents. Since these officers control the status and the salaries of teachers, it is only through them that effective external pressure can be used to limit faculty freedom. To say then, as we must, that the explicit purpose of the tenure system is to protect freedom against the President and Regents, is not to say that these officials are more evil than others.

Theirs is the power by which, unless it is checked by a tenure system, evil may be done.

Under the excellent code adopted at the University of Washington, it is agreed that after a trial period in which the university makes sure that a teacher is competent and worthy of confidence, he is given "permanence" of tenure. This means that he is secure from dismissal unless one or more of five carefully specified charges are proved against him. And the crucial feature of this defense of freedom is that the holding of any set of opinions, however unpopular or unconventional, is scrupulously excluded from the list of proper grounds for dismissal. The teacher who has tenure may, therefore, go fearlessly wherever his search for the truth may lead him. And no officer of the university has authority, openly or by indirection, to abridge that freedom.

When, under the Washington code, charges are made against a teacher, it is provided that prosecution and defense shall be heard by a tenure committee of the faculty, which shall judge whether or not the accusations have been established. In the five cases here under discussion, the only charge made was that of present or past membership in the American Communist Party. Specific evidence of acts revealing unfitness or misconduct in university or other activities was deliberately excluded from the prosecution case. And further, since the alleged fact of party membership was frankly admitted by the defense, the only question at issue was the abstract inquiry whether or not such membership is forbidden under the five provisions of the tenure code.

Upon that issue, the faculty committee decided unanimously that in the cases of the ex-members of the Communist party, there were, under the code, no grounds for dismissal. And by a vote of eight to three, the same conclusion was reached concerning the two men who were still members of the party. In the discussions of the committee, the suggestion was made that the code should be so amended that party membership would give ground for dismissal. But that action was not recommended. In its capacity as the interpreter of the code which now protects academic freedom, the committee, in all five cases, declared the charges to be not supported by the evidence presented.

In response to this judgment upon teachers by their intellectual peers, the Regents, on recommendation of the President, dismissed the two party members. And second, going beyond the recommendation of the President, they placed the three ex-members "on probation" for two years. These actions are clearly a violation of the agreement under which faculty members have accepted or continued service in the university. They deserve the condemnation of everyone who respects the integrity of a covenant, of everyone who values faculty freedom and faculty responsibility for the maintaining of freedom.

The second phase of the general question goes deeper than the forms of university organization. It challenges the wisdom of the tenure code as it now stands. It may be that, though the Regents are wrong in procedure, they are right in principle. Here, then, we must ask whether President Allen is justified in saying that a teacher who is "sincere in his belief in communism" cannot "at the same time be a sincere seeker after truth which is the first obligation of the teacher." In a press interview, Mr. Allen is quoted as saying, "I insist that the Communist party exercises thought control over every one of its members. That's what I object to." Such teachers, he tells us, are "incompetent, intellectually dishonest, and derelict in their duty to find and teach the truth." Can those assertions be verified? If so, then the tenure code should be amended. If not, then the action of the university should be immediately and decisively reversed.

No one can deny that a member of the American Communist Party accepts a "discipline." He follows a party "line." As the policies of the party shift, he shifts with them. That statement is in some measure true of all parties, whose members agree to work together by common tactics toward a common end. But the Communist discipline, it must be added, is unusually rigid and severe. Our question is, then, whether submission to that discipline unfits for university work men who, on grounds of scholarship and character, have been judged by their colleagues to be fitted for it.

For the judging of that issue we must examine the forces by means of which the discipline of the American Communist Party is exercised. It is idle to speak of "thought control" except as we measure the compulsions by which that control is made effective. What then are the inducements, the dominations, which by their impact upon the minds of these university teachers, rob them of the scholar's proper objectivity?

So far as inducements are concerned, good measuring of them requires that we place side by side the advantages offered to a scholar by the Communist Party and those offered by the President and Regents of a university. On the one hand, as seen in the present case, the administration can break a man's career at one stroke. It has power over every external thing he cares for. It can destroy his means of livelihood, can thwart his deepest inclinations and intentions. For example, in very many of our universities it is today taken for granted that a young scholar who is known to be a Communist has not the slightest chance of a faculty appointment. He is barred from academic work. And, as against this, what has the American Communist Party to offer? Its "inducements" are the torments of suspicion, disrepute, insecurity, personal and family disaster.

Why then do men and women of scholarly training and taste choose party membership? Undoubtedly, some of them are, hysterically, attracted by disrepute and disaster. But, in general, the only explanation which fits the facts is that these scholars are moved by a passionate determination to follow the truth where it seems to lead, no matter what may be the cost to themselves and their families. If anyone wishes to unearth the "inducements" which threaten the integrity of American scholarship he can find far more fruitful lines of inquiry than that taken by the administration of the University of Washington.

But Communist controls, we are told, go far deeper than "inducements." The members of the party, it is said, "take orders from Moscow"; they are subject to "thought control by a foreign power." Now here again, the fact of rigid party discipline makes these assertions, in some ambiguous sense, true. But, in the sense in which President Allen and his Regents interpret them, they are radically false.

Let us assume as valid the statement that, in the American Communist Party "orders" do come from Moscow. But by what power are those orders enforced in the United States? In the Soviet Union, Mr. Stalin and his colleagues can, and do, enforce orders by police and military might. But by what form of "might" do they control an American teacher in an American university? What can they do to him? At its extreme limit, their only enforcing action is that of dismissal from the party. They can say to him, "You cannot be a member of this party unless you believe our doctrines, unless you conform to our policies." But, under that form of control, a man's acceptance of doctrines and policies is not "required." It is voluntary.

To say that beliefs are required as "conditions of membership" in a party is not to say that the beliefs are required by force, unless it is shown that membership in the party is enforced. If membership is free, then the beliefs are free.

Misled by the hatreds and fears of the cold war, President Allen and his Regents are unconsciously tricked by the ambiguities of the words "control" and "require" and "free" and "objective." The scholars whom they condemn are, so far as the evidence shows, free American citizens. For purposes of social action, they have chosen party affiliation with other men, here and abroad, whose beliefs are akin to their own. In a word, they do not accept Communist beliefs because they are members of the party. They are members of the party because they accept Communist beliefs.

Specific evidence to support the assertion just made was staring President Allen and his Regents in the face at the very time when they were abstractly denying that such evidence could exist. Three of the five men whom they condemned as enslaved by party orders had already, by their own free and independent thinking, resigned from the party. How could they have done that if, as charged, they were incapable of free and independent thinking? Slaves do not resign.

At the committee hearings, these men explained, simply and directly, that under past conditions, they had found the party the most effective available weapon for attack upon evil social forces, but that with changing conditions, the use of that weapon seemed no longer advisable. Shall we say that the decision to be in the party gave evidence of a lack of objectivity while the decision to resign gave evidence of the possession of it? Such a statement would have no meaning except as indicating our own lack of objectivity.

In these three cases, as in the more famous case of Granville Hicks, who some years ago resigned party membership with a brilliant account of his reasons for doing so, the charge made cannot be sustained. The accusation as it stands means nothing more than that the President and Regents are advocating one set of ideas and are banning another. They are attributing to their victims their own intellectual sins. And the tragedy of their action is that it has immeasurably injured the cause which they seek to serve and, correspondingly, has advanced the cause which they are seeking to hold back.

The third phase of our question has to do with the wisdom, the effectiveness, of the educational policy under which teachers have been dismissed or put on probation. And on this issue, the evidence against the President and Regents is clear and decisive. However good their intention, they have made a fatal blunder in teaching method.

As that statement is made, it is taken for granted that the primary task of education in our colleges and universities is the teaching of the theory and practice of intellectual freedom, as the first principle of the democratic way of life. Whatever else our students may do or fail to do, they must learn what freedom is. They must learn to believe in it, to love it, and most important of all, to trust it.

What then is this faith in freedom, so far as the conflict of opinions is concerned? With respect to the world-wide controversy now raging between the advocates of the freedom of belief and the advocates of suppression of belief, what is our American doctrine? Simply stated, that doctrine expresses our confidence that whenever, in the field of ideas, the advocates of freedom and the advocates of suppression meet in fair and unabridged discussion, freedom will win. If that were not true, if the intellectual program of democracy could not hold its own in fair debate, then that program itself would require of us its own abandonment. That chance we believers in self-government have determined to take. We have put our faith in democracy.

But the President and Regents have, at this point, taken the opposite course. They have gone over to the enemy. They are not willing to give a fair and equal hearing to those who disagree with us. They are convinced that suppression is more effective as an agency of freedom than is freedom itself.

But this procedure violates the one basic principle on which all teaching rests. It is impossible to teach what one does not believe. It is idle to preach what one does not practice. These men who advocate that we do to the Russians what the Russians, if they had the power, would do to us are declaring that the Russians are right and that we are wrong. They practice suppression because they have more faith in the methods of dictatorship than in those of a free self-governing society.

For many years the writer of these words has watched the disastrous educational effects upon student opinion and attitude when suppression has been used, openly or secretly, in our universities and colleges. The outcome is always the same. Dictatorship breeds rebellion and dissatisfaction. High-spirited youth will not stand the double-dealing which prates of academic freedom and muzzles its teachers by putting them "on probation."

If we suggest to these young people that they believe in democracy, then they will insist on knowing what can be said against it as well as what can be said for it. If we ask them to get ready to lay down their lives in conflict against an enemy, they want to know not only how strong or how weak are the military forces of that enemy, but also what he has to say for himself as against what we are saying for ourselves.

Many of the students in our colleges and universities are today driven into an irresponsible radicalism. But that drive does not come from the critics of our American political institutions. It comes chiefly from the irresponsible defenders of those institutions—the men who make a mockery of freedom by using in its service the forces of suppression.

Underlying and surrounding the Washington controversy is the same controversy as it runs through our national life. The most tragic mistake of the contemporary American mind is its failure to recognize the inherent strength and stability of free institutions when they are true to themselves. Democracy is not a weak and unstable thing which forever needs propping up by the devices of dictatorship. It is the only form of social life and of government which today has assurance of maintaining itself.

As contrasted with it, all governments of suppression are temporary and insecure. The regimes of Hitler and Mussolini flared into strength, and quickly died away. The power of the Soviet Union cannot endure unless that nation can find its way into the practices of political freedom. And all the other dictatorships are falling, and will fall, day by day. Free self-government alone gives promise of permanence and peace. The only real danger which threatens our democracy is that lack of faith which leads us into the devices and follies of suppression.

15
Letter to the Federal Bureau of Investigation

The Federal Bureau of Investigation employed a large net-work of informers to ferret out information about what "subversive" people believed. This information was made available to government agencies and congressional investigating committees, and, through them, to employers and prospective employers.

Agents of the FBI visited Meiklejohn's home to ask him to reveal the opinions of his former students and colleagues. When an agent arrived, Meiklejohn would call Mrs. Meiklejohn to station herself on the stairway landing to enjoy the spectacle of his explaining his position to the agent. When agents had difficulty understanding the grounds for his refusal to tell them the opinions of his friends, he wrote their chief the following letter to clear up any misunderstanding.

This letter, held among Meiklejohn's papers at the State Historical Society of Wisconsin, was published by the Meiklejohn Civil Liberties Institute in their 15th Anniversary Journal *(October 1980).*

Dec. 20, 1951

Chief, San Francisco Office
Federal Bureau of Investigation

Dear Sir,

A week or two ago one of your agents called to ask me about a person whom I have known for forty years as pupil, colleague, and friend, and whom I would gladly recommend for any appointment he is willing to take.

When the issue of "Loyalty" was raised, I explained to your agent that the questions he was asking were of two kinds, one of which I am

227

Meiklejohn in 1953.

glad to answer, while the others are such that, as a believer in the Constitution, I find it necessary to refuse to answer them. This was the same attitude which I had expressed to another of your agents, about three years ago. The two young men, especially the later one, found it hard, apparently, to understand the grounds of my decision. It seems desirable, therefore, that I state them, as directly as possible, to you, so that you may have them for reference. If, at any point, the statement is unclear, I shall be very glad to talk it over with you.

1. On the one hand, I am glad to give information concerning a person's abilities, training, character, and, in general, his fitness for the office in question. And if Loyalty be given its proper meaning of "unqualified devotion to the best interests of the nation, as one sees them," I feel both willing and obliged to speak freely about that.

2. But the term "Loyalty" is sometimes used as referring to a man's opinions about our form of government or our national policies, the assumption being that if a man disagrees with prevailing beliefs on these matters, he is "disloyal." When questions seem to imply this constitutionally false and misleading use of terms, I feel bound, under the First Amendment, to refuse to answer them. I cannot, therefore, give information about a man's beliefs, or party affiliations, or organizational connections. To do so seems to me a serious violation of the most significant principle of our form of government.

It is not easy to make, and to hold fast to, such a decision as this, but the other decision is, for me, impossible.

Please let me know if I can be of service in any way.

Yours,

/s/ Alexander Meiklejohn

16

Testimony on the Meaning of the First Amendment

In 1955, when he was eighty-three years old, Meiklejohn was summoned before the Senate Subcommittee on Constitutional Rights to summarize his interpretation of the First Amendment. This was a subcommittee to the Senate Judiciary Committee, also the parent body of the Subcommittee on Internal Security. The Hennings Subcommittee took its

> *name from its chairman, Thomas Carey Hennings, Jr.,
> who had been elected senator from Missouri in 1950 on a
> platform of opposition to McCarthyism and the Internal
> Security Act of 1950. In early 1955, when Hennings was
> named chairman of the Subcommittee on Civil Rights, he
> changed its name to Constitutional Rights, so that the com-
> mittee could examine the whole Bill of Rights to see
> whether it was being violated. The Senate had censured
> Senator Joseph McCarthy in November, 1954, but it was
> still a bad time for the Bill of Rights. Chief Justice Earl
> Warren said in St. Louis in February, 1955, that if the
> nation were asked at that time to ratify the Bill of Rights, it
> would not do so.*
>
> *The Hennings Subcommittee began its hearings on free-
> dom of speech, press, and assembly by inviting four legal
> scholars to discuss the extent to which Congress could con-
> stitutionally limit these freedoms in the interest of national
> security. The subcommittee invited Alexander Meiklejohn;
> Zechariah Chafee, professor of law at Harvard University;
> Thomas I. Cook, professor of political science at Johns
> Hopkins University; and Morris L. Ernst, a leading ACLU
> lawyer in New York City. After these four testified, the sub-
> committee heard testimony from witnesses about actual con-
> ditions. Hennings wanted, by means of these hearings, to
> reduce the size of the security program and to reform its
> procedural failings. But before he could issue a final report
> the Supreme Court, on June 11, 1956, in* Cole v Young,
> *held that the Eisenhower Security Program exceeded the
> authority granted by Congress in Public Law 733 (1950).*
>
> *Meiklejohn's testimony was published in Senate, Com-
> mittee on the Judiciary, Subcommittee on Constitutional
> Rights, Hearings, 84th Congress, 1st Session, 1955, Part
> 1, 1ff, and also in Alexander Meiklejohn,* Political Free-
> dom: The Constitutional Powers of the People *(New
> York: Oxford University Press, 1965), pp. 107-124.*

Mr. Chairman and Members of the Committee:

I deeply appreciate your courtesy in asking me to join with you in
an attempt to define the meaning of the words, "Congress shall make

no law . . . abridging the freedom of speech, or of the press; or the right of the people peaceably to assemble, and to petition the government for a redress of grievances.'' Whatever those words may mean, they go directly to the heart of our American plan of government. If we can understand them we can know what, as a self-governing nation, we are trying to be and to do. Insofar as we do not understand them, we are in grave danger of blocking our own purposes, of denying our own beliefs.

1

It may clarify my own part in our conference if I tell you at once my opinion concerning this much-debated subject. The First Amendment seems to me to be a very uncompromising statement. It admits of no exceptions. It tells us that the Congress and, by implication, all other agencies of the government are denied any authority whatever to limit the political freedom of the citizens of the United States. It declares that with respect to political belief, political discussion, political advocacy, political planning, our citizens are sovereign, and the Congress is their subordinate agent. That agent is authorized, under strong safeguards against the abuse of its power, to limit the freedom of men as they go about the management of their private, their non-political, affairs. But the same men, as they endeavor to meet the public responsibilities of citizenship in a free society, are in a vital sense, which is not easy to define, beyond the reach of legislative control. Our common task, as we talk together today, is to determine what that sense is.

Mr. Chairman, in view of your courtesy to me, I hope you will not find me discourteous when I suggest that the Congress is a subordinate branch of the government of the United States. In saying this I am simply repeating in less passionate words what was said by the writers of the *Federalist* papers when, a century and three-quarters ago, they explained the meaning of the proposed Constitution to a body politic which seemed very reluctant to adopt it. Over and over again the writers of those papers declared that the Constitutional Convention had given to the people adequate protection against a much-feared tyranny of the legislature. In one of the most brilliant statements ever written about the Constitution, the *Federalist* says—

It is one thing to be subject to the laws, and another to be dependent on the legislative body. The first comports with, the last violates, the fundamental principles of good government, and, whatever may be the forms of the Constitution, unites all power in the same hands. (No. 71)

It is chiefly the legislature, the *Federalist* insists, which threatens to usurp the governing powers of the people. In words which unfortunately have some relevance today, it declares that "It is against the enterprising ambition of this department that the people ought to indulge their jealousy and exhaust all their precautions." And, further, the hesitant people were assured that the Convention, having recognized this danger, had devised adequate protections against it. The representatives, it was provided, would be elected by vote of the people. Elections would be for terms brief enough to ensure active and continuous popular control. The legislature would have no law-making authority other than those limited powers specifically delegated to it. A general legislative power to act for the security and welfare of the nation was denied on the ground that it would destroy the basic postulate of popular self-government on which the Constitution rests.

As the *Federalist* thus describes, with insight and accuracy, the Constitutional defenses of the freedom of the people against legislative invasion, it is not speaking of that freedom as an "individual right" which is bestowed upon the citizens by action of the legislature. Nor is the principle of the freedom of speech derived from a law of Nature or of Reason in the abstract. As it stands in the Constitution, it is an expression of the basic American political agreement that, in the last resort, the people of the United States shall govern themselves. To find its meaning, therefore, we must dig down to the very foundations of the self-governing process. And what we shall there find is the fact that when men govern themselves, it is they—and no one else—who must pass judgment upon public policies. And that means that in our popular discussions, unwise ideas must have a hearing as well as wise ones, dangerous ideas as well as safe, un-American as well as American. Just so far as, at any point, the citizens who are to decide issues are denied acquaintance with information or opinion or doubt or disbelief or criticism which is relevant to those issues, just so far the result must be ill-considered, ill-balanced planning for the general good. It is that mutilation of the thinking process of the community against which the First Amendment is directed. That provision neither the Legislature, nor the Executive, nor the Judiciary, nor all of them acting together, has authority to nullify. We Americans have, together, decided to be politically free.

2

Mr. Chairman, I have now stated for your consideration the thesis that the First Amendment is not "open to exceptions"; that our American "freedom of speech" is not, on any grounds whatever, subject to abridgment by the representatives of the people. May I next try to answer two arguments which are commonly brought against that thesis in the courts and in the wider circle of popular discussion?

The first objection rests upon the supposition that freedom of speech may on occasion threaten the security of the nation. And when these two legitimate national interests are in conflict, the government, it is said, must strike a balance between them. And that means that the First Amendment must at times yield ground. The freedom of speech must be abridged in order that the national order and safety may be secured.

In the courts of the United States, many diverse opinions have asserted that "balancing" doctrine. One of these, often quoted, reads as follows:

> To preserve its independence, and give security against foreign aggression and encroachment, is the highest duty of every nation, and to attain these ends nearly all other considerations are to be subordinated. It matters not in what form such aggression comes. . . . The government, possessing the powers which are to be exercised for protection and security, is clothed with authority to determine the occasion on which the powers shall be brought forth.

That opinion tells us that the "government" of the United States has unlimited authority to provide for the security of the nation, as it may seem necessary and wise. It tells us, therefore, that constitutionally, the government which has created the defenses of political freedom may break down those defenses. We, the people, who have enacted the First Amendment, may by agreed-upon procedure modify or annul that amendment. And, since we are, as a government, a sovereign nation, I do not see how any of these assertions can be doubted or denied. We Americans, as a body-politic, may destroy or limit our freedom whenever we choose. But what bearing has that statement upon the authority of Congress to interfere with the provisions of the First Amendment? Congress is not the government. It is only one of four branches to each of which the people have denied specific and limited powers as well as delegated such powers. And in the case before us, the words, "Congress shall make no law . . . abridging the freedom of speech," give plain evidence that, so far as Congress is concerned, the power to limit our political freedom has been explicitly denied.

There is, I am sure, a radical error in the theory that the task of "balancing" the conflicting claims of security and freedom has been delegated to Congress. It is the failure to recognize that the balancing in question was carefully done when, one hundred seventy years ago, the Constitution was adopted and quickly amended. The men who wrote the text of that Constitution knew, quite as well as we do, that the program of political freedom is a dangerous one. They could foresee that, as the nation traveled the ways of self-government, the freedom of speech would often be used irresponsibly and unwisely, especially in the times of war or near-war, and that such talking might have serious consequences for the national safety.

They knew, too, that a large section of the voting population was hostile to the forms of government which were then being adopted. And, further, they had every reason to expect that in a changing world, new dissatisfactions would arise and might in times of stress break out into open and passionate disaffection. All these considerations, I am saying, were as clearly and as disturbingly present to their minds as they are to our minds today. And because of them, the First Amendment might have been written, not as it is, but as the Courts of the United States have re-written it in the war-maddened years since 1919. The Amendment might have said, "Except in times and situations involving 'clear and present danger' to the national security, Congress shall make no law abridging the freedom of speech." Or it might have read, "Only when, in the judgment of the legislature, the interests of order and security render such action advisable shall Congress abridge the freedom of speech." But the writers of the Amendment did not adopt either of these phrasings or anything like them. Perhaps a minor reason for their decision was the practical certainty that the Constitution, if presented in that form, would have failed of adoption. But more important than such questionable historical speculation are two reasons which are as valid today as they were when the Amendment was decreed.

First, our doctrine of political freedom is not a visionary abstraction. It is a belief which is based in long and bitter experience, which is thought out by shrewd intelligence. It is the sober conviction that, in a society pledged to self-government, it is never true that, in the long run, the security of the nation is endangered by the freedom of the people. Whatever may be the immediate gains and losses, the dangers to our safety arising from political suppression are always greater than the dangers to that safety arising from political freedom. Suppression is always foolish. Freedom is always wise. That is the faith, the experimental faith, by which we Americans have undertaken to live. If we, the citizens of today, cannot shake ourselves free from the hysteria which blinds us to that faith, there is little hope for peace and security, either at home or abroad.

Second, the re-writing of the First Amendment which authorizes the legislature to balance security against freedom denies not merely some minor phase of the amendment but its essential purpose and meaning. Whenever, in our Western civilization, "inquisitors" have sought to justify their acts of suppression, they have given plausibility to their claims only by appealing to the necessity of guarding the public safety. It is that appeal which the First Amendment intended, and intends, to outlaw. Speaking to the legislature, it says, "When times of danger come upon the nation, you will be strongly tempted, and urged by popular pressure, to resort to practices of suppression such as those allowed by societies unlike our own in which men do not govern themselves. You are hereby forbidden to do so. This nation of ours intends to be free. 'Congress shall make no law . . . abridging the freedom of speech.' "

The second objection which must be met by one who asserts the unconditional freedom of speech rests upon the well-known fact that there are countless human situations in which, under the Constitution, this or that kind of speaking may be limited or forbidden by legislative action. Some of these cases have been listed by the courts in vague and varying ways. Thus libels, blasphemies, attacks upon public morals or private reputation have been held punishable. So too, we are told that "counselling a murder" may be a criminal act, or "falsely shouting fire in a theatre, and causing a panic." "Offensive" or "provocative" speech has been denied legislative immunity. "Contempt of court," shown by the use of speech or by refusal to speak, may give basis for prosecution. Utterances which cause a riot or which "incite" to it may be subject to the same legal condemnation. And this listing of legitimate legislative abridgments of speech could be continued indefinitely. Their number is legion.

In view of these undoubted facts, the objection which we must now try to meet can be simply stated. In all these cases, it says, inasmuch as speaking is abridged, "exceptions" are made to the First Amendment. The Amendment is thus shown to be, in general, "open to exceptions." And from this it follows that there is no reason why a legislature which has authority to guard the public safety should be debarred from making an "exception" when faced by the threat of national danger.

Now the validity of that argument rests upon the assumed major premise that whenever, in any way, limits are set to the speaking of an individual, an "exception" is made to the First Amendment. But that premise is clearly false. It could be justified only if it were shown that the Amendment intends to forbid every form of governmental control over the act of speaking. Is that its intention? Nothing could be further from the truth. May I draw an example from our own present activities in this room? You and I are here talking about freedom within limits defined by the Senate. I am allowed to speak only because you have invited me to do so. And just now everyone else is denied that privilege. But further, you have assigned me a topic to which my remarks must be relevant. Your schedule, too, acting with generosity, fixes a time within which my remarks must be made. In a word, my speaking, though "free" in the First Amendment sense, is abridged in many ways. But your speaking, too, is controlled by rules of procedure. You may, of course, differ in opinion from what I am saying. To that freedom there are no limits. But unless the chairman intervenes, you are not allowed to express that difference by open speech until I have finished my reading. In a word, both you and I are under control as to what we may say and when and how we may say it. Shall we say, then, that this conference, which studies the principle of free speech, is itself making "exceptions" to that principle? I do not think so. Speech, as a form of human action, is subject to regulation in exactly the same sense as is walking, or lighting a fire, or shooting a gun. To interpret the First Amendment as forbidding such regulation is to so misconceive its meaning as to reduce it to nonsense.

The principle here at issue was effectively, though not clearly, stated by Mr. Justice Holmes when, in the *Frohwerk* case, he said —

The First Amendment, while prohibiting legislation against free speech as such, cannot have been, and obviously was not, intended to give immunity to every form of language. . . . We venture to believe that neither Hamilton nor Madison, nor any other competent person, ever supposed that to make criminal the counselling of a murder would be an unconstitutional interference with free speech.

Those words of the great Justice, by denying that the First Amendment intends to forbid such abridgments of speech as the punishing of incitement to murder, seem to me to nullify completely the supposed evidence that the amendment is "open to exceptions." They show conclusively the falsity of the "exception" theory which has been used by the courts to give basis for the "danger" theory of legislative authority to abridge our political freedom. If, then, the "danger" theory is to stand it must stand on its own feet. And those feet, if my earlier argument is valid, seem to be made of clay.

3

Mr. Chairman, in the first section of this paper I spoke of the negative fact that the First Amendment forbids the legislature to limit the political freedom of the people. May I now, surveying the same ground from its positive side, discuss with you the active powers and responsibilities of free citizens, as these are described or taken for granted in the general structure of the Constitution as a whole? If I am not mistaken, we shall find here the reasons why the words of the great proclamation are so absolute, so uncompromising, so resistant of modification or exception.

The purpose of the Constitution is, as we all know, to define and allocate powers for the governing of the nation. To that end, three special governing agencies are set up, and to each of them are delegated such specific powers as are needed for doing its part of the work.

Now that program rests upon a clear distinction between the political body which delegates powers and the political bodies—Legislative, Executive, and Judicial—to which powers are delegated. It presupposes, on the one hand, a supreme governing agency to which, originally, all authority belongs. It specifies, on the other hand, subordinate agencies to which partial delegations of authority are made. What, then, is the working relation between the supreme agency and its subordinates? Only as we answer that question shall we find the positive meaning of the First Amendment.

First of all, then, what is the supreme governing agency of this nation? In its opening statement the Constitution answers that question. "We, the People of the United States," it declares, "do ordain and establish this Constitution . . ." Those are revolutionary words which define the freedom which is guaranteed by the First Amendment. They mark off our government from every form of despotic polity. The legal powers of the people of the United States are not granted to them by some one else—by kings or barons or priests, by legislators or executives or judges. All political authority, whether delegated or not, belongs, constitutionally, to us. If any one else has political authority, we are lending it to him. We, the people, are supreme in our own right. We are governed, directly or indirectly, only by ourselves.

But now what have we, the people, in our establishing of the Constitution, done with the powers which thus inhere in us? Some of them we have delegated. But there is one power, at least, which we have not delegated, which we have kept in our own hands, for our own direct exercise. Article 1, (2), authorizes the people, in their capacity as "electors," to choose their representatives. And that means that we, the people, in a vital sense, do actively govern those who, by other delegated powers, govern us. In the midst of all our assigning of powers to legislative, executive, and judicial bodies, we have jealously kept for ourselves the most fundamental of all powers. It is the power of voting, of choosing by joint action, those representatives to whom certain of our powers are entrusted. In the view of the Constitution, then, we the people are not only the supreme agency. We are also, politically, an active electorate—a Fourth, or perhaps better, a First Branch which, through its reserved power, governs at the polls. That is the essential meaning of the statement that we Americans are, in actual practice, politically a free people. Our First Amendment freedom is not merely an aspiration. It is an arrangement made by women and men who vote freely and, by voting, govern the nation. That is the responsibility, the opportunity, which the Constitution assigns to us, however slackly and negligently we may at times have exercised our power.

It follows from what has just been said that under the Constitution, we Americans are politically free only insofar as our voting is free. But to get the full meaning of that statement we must examine more closely what men are doing when they vote, and how they do it.

The most obvious feature of activity at the polls is the choosing among candidates for office. But under our election procedures, with their party platforms and public meetings, with the turmoil and passion of partisan debate, the voters are also considering and deciding about issues of public policy. They are thinking. As we vote we do more than elect men to represent us. We also judge the wisdom or folly of suggested measures. We plan for the welfare of the nation. Now it is these "judging" activities of the governing people which the First Amendment protects by its guarantees of freedom from legislative interference. Because, as self-governing women and men, we the people have work to do for the general welfare, we make two demands. First, our judging of public issues, whether done separately or in groups, must be free and independent—must be our own. It must be done by us and by no one else. And second, we must be equally free and independent in expressing, at the polls, the conclusions, the beliefs, to which our judging has brought us. Censorship over our thinking, duress over our voting, are alike forbidden by the First Amendment. A legislative body, or any other body which, in any way, practices such censorship or duress, stands in "contempt" of the sovereign people of the United States.

But, further, what more specifically are the judging activities with which censorship and duress attempt to interfere? What are the intellectual processes by which free men govern a nation, which therefore must be protected from any external interference? They seem to be of three kinds.

First, as we try to "make up our minds" on issues which affect the general welfare, we commonly—though not commonly enough—read the printed records of the thinking and believing which other men have done in relation to those issues. Those records are found in documents and newspapers, in works of art of many kinds. And all this vast array of idea and fact, of science and fiction, of poetry and prose, of belief and doubt, of appreciation and purpose, of information and argument, the voter may find ready to help him in making up his mind.

Second, we electors do our thinking, not only by individual reading and reflection, but also in the active associations of private or public discussion. We think together, as well as apart. And in this field, by the group action of congenial minds, by the controversies of opposing minds, we form parties, adopt platforms, conduct campaigns, hold meetings, in order that this or that set of ideas may prevail, in order that that measure or this may be defeated.

And third, when election day finally comes, the voter, having presumably made up his mind, must now express it by his ballot. Behind the canvas curtain, alone and independent, he renders his decision. He acts as sovereign, one of the governors of his country. However slack may be our practice, that, in theory, is our freedom.

What, then, as seen against this Constitutional background, is the purpose of the First Amendment, as it stands guard over our freedom? That purpose is to see to it that in none of these three activities of judging shall the voter be robbed, by action of other, subordinate branches of the government, of the responsibility, the power, the authority, which are his under the Constitution. What shall be read? What he himself decides to read. With whom shall he associate in political advocacy? With those with whom he chooses to associate. Whom shall he oppose? Those with whom he disagrees. Shall any branch of the government attempt to control his opinions or his vote, to drive him by duress or intimidation into believing or voting this way or that? To do this is to violate the Constitution at its very source. We, the people of the United States, are self-governing. That is what our freedom means.

4

Mr. Chairman, this interpretation of the First Amendment which I have tried to give is, of necessity, very abstract. May I, therefore, give some more specific examples of its meaning at this point or that?

First, when we speak of the Amendment as guarding the freedom to hear and to read, the principle applies not only to the speaking or writing of our own citizens but also to the writing or speaking of every one whom a citizen, at his own discretion, may choose to hear or to read. And this means that unhindered expression must be open to non-citizens, to resident aliens, to writers and speakers of other nations, to anyone, past or present, who has something to say which may have significance for a citizen who is thinking of the welfare of this nation. The Bible, the Koran, Plato, Adam Smith, Joseph Stalin, Gandhi, may be published and read in the United States, not because they have, or had, a right to be published here, but because we, the citizen-voters, have authority, have legal power, to decide what we will read, what we will think about. With the exercise of that "reserved" power, all "delegated" powers are, by the Constitution, forbidden to interfere.

Second, in the field of public discussion, when citizens and their fellow thinkers "peaceably assemble" to listen to a speaker, whether he be American or foreign, conservative or radical, safe or dangerous, the First Amendment is not, in the first instance, concerned with the "right" of the speaker to say this or that. It is concerned with the authority of the hearers to meet together, to discuss, and to hear discussed by speakers of their own choice, whatever they may deem worthy of their consideration.

Third, the same freedom from attempts at duress is guaranteed to every citizen as he makes up his mind, chooses his party, and finally casts his vote. During that process, no governing body may use force upon him, may try to drive him or lure him toward this decision or that, or away from this decision or that. And for that reason, no subordinate agency of the government has authority to ask, under compulsion to answer, what a citizen's political commitments are. The question, "Are you a Republican?" or "Are you a Communist?", when accompanied by the threat of harmful or degrading consequences if an answer is refused, or if the answer is this rather than that, is an intolerable invasion of the "reserved powers" of the governing people. And the freedom thus protected does not rest upon the Fifth Amendment "right" of one who is governed to avoid self-incrimination. It expresses the constitutional authority, the legal power, of one who governs to make up his own mind without fear or favor, with the independence and freedom in which self-government consists.

And fourth, for the same reason, our First Amendment freedom forbids that any citizen be required under threat of penalty to take an oath, or make an affirmation as to beliefs which he holds or rejects. Every citizen, it is true, may be required, and should be required, to pledge loyalty, and to practice loyalty, to the nation. He must agree to support the Constitution. But he may never be required to *believe* in the Constitution. His loyalty may never be tested on grounds of

adherence to, or rejection of, any *belief.* Loyalty does not imply conformity of opinion. Every citizen of the United States has Constitutional authority to approve or to condemn any laws enacted by the
Legislature, any actions taken by the Executive, any decisions rendered by the Judiciary, and any principles established by the Constitution. All these enactments which, as men who are governed, we must
obey, are subject to our approval or disapproval, as we govern. With
respect to all of them, we, who are free men, are sovereign. We are
"The People." We govern the United States.

5

Mr. Chairman, I have tried to state and defend the assertion that
Constitutional guarantee of political freedom is not "open to exceptions." Judgment upon the theoretical validity of that position I now
leave in your hands.

But as between conflicting views of the First Amendment, there is
also a practical question of efficiency. May I, in closing, speaking with
the tentativeness becoming to a non-lawyer, offer three suggestions as
to the working basis on which decisions about political freedom should
rest?

First, the experience of the courts since 1919 seems to me to show
that, as a procedural device for distinguishing forms of speech and
writing and assembly which the Amendment does protect from those
which it does not protect, the "clear and present danger" test has
failed to work. Its basic practical defect is that no one has been able to
give it dependable, or even assignable, meaning. Case by case, opinion
by opinion, it has shifted back and forth with a variability of meaning
which reveals its complete lack of Constitutional basis. In his opinion
confirming the conviction of Eugene Dennis and others for violation
of the Smith Act, Judge Learned Hand reviewed the long series of
judicial attempts to give to the words "clear and present" a usable
meaning. His conclusion reads, in part, as follows:

> The phrase "clear and present danger". . .is a way to describe
> a penumbra of occasions, even the outskirts of which are
> indefinable, but within which, as is so often the case, the courts
> must find their way as they can. In each case they must ask
> whether the gravity of the "evil," discounted by its improbabil-
> ity, justifies such an invasion of free speech as is necessary to
> avoid the danger.

And to this bewildering interpretation of the words, "clear and present," he adds:

That is a test in whose application the utmost differences of opinion have constantly arisen, even in the Supreme Court. Obviously it would be impossible to draft a statute which should attempt to prescribe a rule for each occasion; and it follows, as we have said, either that the Act is definite enough as it stands, or that it is practically impossible to deal with such conduct in general terms.

Those words, coming from the penetrating and powerful mind of Learned Hand, show how intolerable it is that the most precious, most fundamental, value in the American plan of government should depend, for its defense, upon a phrase which not only has no warrant in the Constitution but has no dependable meaning, either for a man accused of crime or for the attorneys who prosecute or defend him or for the courts which judge him. That phrase does not do its work. We need to make a fresh start in our interpreting of the words which protect our political freedom.

Second, as we seek for a better test, it is of couse true that no legal device can transform the making of decisions about freedom into a merely routine application of an abstract principle. Self-government is a complicated business. And yet, the "no-exception" view which I have offered seems to me to promise a more stable and understandable basis for judicial decision than does the 1919 doctrine which the courts have been trying to follow. For example, the most troublesome issue which now confronts our courts and our people is that of the speech and writing and assembling of persons who find, or think they find, radical defects in our form of government, and who devise and advocate plans by means of which another form might be substituted for it. And the practical question is, "How far, and in what respects, are such revolutionary planning and advocacy protected by the First Amendment?"

It is, of course, understood that if such persons or groups proceed to forceful or violent action, or even to overt preparation for such action, against the government, the First Amendment offers them, in that respect, no protection. Its interest is limited to the freedom of judgment-making—of inquiry and belief and conference and persuasion and planning and advocacy. It does not protect either overt action or incitement to such action. It is concerned only with those political activities by which, under the Constitution, free men govern themselves.

From what has just been said it follows that, so far as speech and writing are concerned, the distinction upon which the application of the First Amendment rests is that between "advocacy of action" and "incitement to action." To advocacy the amendment guarantees freedom, no matter what may be advocated. To incitement, on the other hand, the amendment guarantees nothing whatever.

This distinction was sharply drawn by Justice Brandeis when, in the *Whitney* case, he said—

> Every denunciation of existing law tends in some measure to increase the probability that there will be violations of it. Condonation of a breach enhances the probability. Propagation of the criminal state of mind by teaching syndicalism increases it. Advocacy of law-breaking heightens it still further. But even advocacy of violation, however reprehensible morally, is not a justification for denying free speech where the advocacy falls short of incitement and there is nothing to indicate that the advocacy would be immediately acted on.

Those words, I think, point the way which decisions about our political freedom can, and should, follow. An incitement, I take it, is an utterance so related to a specific overt act that it may be regarded and treated as a part of the doing of the act itself, if the act is done. Its control, therefore, falls within the jurisdiction of the legislature. An advocacy, on the other hand, even up to the limit of arguing and planning for the violent overthrow of the existing form of government, is one of those opinion-forming, judgment-making expressions which free men need to utter and to hear as citizens responsible for the governing of the nation. If men are not free to ask and to answer the question. "Shall the present form of our government be maintained or changed?"; if, when that question is asked, the two sides of the issue are not equally open for consideration, for advocacy, and for adoption, then it is impossible to speak of our government as established by the free choice of a self-governing people. It is not enough to say that the people of the United States were free one hundred seventy years ago. The First Amendment requires, simply and without equivocation, that they be free now.

Third, and finally, if we say, as this paper has urged, that in many situations, speech and writing and assembly may be controlled by legislative action, we must also say that such control may never be based on the ground of disagreement with opinions held or expressed. No belief or advocacy may be denied freedom if, in the same situation, opposing beliefs or advocacies are granted that freedom.

If then, on any occasion in the United States, it is allowable to say that the Constitution is a good document, it is equally allowable, in that situation, to say that the Constitution is a bad document. If a public building may be used in which to say, in time of war, that the war is justified, then the same building may be used in which to say that it is not justified. If it be publicly argued that conscription for armed service is moral and necessary, it may be likewise publicly argued that it is immoral and unnecessary. If it may be said that American political institutions are superior to those of England or Russia or Germany, it may, with equal freedom, be said that those of England or Russia or Germany are superior to ours. These conflicting views may be expressed, must be expressed, not because they are valid, but because they are relevant. If they are responsibly entertained by anyone, we, the voters, need to hear them. When a question of policy is "before the house," free men choose to meet it, not with their eyes shut, but with their eyes open. To be afraid of any idea is to be unfit for self-government. Any such suppression of ideas about the common good, the First Amendment condemns with its absolute disapproval. The freedom of ideas shall not be abridged.

17
The First Amendment
Is an Absolute

Meiklejohn wrote this paper largely due to the urging of his friend, Professor Harry Kalven, Jr., of the Law School of the University of Chicago. Kalven challenged Meiklejohn by saying he was not sure that Meiklejohn's interpretation could stand the test of lawyer-like application to the many specific situations that the courts must handle.

Meiklejohn was never intimidated by his friends with law degrees who sometimes behaved as if the Constitution and its interpretation were their private domain. In this article he brought his principles to bear, as nearly as he could, in as lawyer-like a form as he could, on the issues facing the courts. It appeared in an annual compilation of legal argument: Philip B. Kurland, ed., The Supreme Court Review 1961 *(Chicago: University of Chicago Press, 1961), pp. 245-266. What follows constitutes the final half of Meiklejohn's argument.*

. . . . The freedom that the First Amendment protects is not, then, an absence of regulation. It is the presence of self-government. Our argument now proceeds to define, as clearly as it can, the intention of the Constitutional provision that begins with the words: "Congress shall make no law abridging. . . ."

Rational Principles To Mark the Limits of Constitutional Protection

In his *Free Speech in the United States*[1] Professor Chafee stated the dilemma which confronts our inquiry and which divides the Supreme Court so evenly: "The question whether such perplexing cases are within the First Amendment or not cannot be solved by the multiplication of obvious examples, but only by the development of a rational principle to mark the limits of constitutional protection." Professor Chafee was too much involved in the complexities of balancing to

246

formulate the needed principle of which absolutists speak. But he indicated the goal toward which every interpreter of the First Amendment should now be trying to make his way.[2] We are looking for a principle which is not in conflict with any other provision of the Constitution, a principle which, as it now stands, is "absolute" in the sense of being "not open to exceptions," but a principle which also is subject to interpretation, to change, or to abolition, as the necessities of a precarious world may require.

Apart from the First Amendment itself, the passages of the Constitution which most directly clarify its meaning are the Preamble, the Tenth Amendment, and Section two of Article I. All four provisions must be considered in their historical setting, not only in relation to one another but, even more important, in relation to the intention and structure of the Constitution as a whole. Out of such consideration the following principles seem to emerge:

1. All constitutional authority to govern the people of the United States belongs to the people themselves, acting as members of a corporate body politic. They are, it is true, "the governed." But they are also "the governors." Political freedom is not the absence of government. It is self-government.

2. By means of the Constitution, the people establish subordinate agencies, such as the legislature, the executive, the judiciary, and delegate to each of them such specific and limited powers as are deemed necessary for the doing of its assigned governing. These agencies have no other powers.

3. The people do not delegate all their sovereign powers. The Tenth Amendment speaks of powers that are reserved "to the people," as well as of powers "reserved to the States."

4. Article I, § 2, speaks of a reserved power which the people have decided to exercise by their own direct activity: "The House of Representatives shall be composed of members chosen every second year by the people of the several States. . . ." Here is established the voting power through which the people, as an electorate, actively participate in governing both themselves, as subjects of the laws, and their agencies, as the makers, administrators, and interpreters of the laws. In today's government, the scope of direct electoral action is wider than the provisions made when Article I, § 2, was adopted, but the constitutional principle or intention is the same.

5. The revolutionary intent of the First Amendment is, then, to deny to all subordinate agencies authority to abridge the freedom of the electoral power of the people.

For the understanding of these principles it is essential to keep clear the crucial difference between "the rights" of the governed and "the powers" of the governors. And at this point, the title "Bill of Rights" is lamentably inaccurate as a designation of the first ten amendments. They are not a "Bill of Rights" but a "Bill of Powers and Rights." The Second through the Ninth Amendments limit the powers of the subordinate agencies in order that due regard shall be paid to the private "rights of the governed." The First and Tenth Amendments protect the governing "powers" of the people from abridgment by the agencies which are established as their servants. In the field of our "rights," each one of us can claim "due process of law." In the field of our governing "powers," the notion of "due process" is irrelevant.

The Freedom of Thought and Communication by Which We Govern

The preceding section may be summed up thus: The First Amendment does not protect a "freedom to speak." It protects the freedom of those activities of thought and communication by which we "govern." It is concerned, not with a private right, but with a public power, a governmental responsibility.

In the specific language of the Constitution, the governing activities of the people appear only in terms of casting a ballot. But in the deeper meaning of the Constitution, voting is merely the external expression of a wide and diverse number of activities by means of which citizens attempt to meet the responsibilities of making judgments, which that freedom to govern lays upon them. That freedom implies and requires what we call "the dignity of the individual." Self-government can exist only insofar as the voters acquire the intelligence, integrity, sensitivity, and generous devotion to the general welfare that, in theory, casting a ballot is assumed to express.

The responsibilities mentioned are of three kinds. We, the people who govern, must try to understand the issues which, incident by incident, face the nation. We must pass judgment upon the decisions which our agents make upon those issues. And, further, we must share in devising methods by which those decisions can be made wise and effective or, if need be, supplanted by others which promise greater wisdom and effectiveness. Now it is these activities, in all their diversity, whose freedom fills up "the scope of the First Amendment." These are the activities to whose freedom it gives its unqualified protection. And it must be recognized that the literal text of the Amendment falls far short of expressing the intent and the scope of that protection. I have previously tried to express that inadequacy:[3]

We must also note that, though the intention of the Amendment is sharp and resolute, the sentence which expresses that intention is awkward and ill-constructed. Evidently, it was hard to write and is, therefore, hard to interpret. Within its meaning are summed up centuries of social passion and intellectual controversy, in this country and in others. As one reads it, one feels that its writers could not agree, either within themselves or with each other, upon a single formula which would define for them the paradoxical relation between free men and their legislative agents. Apparently, all that they could make their words do was to link together five separate demands which had been sharpened by ages of conflict and were being popularly urged in the name of the "Freedom of the People." And yet, those demands were, and were felt to be, varied forms of a single demand. They were attempts to express, each in its own way, the revolutionary idea which, in the slowly advancing fight for freedom, has given to the American experiment in self-government its dominating significance for the modern world.

What I have said is that the First Amendment, as seen in its constitutional setting, forbids Congress to abridge the freedom of a citizen's speech, press, peaceable assembly, or petition, whenever those activities are utilized for the governing of the nation. In these respects, the Constitution gives to all "the people" the same protection of freedom which, in Article I, § 6(1), it provides for their legislative agents: "and for any speech or debate in either House, they shall not be questioned in any other place." Just as our agents must be free in their use of their delegated powers, so the people must be free in the exercise of their reserved powers.

What other activities, then, in addition to speech, press, assembly, and petition, must be included within the scope of the First Amendment? First of all, the freedom to "vote," the official expression of a self-governing man's judgment on issues of public policy, must be absolutely protected. None of his subordinate agencies may bring pressure upon him to drive his balloting this way or that. None of them may require him to tell how he has voted; none may inquire by compulsory process into his political beliefs or associations. In that area, the citizen has constitutional authority and his agents have not.

Second, there are many forms of thought and expression within the range of human communications from which the voter derives the knowledge, intelligence, sensitivity to human values: the capacity for sane and objective judgment which, so far as possible, a ballot should express. These, too, must suffer no abridgment of their freedom. I list four of them below.

1. Education, in all its phases, is the attempt to so inform and cultivate the mind and will of a citizen that he shall have the wisdom, the independence, and, therefore, the dignity of a governing citizen. Freedom of education is, thus, as we all recognize, a basic postulate in the planning of a free society.

2. The achievements of philosophy and the sciences in creating knowledge and understanding of men and their world must be made available, without abridgment, to every citizen.

3. Literature and the arts must be protected by the First Amendment. They lead the way toward sensitive and informed appreciation and response to the values out of which the riches of the general welfare are created.

4. Public discussions of public issues, together with the spreading of information and opinion bearing on those issues, must have a freedom unabridged by our agents. Though they govern us, we, in a deeper sense, govern them. Over our governing, they have no power. Over their governing we have sovereign power.

A Paradox

Out of the argument thus far stated, two apparently contradictory statements emerge. Congress may, in ways carefully limited, "regulate" the activities by which the citizens govern the nation. But no regulation may abridge the freedom of those governing activities. I am sure that the two statements are not contradictory. But their combination is, to say the least, paradoxical. It is that paradox that I must now face as I try to respond to Professor Kalven's challenge.[4] As a non-lawyer, I shall not discuss in detail the difficulties and puzzlements with which the courts must deal. I can only suggest that, here and there, seeming contradictions are not real.

First. A distinction must be drawn between belief and communication in their relations to Congressional authority. A citizen may be told when and where and in what manner he may or may not speak, write, assemble, and so on. On the other hand, he may not be told what he shall or shall not believe. In that realm each citizen is sovereign. He exercises powers that the body politic reserves for its own members. In 1953, testifying before the Senate Committee on Constitutional Rights, I said:[5]

> . . . our First Amendment freedom forbids that any citizen be required, under threat of penalty, to take an oath, or make an affirmation, as to beliefs which he holds or rejects. Every citizen, it is true, may be required and should be required, to pledge loyalty, and to practice loyalty, to the nation. He must agree to support the Constitution. But he may never be required to *believe* in the Constitution. His loyalty may never be tested on grounds of adherence to, or rejection of, any *belief.* Loyalty does not imply conformity of opinion. Every citizen of the United States has Constitutional authority to approve or to condemn any laws enacted by the Legislature, any actions taken by the Executive, and judgments rendered by the Judiciary, any principles established by the Constitution. All these enactments which, as men who are governed, we must obey, are subject to our approval or disapproval, as we govern. With respect to all of them we, who are free men, are sovereign. We are "The People." We govern the United States.

However far our practice falls short of the intention expressed by those words, they provide the standard by which our practice must be justified or condemned.

Second. We must recognize that there are many forms of communication which, since they are not being used as activities of governing, are wholly outside the scope of the First Amendment. Mr. Justice Holmes has told us about these, giving such vivid illustrations as "persuasion to murder."[6] and "falsely shouting fire in a theatre and causing a panic."[7] And Mr. Justice Harlan, referring to Holmes and following his lead, gave a more extensive list:[8] "libel, slander, misrepresentation, obscenity, perjury, false advertising, solicitation of crime, complicity by encouragement, conspiracy. . . ." Why are these communications not protected by the First Amendment? Mr. Justice Holmes suggested an explanation when he said of the First Amendment in *Schneck:*[9] "It does not even protect a man from an injunction against uttering words that may have all the effect of force."

Now it may be agreed that the uttering of words cannot be forbidden by legislation, nor punished on conviction, unless damage has been done by them to some individual or to the wider society. But that statement does not justify the imputation that all "words that may have all the effect of force" are denied the First Amendment's protection. The man who falsely shouts "Fire!" in a theatre is subject to prosecution under validly enacted legislation. But the army officer who, in command of a firing squad, shouts "Fire!" and thus ends a life, cannot be prosecuted for murder. He acts as an agent of the government. And, in fact, all governing communications are intended to have, more or less directly, "the effect of force." When a voter casts his ballot for a tax levy, he intends that someone shall be deprived of property. But his voting is not therefore outside the scope of the First Amendment. His voting must be free.

The principle here at stake can be seen in our libel laws. In cases of private defamation, one individual does damage to another by tongue or pen; the person so injured in reputation or property may sue for damages. But, in that case, the First Amendment gives no protection to the person sued. His verbal attack has no relation to the business of governing. If, however, the same verbal attack is made in order to show the unfitness of a candidate for governmental office, the act is properly regarded as a citizen's participation in government. It is, therefore, protected by the First Amendment. And the same principle holds good if a citizen attacks, by words of disapproval and condemnation, the policies of the government, or even the structure of the Constitution. These are "public" issues concerning which, under our form of government, he has authority, and is assumed to have competence, to judge. Though private libel is subject to legislative control, political or seditious libel is not.

Third In discussions of the First Amendment too little attention has been given to the regulatory word "peaceable" in relation to "assembly." It suggests principles of limitation which apply also to speech, press, petition, and to the other forms of communication which support them. This limitation is significant in demonstrating that a citizen's governing is often both "regulated" and "free."

Peaceableness in governing may serve either one or both of two purposes. It provides protection for an assembly against external violation of rules of public order. It also seeks to ensure that relations within the assembly shall succeed in serving the governing function which warrants its protection by the First Amendment. The first of these purposes has to do with relations between the assembly and "outsiders" who, disagreeing with its ideas and intentions, may seek to disrupt the discussion and, in various ways, to render it ineffectual. In this situation, both the local authorities which have authority to "regulate" and the police who seek to apply the regulations are held responsible by the intention of the First and Fourteenth Amendments. No ordinance may be based upon disapproval of policies to be discussed or decreed by the assembly. And the police must, to the limit of their power, defend the meeting from interruption or interference by its enemies. But basically more important are the conditions of peaceableness within an assembly itself. It is, of course, impossible that everyone should be allowed to express his point of view whenever and however he chooses. In a meeting for discussion, as contrasted with a lecture, however, no one may be "denied the floor" on the ground of disapproval of what he is saying or would say. And, if the interests of a self-governing society are to be served, vituperation which fixes attention on the defects of an opponent's character or intelligence and thereby distracts attention from the question of policy under discussion may be foridden as a deadly enemy of peaceable assembly. Anyone who persists in it should be expelled from the meeting, and, if need be, the police should give help in getting it done.

I cannot, however, leave those words on record without noting how inadequate, to the degree of non-existence, are our public provisions for active discussions among the members of our self-governing society. As we try to create and enlarge freedom, such universal discussion is imperative. In every village, in every district of every town or city, there should be established at public expense cultural centers inviting all citizens, as they may choose, to meet together for the consideration of public policy. And conditions must be provided under which such meetings could be happily and successfully conducted. I am not thinking of such lunatic-fringe activities as those in Hyde Park in London. I am thinking of a self-governing body politic, whose freedom of individual expression should be cultivated, not merely because it serves to prevent outbursts of violence which would result from suppression, but for the positive purpose of bringing every citizen into active and intelligent sharing in the government of his country.

Fourth. Largely because of our failure to make adequate provision for free and unhindered public discussion, the courts are called upon to judge the constitutionality of local ordinances which forbid or limit the holding of public meetings in public places. Such ordinances come into effect when individuals or groups assemble in such a way as to interfere with other interests of the community or of its members. The most striking and perplexing cases of this kind occur when meetings are held on public streets or in parks whose primary use is, in the opinion of the authorities, blocked or hindered to a degree demanding action. Now if such ordinances are based upon official disapproval of the ideas to be presented at the meeting, they clearly violate the First Amendment. But if no such abridgment of freedom is expressed or implied, regulation or prohibition on other grounds may be enacted and enforced.

It must not be assumed that every governmental regulation of a public meeting is, under current conditions, destructive of political freedom. Conditions of traffic on a city street are very different from those in the relatively open spaces of a country village. Parks may be needed for rest, quiet, and release from excitement and strain. Just as an individual, seeking to advocate some public policy may not do so, without consent, by interrupting a church service, or a classroom, or a sickroom, or a session of Congress or of the Supreme Court, or by ringing a doorbell and demanding to be heard, so meetings must conform to the necessities of the community, with respect to time, place, circumstance, and manner of procedure. And, unless those considerations are dishonestly used as a cover for unconstitutional discrimination against this idea or that, there is no First Amendment complaint against the ordinances which express them. The Amendment, I repeat, does not establish an "unlimited right to talk."

It must further be noted that in "emergency" situations, when something must be said and no other time, place, circumstance, or manner of speech will serve for the saying of it, a citizen may be justified in "taking the law into his own hands." In the famous example of Mr. Justice Holmes, a man is not allowed to shout "Fire!" *falsely* in a theatre. But, if, during a performance in a theatre, a person sees a fire which threatens to spread, he is not only allowed, he is duty-bound, to try to find some way of informing others so that a panic may not ensue with its disastrous consequences. The distinction between "falsely" and "truly" is here fundamental to an understanding of what freedom is.

Fifth. In the current discussions as to whether or not "obscenity" in literature and the arts is protected by the First Amendment, the basic principle is, I think, that literature and the arts are protected because they have a "social importance" which I have called a "governing" importance. For example, the novel is at present a powerful determinative of our views of what human beings are, how they can be influenced, in what directions they should be influenced by many forces, including, especially, their own judgments and appreciations. But the novel, like all the other creations of literature and the arts, may be produced wisely or unwisely, sensitively or coarsely, for the building up of a way of life which we treasure or for tearing it down. Shall the government establish a censorship to distinguish between "good" novels and "bad" ones? And, more specifically, shall it forbid the publication of novels which portray sexual experiences with a frankness that, to the prevailing conventions of our society, seems "obscene"?

The First Amendment seems to me to answer that question with an unequivocal "no." Here, as elsewhere, the authority of citizens to decide what they shall write and, more fundamental, what they shall read and see, has not been delegated to any of the subordinate branches of government. It is "reserved to the people," each deciding for himself to whom he will listen, whom he will read, what portrayal of the human scene he finds worthy of his attention. And at this point I feel compelled to disagree with Professor Kalven's interpretation of what I have tried to say. In his recent article on obscenity, he wrote:[10]

> The classic defense of John Stuart Mill and the modern defense
> of Alexander Meiklejohn do not help much when the question

is why the novel, the poem, the painting, the drama, or the piece of sculpture falls within the protection of the First Amendment. Nor do the famous opinions of Hand, Holmes, and Brandeis. The emphasis is all on truth winning out in a fair fight between competing ideas. The emphasis is clearest in Meiklejohn's argument that free speech is indispensable to the informed citizenry required to make democratic self-government work. The people need free speech because they vote. As a result his argument distinguishes sharply between public and private speech. Not all communications are relevant to the political process. The people do not need novels or dramas or paintings or poems because they will be called upon to vote. Art and belles-lettres do not deal in such ideas—at least not good art or belles-lettres. . . .

In reply to that friendly interpretation, I must, at two points, record a friendly disavowal. I have never been able to share the Miltonian faith that in a fair fight between truth and error, truth is sure to win. And if one had that faith, it would be hard to reconcile it with the sheer stupidity of the policies of this nation— and of other nations— now driving humanity to the very edge of final destruction. In my view, "the people need free speech" because they have decided, in adopting, maintaining and interpreting their Constitution, to govern themselves rather than to be governed by others. And, in order to make that self-government a reality rather than an illusion, in order that it may become as wise and efficient as its responsibilities require, the judgment-making of the people must be self-educated in the ways of freedom. That is, I think, the positive purpose to which the negative words of the First Amendment gave a constitutional expression. Moreover, as against Professor Kalven's interpretation, I believe, as a teacher, that the people do need novels and dramas and paintings and poems, "because they will be called upon to vote." The primary social fact which blocks and hinders the success of our experiment in self-government is that our citizens are not educated for self-government. We are terrified by ideas, rather than challenged and stimulated by them. Our dominant mood is not the courage of people who dare to think. It is timidity of those who fear and hate whenever conventions are questioned.

Conclusion

Professor Leonard W. Levy, in a stimulating book,[11] has recently given strong evidence that the Framers of the Constitution were not, for the most part, explicitly concerned with those aspects of the First Amendment's meaning and application which now especially concern us. If we asssume that his thesis has been established, what bearing does it have upon the contentions of this paper?

In answer to that question, two different statements can be made which properly supplement each other. First, the Framers initiated a political revolution whose development is still in process throughout the world. Second, like most revolutionaries, the Framers could not foresee the specific issues which would arise as their "novel idea" exercised its domination over the governing activities of a rapidly developing nation in a rapidly and fundamentally changing world. In that sense, the Framers did not know what they were doing. And in the same sense, it is still true that, after two centuries of experience, we do not know what they were doing, or what we ourselves are now doing.

In a more abstract and more significant sense, however, both they and we have been aware that the adoption of the principle of self-govenment by "The People" of this nation set loose upon us and upon the world at large an idea which is still transforming men's conceptions of what they are and how they may best be governed. Wherever it goes, that idea is demanding—and slowly securing—a recognition that, with respect to human dignity, women have the same status as men, that people of all races and colors and creeds must be treated as equals, that the poor are at least the equals of the rich. In popular language the idea finds expression in such phrases as "the land of the free," or "government by consent of the governed," or "government of the people, by the people, for the people shall not perish from the earth."

In our discussions of the Constitution, we commonly think that the clearest and most compelling expression of the "idea" of political freedom is given by the First Amendment. But in theory, and perhaps in practice, more penetrating insights are given by the Preamble's declaration that "We, the people of the United States . . .do ordain and establish this Constitution. . . ," or by the Tenth Amendment's assertion that, while we have delegated some limited governing

Meiklejohn and James Baldwin celebrating the 172nd anniversary of the ratification of the Bill of Rights at a dinner, organized by the Emergency Civil Liberties Committee in New York City, in December, 1963.

powers to our agents, we have reserved other powers to ourselves, or, finally, by the provision of Article I, Section 2, that we have authority to exercise direct governing power in electing our representatives.

If what we are saying here is true, then *Robertson v. Baldwin* seems to me to contain the most disastrous judicial pronouncement that I have found:[12] "The law is perfectly well settled that the first ten amendments to the Constitution, commonly known as the Bill of Rights, were not intended to lay down any novel principles of government, but simply to embody certain guaranties and immunities which we had inherited from our English ancestors. . . ." In 1951, in his opinion in *Dennis,* Mr. Justice Frankfurter, in quoting that statement, said of it,[13] "That this represents the authentic view of the Bill of Rights and the spirit in which it must be construed has been recognized again and again in cases that have come here within the last fifty years."

In 1953, in a comment on that concurring opinion,[14] I quoted that dictum and criticized it. To sum up what I have been trying to say in this paper, I wish to repeat some part of that criticism. Mr. Justice Frankfurter, it must be noted, does not here speak as one expressing his own opinion. He is telling us of a contention which has prevailed for a long time in the Court. Is that contention valid? Is it true, for example, that the religion clause of the First Amendment was "inherited" from a nation which had, and still has, an established church? However that may be, a ringing dissent by the first Mr. Justice Harlan in *Robertson v. Baldwin* seems to me to cut into meaningless bits the assertion that no "novel principles of government" were in mind when the Bill of Rights was adopted. Arguing, in his dissent, about the constitutionality of involuntary servitude, he said:[15] "Nor, I submit, is any light thrown upon the question by the history of legislation in Great Britain. The powers of the British Parliament furnish no test for the powers that may be exercised by the Congress of the United States." The distinctive feature of our Constitution, he declared, that marks it off from British political institutions, is that it is established, not by the legislature, but by the people. And he summed up the novelty of our system:[16] "No such powers have been or can be exercised by any legislative body under the American system. Absolute, arbitrary power exists nowhere in this free land. The authority for the exercise of power by the Congress of the United States must be found in the Constitution. Whatever it does in excess of the powers granted it, or in violation of the injunctions of the supreme law of the land, is a nullity, and may be so treated by every person." To a teacher of freedom in the United States that seems to be good law. I wish it would seem so to those who now have authority to determine what good law is.

Footnotes

1. 15 (1941).

2. That Chafee was, in 1942, a "balancer" is shown by the first chapter of his book to which I already have made reference. There he said in summation: "That is, in technical language, there are individual interests and social interests, which must be balanced against each other, if they conflict, in order to determine which interest shall be sacrificed under the circumstances and which shall be protected and become the foundation of a legal right." *Id.* at 32. On the other hand, his absolutist demand for a "rational principle" was never fully abandoned, though never fully satisfied. It reappears in tentative form in a personal letter to Ernest Angell: "Penning a longhand letter from a hospital bed in 1953, he [Chaffee] wrote: 'In court cases fine lines have to be drawn—it's unavoidable once you get that far. Yet Meiklejohn is right in a way—things ought never to have got to this pass where freedom of thought and expression depend on distinctions as thin as a hair.' And: 'The upshot of all this is that I see little prospect of a recovery of freedom and sanity through any particular court decision. There will have to be a real repudiation of the whole darned business—but by whom? Or else, which seems more probable, it will die out because people are sick of it, the way censorship expired in 1695 in England.' " Angell, *Zechariah Chafee, Jr.—Individual Freedoms,* 70 Harv. L. Rev. 1341, 1343 (1957).

3. Meiklejohn, "What Does the First Amendment Mean?" 20 U. Chi. Law. Rev. 461, 463 (1953).

4. The writing of this paper is largely due to the friendly insistence of Professor Harry Kalven, Jr., of the Law School of the University of Chicago. He and I have had, in recent years, a continuing exchange of ideas. Professor Kalven tells me that he is not sure that my interpretation of the First Amendment can stand the test of lawyer-like application to the many specific situations which the courts must handle. In response to that challenge, I cannot presume to offer fully specific answers to specific problems. I can only suggest principles, bringing them as near as I can to the actual issues with which the courts deal.

5. Hearings before the Subcommittee on Constitutional Rights of the Senate Committee on the Judiciary, 84th Cong., 2d Sess., at p. 20 (1955).

6. *Abrams v. United States,* 250 U.S. 616,627 (1919).

7. *Schenck v. United States,* 249 U.S. 47,52 (1919).

8. 366 U.S. at 49 n. 10.

9. 249 U.S. at 52.

10. Kalven, *Metaphysics of the Law of Obscenity,* 1960 Sup. Ct. Rev. 1, 15-16.

11. *Legacy of Suppression* (1960).

12. 165 U.S. 275,281 (1897).

13. 341 U.S. at 524.

14. Meiklejohn, "What Does the First Amendment Mean?" 20 U. Chi. Law. Rev. 461 (1953).

15. 165 U.S. at 296.

16. *Ibid.*

Meiklejohn's Publications

Books

The Liberal College. Boston: Marshall Jones Co., 1920.

Freedom and the College. New York: Century Co., 1923.

Philosophy. Chicago: American Library Association, 1926.

The Experimental College. New York: Harper Brothers, 1932; reprinted by Arno Press, 1971.

What Does America Mean? New York: W.W. Norton, 1935.

Education Between Two Worlds. New York: Harper & Brothers, 1942.

Free Speech and Its Relation to Self-Government. New York: Harper & Brothers, 1948.

Education for a Free Society: Selected Papers. 2 vols. Pasadena, Calif.: Fund for Adult Education, 1957. (A mimeographed collection of articles and excerpts from Meiklejohn's books and articles).

Political Freedom: The Constitutional Powers of the People. New York: Oxford University Press, 1960, reprinted 1965 (a new edition, revised with additional material, of *Free Speech and Its Relation to Self-Government*).

Articles, Reviews, and Pamphlets

Review of *La modalite du jugement,* by Leon Brunschvieg. *Philosophical Review* 6 (November 1897): 677-79.

Review of *Les principes du positivisme contemporain,* by Jean Halleux. *Philosophical Review* 8 (March 1899): 212-13.

Review of *The Relation of Berkeley's Later to His Earlier Idealism,* by Carl V. Tower. *Philosophical Review* 10 (January 1901): 102-04.

Review of *A Syllabus of an Introduction to Philosophy,* by Walter G. Marvin. *Philosophical Review* 10 (May 1901): 322-24.

Review of *Kant contra Haeckel,* by Erich von Adickes. *Philosophical Review* 10 (November 1901): 668-70.

"The Evils of College Athletics." *Harper's Weekly* 49 (December 2, 1905): 1751-52.

"College Education and the Moral Ideal." *Education* 28 (May 1908): 552-67.

"Is Mental Training a Myth?" *Educational Review* 37 (February 1909): 126-41.

"Are College Entrance Requirements Excessive?" *Education* 29 (May 1909): 561-66.

"Competition in College." *Brown Alumni Monthly* 10 (November 1909): 75-78.

"Fraternities and Scholarship." *Brown Alumni Monthly* 11 (November 1910): 89-91.

"What Constitutes Preparation for College: The College View." *Education* 31 (May 1911): 578-84.

"The Values of Logic and the College Curriculum." *Religious Education* 7 (April 1912): 62-68.

"Inaugural Address." *Amherst Graduates' Quarterly* 2 (November 1912): 56-73. Reprinted in *The Liberal College*, pp. 29-50; *Freedom and the College*, pp. 155-89; *Essays for College Men*, pp. 28-59. New York: Holt, 1913; *American Higher Education: A Documentary History, II*, 897-903. (Edited by Richard Hofstadter and Wilson Smith. Chicago: University of Chicago Press, 1961.)

"The Goal and the Game." *Amherst Graduates' Quarterly* 3 (October 1913): 11-20.

"Report of the President to the Trustees." *Amherst College Bulletin* 3 (January 1914): 3. Reprinted in part in *The Liberal College*, pp. 135-48.

"The Challenge of the College." *Amherst Monthly* (October 1914).

"The Purpose of the Liberal College." National Education Association. *Proceedings and Addresses of the. . .Annual Meeting. . .1914*, pp. 102-3. Ann Arbor, Mich.: N.E.A., 1914.

"The Place of Student Activities in the College." *Amherst Graduates' Quarterly* 4 (January 1915): 110-18; also in *Education* 35 (January 1915): 312-19. Reprinted in *The Liberal College*, pp. 97-106; and in *College Years*, pp. 157-65. Edited by J. B. Heidler. New York: Ray Long and Richard R. Smith, 1933.

"The Function of the College as Distinct from the High School, the Professional School, and the University." Address at Allegheny College, June 23, 1915. *The American College,* pp. 147-69. Edited by W. H. Crawford. New York: Holt, 1915. Reprinted as "What the College Is Not," *The Liberal College,* pp. 13-28.

"Address at Inauguration of Hermon C. Bumpus as President of Tufts College." *Tufts College Graduate* 14 (Autumn 1915): 69-75.

"A Schoolmaster's View of Compulsory Military Training." *School and Society* 4 (July 1, 1916): 9-14; also in *Amherst Monthly* (June 1916), pp. 93-100; also in *Proceedings of Academy of Political Science* 6 (July 1916): 171-78.

"Tenure of Office and Academic Freedom." *Proceedings of the Association of American Colleges* (April 1916), pp. 179-87.

"Fiat Justitia—The College as Critic." *Harvard Graduate Magazine* (September 1917); also in *Amherst Monthly* 32 (October 1917): 419-32; *The Liberal College,* pp. 66-83.

"Faith." *The Amherst Student* (June 19, 1917).

Chapel Address. *Amherst Graduates' Quarterly* 7 (November 1917): 8-12.

"The Freedom of the College." *Atlantic Monthly* 121 (January 1918): 83-89. Reprinted in *The Liberal College,* pp. 84-96.

"Last Two Years of the College Course." Association of American Colleges. *Bulletin* 24 (April 1918): 22-32.

"Keep on in College." *The Christian Endeavor World* (July 18, 1918), p. 811.

"Report of the President to the Trustees." *Amherst College Bulletin* 8 (December 1918). Extracts reprinted: "A Reorganization of the College Curriculum," *The Liberal College,* pp. 149-63; "Reorganizing the College Curriculum," *Freedom and the College,* pp. 207-31; "The Colleges and the S.A.T.C.," *Nation* 107 (December 7, 1918): 697-98.

"The Four Year American Cultural College." Association of Colleges and Preparatory Schools of the Middle States and Maryland. *Proceedings* (1919), pp. 48-60.

"Future of Our Liberal Colleges." *New York Sun* (October 19, 1919).

"English Impressions." *Amherst Graduates' Quarterly* 9 (November 1919): 7-11.

"Production, Distribution, and Use." Association of Urban Universities. *Fourth Report* (December 1919): 54-59.

"Administration of the College," "The Educational Work of the College," and "Faculty Supervision of Student Activities." *Proceedings of the Alumni Council of Amherst College,* 1919, pp. 28-35; 8-14; and 45-48. Amherst, Mass.: The Alumni Council, 1920.

"The Trustee" (a tribute to John Woodruff Simpson). *Amherst Graduates' Quarterly* 10 (November 1920): 24-25.

"What Does the College Hope to Be During the Next One Hundred Years?" *Amherst Graduates' Quarterly* 10 (August 1921): 327-47. Reprinted in *Freedom and the College,* pp. 101-42.

"The Machine City." *Brown Alumni Monthly* (November 1921). Reprinted in *Freedom and the College,* pp. 145-52.

"For Athletic Disarmament." *Amherst Graduates' Quarterly* 11 (May 1922): 171-73. Also in *Outdoor* (March 8, 1922) as "Intercollegiate Athletics."

"The Unity of the Curriculum." *New Republic* 32 (October 25, 1922): 2-3 (supp.). Reprinted in *Freedom and the College,* pp. 193-203.

"What Are College Games For?" *Atlantic Monthly* 30 (November 1922): 663-71. Reprinted in *Freedom and the College,* pp. 71-97.

"Democracy Held Success Not a Popular Delusion." *New York Times* (December 7, 1922), sec. 8, p. 2.

"The Measure of a College." *Amherst Graduates' Quarterly* 12 (February 1923): 85-92.

"Unifying the Liberal College Curriculum." Association of American Colleges. *Bulletin* 9 (March 1923): 79-90.

"Is Our World Christian?" *Amherst Graduates' Quarterly* 12 (August 1923): 224-33. Also published in part as "Pharisees and Reformers," *Nation* 117 (July 4, 1923): 13. Reprinted in *Freedom and the College,* pp. 27-45.

"Letter of Resignation." *Amherst Graduates' Quarterly* 12 (August 1923): 219-20. Also in *School and Society* 17 (June 30, 1923): 714.

"The College and the Common Life." *Harper's* 147 (November 1923): 721-26.

"The Return to the Book." An address delivered to the American Library Association in 1924. In *American Ideas About Adult Education 1710-1951,* pp. 124-28. Edited by C. Hartley Grattan. New York: Teachers College, Columbia University, 1959.

"The Devil's Revenge." *Century* 107 (March 1924): 718-23.

"A New College, Notes on the Next Step in Higher Education." *Century* 109 (January 1925): 312-20.

"Philosophers and Others." *Philosophical Review* 34 (May 1925): 262-80.

"Woodrow Wilson, Teacher." *Saturday Review* 1 (May 30, 1925): 785-86.

"A New College." *New Republic* 46 (April 14, 1926): 215-18.

"The College of the Future." In *The Intercollegiate Parley on American College Education,* pp. 11-13. Middletown, Conn.: Wesleyan University, 1926.

"Outstanding Problems in American Education." In *Address at the Second Annual Congress,* December 2-4, 1926, National Student Federation of America, pp. 5-10.

"A New College with a New Idea." *New York Times Magazine* (May 29, 1927), sec. 4, pp. 1-2, 21.

"Wisconsin's Experimental College." *Survey* 58 (June 1, 1927): 268-70, 294-5.

"The Experimental College." *Bulletin of the University of Wisconsin.* Serial No. 1454, General Series No. 1230. Madison, 1927.

"From the Chairman to the Students." In *The First Year of the Experimental College,* pp. 45-48. Madison: The Pioneer Class of the Experimental College, 1928.

"The Experimental College." *Bulletin of the University of Wisconsin.* Serial No. 1510, General Series No. 1284. Madison, 1928.

"The Experimental College." *Wisconsin Alumuni Magazine* (April 1928), p. 237.

"In Memoriam: Address Delivered in Boston on First Anniversary of Sacco and Vanzetti." *New Republic* 56 (September 5, 1928): 69-71.

"The Experimental College After a Year." *Wisconsin Journal of Education* 61 (September 1928): 14-16. Reprinted in *Chicago School Journal* 11 (February 1929): 201-4.

"The Experimental College." *Bulletin of the University of Wisconsin.* Serial No. 1555, General Series No. 1329. Madison, 1928.

"Who Should Go to College?" Review of *College or Kindergarten,* by Max McConn. *New Republic* 57 (January 16, 1929): 238-41.

"What Next in Progressive Education?" *Progressive Education* 6 (April-June 1929): 99-110. Reprinted in slightly altered form in *Higher Education Faces the Future.* Edited by Paul Schil. New York: Horace Liveright, 1930.

"Educational Leadership in America." *Harper's* 160 (March 1930): 44-47.

"Philosophers Join in a Plea for Peace." *New York Times* (September 7, 1930), Sec. 3, p. 4.

"What Ought We to Think About?" *Executives' Club* (of Chicago) *News* (November 1930).

"Wisconsin's Experimental College." *Journal of Higher Education* (December 1930), pp. 485-90.

"Rejoinder" to Vivas article on the Experimental College. *Nation* 132 (March 25, 1931): 325-26.

"Some Notes on the Technique of Experimentation in a Liberal Arts College." In *Liberal Arts Education.* Edited by F. W. Reeves. Chicago: University of Chicago, 1932. Also in *Changes and Experiments in Liberal Arts Education,* Part II, pp. 213-20. National Society for the Study of Education. Thirty-First Yearbook, Bloomington, Ill.: Public School Publishers Co., 1932.

"The Reorganization of Content to Emphasize Fields of Learning or the Relation of Branches to Knowledge." In *Changes and Experiments in Liberal Arts Education,* pp. 162-64. Bloomington, Ill.: Public School Publishers Co., 1932.

"Letter of Greeting to President Stanley King." *Amherst Graduates' Quarterly* 73 (November 1932): 12.

"Education and the Social Order." *The Argonaut* (May 1933).

"Adult Education: A Fresh Start." *New Republic* 80 (August 15, 1934): 14-17.

"Liberty—For What?" *Harper's* 171 (August 1935): 364-72. (Extract from *What Does America Mean?*)

Interview. *Providence Journal & Evening Bulletin.* April 20, 1937.

Foreword to *Selected Supreme Court Decisions.* Edited by Myer Cohen. New York: Harper Brothers, 1937.

"Teachers and Controversial Questions." *Harper's* 177 (June 1938): 15-22.

Review of *Out of Revolution,* by Eugen Rosenstock-Huessy. *Dartmouth Alumni Magazine* (December 1938).

"Higher Education in a Democracy." *North Central Association Quarterly* 16 (October 1941): 149-54.

"The Role of the Liberal Arts College in American Life." In *Learning and Living: Proceedings of an Anniversary Celebration in Honor of Alexander Meikljohn,* pp. 31-48. Edited by Walker H. Hill. Chicago, Ill.: By the Editor, 1942.

"Congress and the People." *Nation* 155 (November 7, 1942): 469-71.

"Education as a Factor in Post-War Reconstruction." *Free World* 5 (January 1943): 27-31. Also in *Beyond Victory.* Edited by Ruth Nander Anshen. New York: Harcourt, 1943.

"The Future of Liberal Education." *New Republic* 108 (January 25, 1943): 113-15.

"For International Citizenship." *Adult Education Journal* 2 (January 1943): 44-47.

"Reply to Sidney Hook's Review of *Education Between Two Worlds.*" *Nation* 156 (March 13, 1943): 393.

"Teacher, Teach Thyself." *Adult Education Journal* 2 (July 1943): 120-29.

"Reason or Violence." *Common Sense* 12 (August 1943): 283-86.

"Mr. Hutchins' Dogma." Review of *Education for Freedom,* by Robert Maynard Hutchins. *New Republic* 109 (August 2, 1943): 147-48.

"Unity with the Communists?" *New Masses* (October 19, 1943), pp. 16-18.

"Free Speech for Fascists?" Reply to Earl Browder. *New Masses* (December 7, 1943).

"Reason and Education." Review of *Liberal Education,* by Mark Van Doren. *New Republic* (January 3, 1944).

Review of *Education for a World Adrift,* by Richard Livingstone, and *Universities Look for Unity,* by John U. Nef. *Journal of Higher Education* (January 1944).

"Required Education for Freedom." *American Scholar* 13 (October 1944): 393-95.

"A Reply to John Dewey." *Fortune* 31 (January 1945): 207, and "Rejoinder," 31 (March 1945): 14.

"Education Under the Charter." *Free World* 10 (October 1945): 37-39.

"To Teach the World to Be Free." *Social Progress* (November 1946). Also in *New York Times Magazine* (August 11, 1946), pp. 5, 48-50.

Review of *Philosophy in American Education,* by Blanshard, Ducasse, Hendel, Murphy and Otto. *Philosophical Review* 55 (November 1946): 687-94.

"Inclinations and Obligations." Howison Lecture, 1947. *University of California Publications in Philosophy* 16 (October 1948): 203-23.

"Everything Worth Saying Should Be Said." *New York Times Magazine* (July 18, 1948), pp. 8, 32.

"Brief Comment on the 90th Birthday of John Dewey." *New Republic* 121 (October 17, 1949): 22.

"Educational Cooperation Between Church and State." *Law and Contemporary Problems* 14 (Winter 1949): 61-72.

"Should Communists Be Allowed To Teach?" *New York Times Magazine* (March 27, 1949), pp. 10, 64-66. Reprinted in *Political Freedom,* pp. 133-41.

Crisis at the University of California, I: *A Statement to the People of California.* San Francisco: American Civil Liberties Union of Northern California, 1949.

"Freedom to Hear and to Judge." *Lawyers Guild Reveiw* 10 (Spring 1950): 26-30.

Crisis at the University of California, II: *A Further Statement to the People of California.* San Francisco: American Civil Liberties Union of Northern California, 1950.

"At Odds With Plato." Review of *The Art of Teaching,* by Gilbert Highet. *New Republic* (June 1950).

"The First Amendment and Evils that Congress Has a Right to Prevent." *Indiana Law Journal* 26 (Summer 1951): 477-93.

"Hockey Pioneers." *Brown Alumni Monthly* (April 1951).

"The Teaching of Intellectual Freedom." *Bulletin of the American Association of University Professors* 38 (Spring 1952): 10-25. Reprinted in *Political Freedom,* pp. 125-33, and in part in *Rights* 3 (April 1956): 6-7.

"The Crisis in Freedom." *The Progressive* 16 (June 1952): 15-18.

"Food for Thought." *Spectator* 169 (July 11, 1952): 58-59.

"A Plea for World Citizenship." Review of *Citizen of the World,* by Stringfellow Barr. *This World* (November 9, 1952).

"What Does the First Amendment Mean?" *University of Chicago Law Review* 20 (Spring 1953): 461-79.

"Integrity of the Universities—How to Defend It." *Bulletin of the Atomic Scientists* 9 (June 1953): 193-94. Also in *ACLU News* (May 1953), pp. 1-2.

"Under the Elms," published as "1893, 1953, and 2013." *Brown Alumni Monthly* 53 (July 1953): 15-16.

"The Priority of the Marketplace of Ideas." In Thurmond Arnold and others. *Conference on Freedom and the Law, May 7, 1953,* pp. 3-15. Conference Series IV, v. 13. Chicago: University of Chicago, 1953.

"The Limits of Congressional Authority: Freedom and the People." *Nation* 177 (December 1953): 500-503. Reprinted in *Political Freedom,* pp. 101-06.

"Education and the Brotherhood of Man." *Gadfly* (November 1954).

Letter to *The Harvard Crimson,* February 25, 1954. Reprinted in *Political Freedom,* pp. 148-55.

"Sedition Circa 400 B.C." Review of *The State Versus Socrates,* by John D. Montgomery. *Nation* 180 (April 23, 1955): 349-52.

U.S. Congress. Senate. Committee on the Judiciary. *Testimony on the Meaning of the First Amendment. Hearings before a Subcommittee on Constitutional Rights,* 84th Cong., 1st sess., 1955. Reprinted in *Political Freedom,* pp. 107-24.

U.S. Congress. Senate. "The American College and American Freedom." 85th Cong., 1st sess., 7-20 June 1957. *Congressional Record,* vol. 103, part 7, pp. 8751-55.

"Chapel Address, 1957." *Amherst Alumni News* 10 (July 1957): 3-5.

"Liberty or Freedom." In *Meiklejohn Library Anniversary Journal,* pp. 9-18. Berkeley, Calif.: Meiklejohn Civil Liberties Library, 1957. Issued as a pamphlet by Northern California American Civil Liberties Union, October 1957.

"Petition for Redress of Grievance, December 12, 1957." *ACLU News* (January 1958), p. 1. Reprinted in *Political Freedom,* pp. 156-58.

"Constitutional Limits to Congressional Investigations." *Rights* 6 (October 1959): 3.

"The Barenblatt Opinion." *University of Chicago Law Review* 27 (Winter 1960): 329-40.

"Legal Status of Our Freedom." *Lawyers Guild Review* 10 (Winter 1960): 106-08.

"The Balancing of Self-Preservation Against Political Freedom." *California Law Review* 49 (March 1961): 4-14.

"The First Amendment Is an Absolute." In *Supreme Court Review 1961,* pp. 245-66. Edited by Philip Kurland. Chicago, Ill.: University of Chicago Press, 1961.

"Rights and Powers Under the First Amendment." *Rights* (Jan-Feb., 1962).

"A Mirror of Friendship." In *Felix Frankfurter, A Tribute,* pp. 87-88. Edited by Wallace Mendelson. New York: Reynal, 1964.

"Words of Advice to the Graduates of Any Class at Any Time." *The Bill of Rights Journal* 1 (December 1968): 32-33 (posthumously).

Sources

This study is based primarily on the published writing of Alexander Meiklejohn and on two archival collections. The basic one, held by the State Historical Society of Wisconsin, consists of sixty-nine boxes entitled "The Papers of Alexander Meiklejohn." The second collection consists of seventy boxes held in the archives of the University of Wisconsin under the heading "Experimental College." Both collections are located in Madison, Wisconsin.

For more than three years, from 1977 to 1980, Helen Meiklejohn met weekly with me. Together we examined Meiklejohn's books and papers still in her possession. She introduced me to key people in his life and shared not only her memory of his life, in which she participated to an extraordinary degree, but also her comprehension of it.

The following people shared their memories of Meiklejohn either in person or by correspondence: Walter Raymond Agard, John Beecher, John Bergstresser, R. Freeman Butts, Paul Clarke, Wilbur Cohen, Kenneth Decker, Alvin J. Gordon, Elizabeth Faragoh, Marge Frantz, Charles Hogan, Myles Horton, Sydney Kasper, Edith Katten, Donald Meiklejohn, Josephine Miles, Elizabeth Nason, David Parsons, John Powell, David Riesman, H. Michael Sapir, Ann Stout, and Joseph Tussman.

James M. Green generously loaned me transcripts of the following interviews: Alexander Meiklejohn, by Theodore Crane, associate professor of history, University of Denver, 19 October 1963 and 22 January 1964; Louis Lyons, reporter who broke the story of the crisis at Amherst in 1923 for the *Springfield Republican,* by Theodore Crane, 26 June 1964; Gordon Meiklejohn, by Theodore Crane, 6 July 1965; Alexander Meiklejohn, by George Wallerstein, professor of astronomy at the University of Washington, 8 August 1963.

Selected Bibliography

Abbot, Scott. "Philosopher and Dean: Alexander Meiklejohn at Brown (1901-1912)." M.A. thesis, University of Denver, 1967.

Adam, T. R. *The Worker's Road to Learning.* New York: American Association for Adult Education, 1940.

Adams, George P., and Montague, William Pepperell, eds. *Contemporary American Philosophy: Personal Statements.* 2 vols. New York: Macmillan Co., 1930; reprint ed., New York: Russell & Russell, 1962.

American Civil Liberties Union. One hundred and fifty-six reports, statements, and pamphlets published from 1920 to 1957.

American Civil Liberties Union of Northern California. *Annual Reports* from 1945 to 1954.

"Alexander Meiklejohn Returns to Amherst." *Amherst Alumni News* 10 (July 1957): 3.

"Amherst College and President Meiklejohn." *School and Society* 17 (June 23, 1923): 687.

Andrews, E. Benjamin. "Modern College Education—Two Educational Ideals." *Cosmopolitan* XXIII (September 1897): 568-76.

Baldwin, Roger. "Dissident Pioneer." *Rights* XII (February 1965): 31-33.

Barth, Allen. "Tribute to Alexander Meiklejohn." *American Association of University Professors Bulletin* 51 (Autumn 1965): 366-73.

Bixler, J. Seelye. "Alexander Meiklejohn and the Making of the Amherst Mind." *Amherst: The College and Its Alumni* (Spring 1973), pp. 1-6.

Bogue, Allen G., and Taylor, Robert, eds. *The University of Wisconsin: One Hundred and Twenty-Five Years.* Madison: University of Wisconsin Press, 1975.

Brameld, Theodore. *Philosophies of Education in Cultural Perspective.* New York: Dryden Press, 1955.

————, ed. *Workers' Education in the United States.* Fifth Yearbook of the John Dewey Society. New York and London: Harper & Brothers, 1941.

Bronson, Walter C. *The History of Brown University 1764-1914.* Providence, R.I.: Brown University, 1914.

Buchanan, Scott. "Both Socrates and Plato." *Rights* XII (February 1965): 13-14.

Burgess, W. Randolph. "What Is Truth?" *Rights* XII (February 1965): 28-29.

Butts, R. Freeman. *The College Charts Its Course: Historical Conceptions and Current Proposals.* New York and London: McGraw-Hill, 1939.

Caldwell, James. "Tribute to Dr. Meiklejohn." *ACLU News* (December 1957): 1.

Cartwright, Morse Adams. *Ten Years of Adult Education.* New York: Macmillan Co., 1935.

Cohen, Myer. *Selected Supreme Court Decisions.* New York: Harper Brothers, 1937.

Commons, John R. *The Economics of Collective Action.* Edited with an introduction by Kenneth H. Parsons. Madison: University of Wisconsin Press, 1970.

————. *Myself.* New York: Macmillan Co., 1934.

Cooper, Charles J. "Alexander Meiklejohn: Absolutes of Intelligence in Political and Constitutional Theory." Ph.D. dissertation, Bryn Mawr, 1967.

Crisis in the Civil Liberties Union: A Statement, Including the Basic Documents Concerned, Giving the Minority Position in the Current Controversy in the American Civil Liberties Union. New York: American Civil Liberties Union, 1940.

Derleth, August. *Still Small Voice: The Biography of Zona Gale.* New York: D. Appleton-Century Co., 1940.

Dewey, John. "Challenge to Liberal Thought." *Fortune* XXX (August 1944): 155. Rejoinder to Meiklejohn, *Fortune* XXXI (March 1945): 10, 14.

————. *Education and the Social Order.* New York: League for Industrial Democracy, 1934.

————. "The Meiklejohn Experiment." *New Republic* LXXII (August 17, 1932): 23-24.

————. "The Problem of the Liberal Arts College." *American Scholar* XIII (October 1944): 391-93.

Donnan, Elizabeth. "A Nineteenth-Century Academic Cause Celebre." *New England Quarterly* XXV (March 1952): 23-46.

276   *Brown*

Dorsen, Norman; Bender, Paul; and Neuborne, Burt. *Political and Civil Rights in the United States.* 4th ed. Vol. 1. Boston: Little, Brown and Co., 1976.

Duberman, Martin. *Black Mountain: An Exploration in Community.* New York: E.P. Dutton & Co., 1972.

Everett, Walter Goodnow. *Moral Values: A Study of the Principles of Conduct.* New York: Henry Holt & Co., 1918.

The First Year of the Experimental College. Written by the Pioneer Class of the Experimental College. Madison: University of Wisconsin Press, 1928.

Foner, Philip S. *History of the Labor Movement in the United States.* Vol. 1: *From Colonial Times to the Founding of the American Federation of Labor.* New York: International Publishers, 1947.

Fuess, Claude Moore. *Amherst: The Story of a New England College.* Boston: Little, Brown & Co., 1935.

Gardner, David P. *The California Oath Controversy.* Berkeley and Los Angeles: University of California Press, 1967.

Gaus, John Merriman. "The Issues at Amherst." *Nation* 117 (July 4, 1923): 12.

George Herbert Palmer (1842-1933): Memorial Addresses. Cambridge, Mass.: Harvard University Press, 1935.

Graham, Patricia Albjerg. *Progressive Education from Arcady to Academe: A History of the Progressive Education Association 1919-1955.* New York: Teachers College Press, 1967.

Grant, Gerald, and Riesman, David. *The Perpetual Dream: Reform and Experiment in the American College.* Chicago: University of Chicago Press, 1978.

Green, James M. "Alexander Meiklejohn—Innovator in Undergraduate Education." Ph.D. dissertation, University of Michigan, 1970.

Harvard University. Committee on the Objectives of a General Education in a Free Society. *General Education in a Free Society.* Cambridge, Mass.: Harvard University Press, 1945.

Hill, Walker H., ed. *Learning and Living: Proceedings of an Anniversary Celebration in Honor of Alexander Meiklejohn, Chicago May 8-10, 1942.* Chicago: By the Editor, 1942.

Hoan, Daniel W. *City Government: The Record of the Milwaukee Experiment.* New York: Harcourt Brace & Co., 1936.

Hofstadter, Richard, and Metzger, Walter P. *The Development of Academic Freedom in the United States.* New York: Columbia University Press, 1955.

Hofstadter, Richard, and Smith, Wilson, eds. *American Higher Education: A Documentary History.* 2 vols. Chicago: University of Chicago Press, 1961.

Howe, Irving, and Coser, Lewis. *The American Communist Party: A Critical History (1919-1957).* Boston: Beacon Press, 1957.

Iversen, Robert W. *The Communists and the Schools.* New York: Harcourt Brace & Co., 1959.

Johnson, Harriet M. Review of *The Experimental College,* by Alexander Meiklejohn. *Progressive Education* (October 1932), pp. 454-58.

Johnson, Roger T. *Robert M. La Follette, Jr., and the Decline of the Progressive Party in Wisconsin.* Madison: State Historical Society of Wisconsin, 1964.

Jones, Richard M. *Experiment at Evergreen.* Cambridge, Mass.: Schenkman Publishing Co., forthcoming.

Journal of Adult Education. 13 vols., 1929-41. Thereafter known as *Adult Education Journal.* 9 vols., 1942-50.

Kalven, Harry. "A Tribute to Alexander Meiklejohn." In *Alexander Meiklejohn, 1872-1964.* Berkeley: Privately printed, 1965.

Kemper, Donald J. *Decade of Fear: Senator Hennings and Civil Liberties.* Columbia, Mo.: University of Missouri Press, 1965.

King, Stanley. *A History of the Endowment of Amherst College.* Amherst, Mass.: Amherst College, 1950.

Koch, Raymond, and Koch, Charlotte. *Educational Communes: The Story of Commonwealth College.* New York: Schocken, 1972.

Laidler, Harry W. *Forty-Five Years of Social Education.* New York: League for Industrial Democracy, 1950.

————. *Socialism in the United States: A Brief History.* New York: League for Industrial Democracy, 1952.

Lamont, Corliss, ed. *The Trial of Elizabeth Gurley Flynn by the American Civil Liberties Union.* New York: Horizon Press, 1968.

Lamson, Peggy. *Roger Baldwin: Founder of the American Civil Liberties Union.* Boston: Houghton Mifflin Co., 1976.

Larrowe, Charles P. *Harry Bridges: The Rise and Fall of Radical Labor in the United States.* Westport, Conn.: Lawrence Hill & Co., 1972.

Larsen, Lawrence H. *The President Wore Spats.* Madison: State Historical Society of Wisconsin, 1965.

Le Duc, Thomas. *Piety and Intellect at Amherst College 1865-1912.* New York: Columbia University Press, 1946.

Leichman, Nathan S. "Meiklejohn's Experiment Ends." *Forward* (May 4, 1930).

Lippmann, Walter. "The Fall of President Meiklejohn." *New York World,* 24 June 1923, editorial section, p. 1.

Lovejoy, A. O. "Organization of the American Association of University Professors." *Science* 41 (January 29, 1915).

Lovett, Robert Morss. *All Our Years.* New York: Viking Press, 1948.

————. "Meiklejohn of Amherst." *New Republic* (July 4, 1923), pp. 146-48.

Lynd, Helen Merrell. "The Conflict in Education." *New Republic* 110 (May 22, 1944): 700-03.

Lynd, Robert. *Knowledge for What?: The Place of Social Science in American Culture.* Princeton, N.J.: Princeton University Press, 1939.

Lynd, Robert S., and Lynd, Helen Merrell. *Middletown: A Study in American Culture.* New York: Harcourt, Brace & Co., 1929.

Markmann, Charles Lam. *The Noblest Cry: A History of the American Civil Liberties Union.* New York: St. Martin's Press, 1965.

Maxwell, Robert S. *La Follette and the Rise of the Progressives in Wisconsin.* Madison: State Historical Society of Wisconsin, 1956.

McGilvary, Evander B. "The Warfare of Moral Ideas." In *Toward a Perspective Realism,* ch. viii. Edited by Albert G. Ramsperger. LaSalle, Ill.: Open Court Publishing Co., 1956.

McIlhany, William H. *The ACLU on Trial.* New Rochelle, N.Y.: Arlington House, 1976.

"The Meiklejohn Experiment." *New Republic* (March 11, 1931): 85-87.

Meiklejohn Library Anniversary Journal. Berkeley, Calif.: Meiklejohn Civil Liberties Library, 1975.

Milner, Lucille. *Education of An American Liberal.* New York: Horizon Press, 1954.

Morison, Samuel Eliot. *Three Centuries of Harvard.* Cambridge, Mass.: Harvard University Press, 1946.

Mitford, Jessica. *A Fine Old Conflict.* London: Michael Joseph, 1977.

Nason, John W. "Man in His Family." *Rights* XII (February 1965).

"The New President of Amherst." *Outlook* 101 (July 27, 1912): 669.

"An Open Letter to Dwight Morrow." *New Republic* (July 25, 1923).

Otto, Max C. *Things and Ideals: Essays in Functional Philosophy.* New York: Henry Holt & Co., 1924.

Palmer, George Herbert. *The Autobiography of a Philosopher.* Boston and New York: Houghton Mifflin & Co., 1930.

Palmer, Mack Redburn. "The Qualified Absolute: Alexander Meiklejohn and Freedom of Speech." Ph.D. dissertation, University of Wisconsin-Madison, 1979.

Plimpton, Calvin H. "Minority Man." *Rights* XII (February 1965): 30.

Pope, Arthur Upham. "Alexander Meiklejohn." *American Scholar* (Autumn 1965): 644.

Powell, John Walker. *Education for Maturity: An Empirical Essay on Adult Group Study.* New York: Hermitage House, 1949.

――――. "Education and Henry Adams." *The Standard* XVII (February 1932): 172-79.

――――. "A Tribute to Alexander Mciklejohn." In *Alexander Meiklejohn 1872-1964.* Berkeley, Calif.: Privately printed, 1965.

Price, Lucien. *Prophet Unawares: The Romance of an Idea.* New York: Century Co., 1924.

Pritchett, C. Herman. *Civil Liberties and the Vinson Court 1946-1953.* Chicago: University of Chicago Press, 1954.

Reeves, Joseph. *A Century of Rochdale Cooperation 1844-1944.* London: Lawrence & Wishart, 1944.

The Reply of the Trustees to the Class of Eighteen Eighty-Five. Amherst, Mass.: Plimpton Press, 1911.

Sellery, George C. *Some Ferments at Wisconsin, 1901-1941: Memories and Reflections.* Madison: University of Wisconsin Press, 1960.

Selvin, David F. *Sky Full of Storm: A Brief History of California Labor.* Berkeley, Calif.: Center for Labor Research and Education, 1966; reprint ed., San Francisco, Calif.: California Historical Society, 1975.

Shannon, David A. *The Socialist Party of America.* New York: Macmillan Co., 1955.

Shantz, Hermione. "The Social and Educational Theory of Alexander Meiklejohn." Ph.D. dissertation, Michigan State University, 1969.

Sharp, Malcolm. "The Experimental College Opens." *Wisconsin Alumni Magazine* (October 1927): 8.

Sinclair, Upton. *The Goose-Step.* Pasadena, Calif.: By the Author, 1923.

Stephens, James. *Songs from the Clay.* New York: Macmillan Co., 1915.

Still, Bayrd. *Milwaukee: The History of a City.* Madison: State Historical Society of Wisconsin, 1948.

Stone, I. F. *The Truman Era.* London: Turnstile Press, 1953.

Strachey, John. *The Coming Struggle for Power.* London: Victor Gollancz Ltd., 1934.

"Student Views of Wisconsin's Experimental College." *Milwaukee Journal,* 13 September 1931, p. 2.

Summary Proceedings of the Experimental College Reunion with Alexander Meiklejohn. Annapolis, Md.: Privately printed, 1957.

Swanberg, W. A. *Norman Thomas: The Last Idealist.* New York: Charles Scribner's Sons, 1976.

Taft, Philip. *Movements for Economic Reform.* New York: Rinehart & Co., 1950.

Tawney, Richard H. *The Acquisitive Society.* New York: Harcourt Brace & Co., 1920.

————. *The Radical Tradition.* Edited by Rita Hinden. London: G. Allen & Unwin, 1964.

Terrill, Ross. *R. H. Tawney and His Times: Socialism As Fellowship.* London: Andre Deutsch, 1973.

Thirty-Five Years of Educational Pioneering. New York: League for Industrial Democracy, 1941.

Tussman, Joseph. *Experiment at Berkeley.* New York: Oxford University Press, 1969.

————. "A Tribute to Alexander Meiklejohn." In *Alexander Meiklejohn 1872-1964.* Berkeley, Calif.: Privately printed, 1965.

Twenty Years of Social Pioneering: The League for Industrial Democracy Celebrates Its Twentieth Anniversary December 30, 1925. New York: League for Industrial Democracy, 1926.

Vivas, Eliseo. "Wisconsin's Experimental College." *Nation* (March 25, 1931), pp. 322-26.

Weigle, Richard D. *St. John's College Annapolis: Pilot College in Liberal Arts Education.* New York, San Francisco, and Montreal: Newcomen Society, 1953.

Weiss, Peter. "Eyeopener for Students." *Rights* XII (February 1965): 17-18.

Wofford, Harris L., Jr., ed. *Embers of the World: Conversations with Scott Buchanan.* Santa Barbara, Calif.,: Center for the Study of Democratic Institutions, 1970.

About the Editor

Cynthia Stokes Brown grew up in Madisonville, Kentucky. She received a B.A. from Duke University in 1960 and a Ph. D. in the history of education from Johns Hopkins University in 1964, supported by a fellowship from the American Association of University Women and an honorary Woodrow Wilson Fellowship. She taught high school history in Baltimore and co-directed a credential program for elementary teachers at the University Without Walls—Berkeley. Currently she teaches at Antioch University—San Francisco and serves as a director of the Coastal Ridge Research and Education Center in Point Arena, California. Her writing includes *Literacy in Thirty Hours: Paulo Freire's Process in Northeast Brasil* (London: Writers and Readers Publishing Cooperative, 1975).

About Meiklejohn Civil Liberties Institute

Meiklejohn Civil Liberties Institute (MCLI) collects and makes available significant source materials on human rights law in the belief that this sharing of experience and knowledge contributes to a useful and realistic approach to dealing with today's problems as they arise in the legal arena.

MCLI defines human rights broadly: **civil liberties** (First Amendment rights—freedom of speech, press, assembly); **due process of law** (trial by jury, right to counsel, fair procedures); **civil rights** (equal protection regardless of race, sex, age, religion, class); **social and economic rights** (unwritten New Deal "amendments" on the right to eat, to unionize, to get a job); and **national, international, and citizenship rights** (in the U.N. Charter, a treaty signed by the U.S.).

Our goal is to teach people how to defend and extend these human rights, as we did at our October, 1980 symposium on McCarthyism and the Cold War: " 'Are You Now Or Have You Ever Been. . . ?,' A Critical Look at Matters of Conscience and the Body Politick."

Our collections—current case file holdings and historical archives—serve both the attorney's need for current practice materials and the scholar's need for primary source documents. We use these materials to answer reference questions from all over the country, responding to telephone, correspondence, and in-person requests for information. We also rely on our collections to produce published materials for the general public, as well as specialized legal materials for lawyers and social scientists.

This book reflects our commitment to share Alexander Meiklejohn's philosophical and practical approaches to issues concerning *freedom* that engaged his intellectual energies for nearly seven decades.

We are anxious to get this book into the hands of every educator and student who will be inspired by it. Despite sixteen years of work, our financial resources and our mailing lists are not extensive enough to achieve this goal without your assistance. Please help by sending us the names and addresses of innovative teachers, experimental colleges, adult education programs, or potential students of Alexander Meiklejohn's theories.